RELATIONAL SUICIDE ASSESSMENT

RELATIONAL SUICIDE ASSESSMENT

Risks, Resources, and Possibilities for Safety

Douglas Flemons
Leonard M. Gralnik

Foreword by Donald Meichenbaum

W. W. Norton & Company
New York • London

For information about permission to reproduce selections from this book, write to
Permissions, W. W. Norton & Company, Inc., 500 Fifth Avenue,
New York, NY 10110

For information about special discounts for bulk purchases, please contact
W. W. Norton Special Sales at specialsales@wwnorton.com or 800-233-4830

Manufacturing by Quad Graphics, Fairfield
Production manager: Leeann Graham

Library of Congress Cataloging-in-Publication Data

Flemons, Douglas G.
  Relational suicide assessment : risks, resources, and possibilities for safety /
Douglas Flemons, Leonard M. Gralnik. — First edition.
    pages cm
  "A Norton professional book."
  Includes bibliographical references and index.
  ISBN 978-0-393-70652-9 (hardcover)
  1. Suicidal behavior—Treatment.   2. Therapeutic alliance.   3. Suicide—
Prevention.   I. Gralnik, Leonard M.   II. Title.
  RC569.F594   2013
  616.85'8445—dc23   2012039472

ISBN: 978-0-393-70652-9

W. W. Norton & Company, Inc., 500 Fifth Avenue, New York, N.Y. 10110
www.wwnorton.com
W. W. Norton & Company Ltd., Castle House, 75/76 Wells Street,
London W1T 3QT

1 2 3 4 5 6 7 8 9 0

Douglas
To the memory of Ian Bebensee, Ken Weaver, Peter Lauritzen,
Peter Wheatley, and Brent Mayer. Reverberations from their lives
and untimely deaths are still felt by those who loved and
continue to miss them.

Len
To my parents, Pearl and Sidney Gralnik, for giving me
a lifetime of inspiration, support, and unwavering love.
To all of my teachers over the years, who gave me the tools
to do my best in attempting to help my patients. And to my patients,
who are the best teachers of all.

CONTENTS

ACKNOWLEDGMENTS

THIS BOOK WOULDN'T exist if we hadn't had the opportunity to work together in our Student Counseling Center, and the center wouldn't have existed were it not for the initial vision of Irv Rosenbaum and Brad Williams and the inspired and supportive oversight of Robert Oller and Henry Del Riego.

The clinic came to life every day and maintained a lifeline every night through the dedicated efforts of our remarkable staff. Mirna Gonzalez electrified our operation with multitasking genius. Roxanne Bamond, who collaborated with us on many suicide assessments, provided inspired clinical supervision for a talented and caring group of clinicians—Lisa Louth Alleva, Holly Carbone, Lisa Waid McKenna, Lisa Kelledy, marcela polanco, Jennifer Sneeden, Mike Rhodes, Andrea Gonzalez, Danielle Hadeed, Jessica Parker, Gloria Petruzzelli, Chris Carbo, Carrie Park, Abigail Patterson, Jessica Ruiz, Anaeli Ramos, Lauren Yerkes, Tyon Hall, Limor Ast, Nura Mowzoon, Siva Jeya, Tali Yuz, Shay Alexander, Laura Mantell, and Kimberley Dockery. All of the staff, including our receptionist, Maryann Sargeant, helped us hone and further develop our thinking. Early on, Jennifer Sneeden found and summarized portions of the research literature, and she contributed significantly to Chapter 5.

Colleagues, friends, and family members provided expert advice and consultation, read and commented on drafts of various chapters, and offered ongoing support. We are grateful for the contributions of Shelley Green, Eric Flemons, Jenna Flemons, William Rambo, Honggang Yang, Scott Poland, Erin Procacci, Arnold Hartman, Daniel Castellanos, Arlene Gordon, Jim Hibel, John Miller, Ward Flemons, Tom Flemons, Don and Isabel Flemons, Pearl and Sidney Gralnik, Jordan Gralnik, Herb and D'Aun Tavenner, Bill and Judy Brown, Valerie Judd, Stan Weaver, David Prentice, Suzanne Rouleau, Michael O'Neill, Jerry Gale, Ron Chenail, Pat Cole, Genevieve LaFleur, Jon Brunner, Terry DiNuzzo, and Pete Musso.

Graduate students—Mike Pusateri, Amy Heinowitz, and Oren Schwartz—helped locate articles and other background material. Douglas's graduate assistant, Nozomu Ozaki, found new articles for us and, using digital bibliographic software, upgraded the reference list and double-checked it for accuracy.

We were fortunate that several clinic directors, program administrators, and clinical supervisors—Arlene Gordon, Tommie Boyd, Martha Marquez, Martha Laughlin, Kate Warner, Mary Neal, Randy Heller, and Shelley Green—generously offered to adopt and road-test early versions of our Risk and Resource Interview Guide. We found their feedback invaluable.

Colleagues, as well as conference and workshop organizers—Eugenio Rothe, Karl Tomm, Rich Simon, Nicole Ovedia, Vicente Martínez, and Jackie Rosen—invited us to present our work-in-progress in Canada, Mexico, and the United States. Preparing for and delivering these talks helped us to better organize and refine our ideas.

Our students, staff, and supervisees challenged us to reflect more deeply and explain more clearly; our clients and patients challenged us to listen and engage more empathically.

As usual, the wonderful folks at Norton—Deborah Malmud, Kevin Olsen, Sophie Hagen, Margaret Ryan, and their assistants—managed to balance professional insight and perspective with patience and warm encouragement: a most welcoming combination.

We are deeply grateful to everyone.

FOREWORD

WHEN I WAS a graduate student in clinical psychology, the very first client I worked with at the local VA hospital took his life. In my 35 years of clinical work since then, I have worked with countless suicidal clients, supervised clinical graduate students who have had clients who died by suicide, and consulted at many residential treatment centers where the need for suicide risk assessment was warranted (Meichenbaum, 2005, 2012).

As noted in Table 1, I am not alone in addressing this clinical challenge. Work with suicidal clients is considered the most stressful of all clinical endeavors. Therapists who lose a client to suicide experience that loss as they would the death of a family member. It can be a career-ending event. Such distress to psychotherapists can be further exacerbated by possible legal entanglements. Twenty-five percent of family members of clients who die by suicide take legal action against the client's mental health treatment team (Bongar, 2002).

TABLE 1. CLINICAL PRACTICE AND CLIENT SUICIDE

- Full-time psychotherapists average 5 suicidal patients per month.
- 1 in 3 psychiatrists and 1 in 7 psychologists report losing a patient to suicide.
- 1 in 3 clinical graduate students will have a client who attempts suicide, and 1 in 6 will experience a client's suicide at some point during their careers.
- 1 in 6 psychiatric patients who die by suicide die while in active treatment with a health care provider.
- Completed suicides often take place soon after individuals are treated by a mental health provider.

I wish that when I was a graduate student in clinical psychology, beginning my work with suicidal clients, I had had this book on relational suicide assessment by Douglas Flemons and Leonard Gralnik. Even now, as a seasoned clinician, I learned from their clinical perspicacity, their ability to weave clinical case vignettes with scholarly critical literature reviews, and their practical suggestions for conducting relational assessments. In their relational approach, they highlight the contextual nature of suicidal behavior and the value of a resource-guided framework.

Flemons and Gralnik emphasize the need to consider both risks and protective factors (or, as they say, resources) in any suicide assessment. In particular, what I found most valuable was the systematic way they offered an explanatory model of how four classes of variables can guide the interviewing and assessment processes: 1) the *disruptions and demands* affecting the client, 2) the client's subsequent *suffering*, and 3) the nature of the client's *troubling behaviors* that can contribute to his or her sense of 4) *desperation* and desire for relief. These concepts come alive as they are continually illustrated with clinical case vignettes and by the inclusion of artful questioning.

Flemons and Gralnik are talented clinicians who think aloud throughout their book. This is particularly evident in Chapter 5, where they demonstrate in detail how to formulate a collaborative, client-generated safety plan. All clinicians should have their eight-step safety plan guidelines on their desks (if not in their heads) when working with suicidal clients:

1) Identifying Resourceful Significant Others (SO)
2) Restricting Access to the Means of Suicide (RA)
3) Exploring Alternatives to Troubling Behaviors (TB)
4) Establishing Safe Havens (SH)
5) Helping Alter Demanding Schedules (DS)
6) Encouraging Treatment (ET)
7) Mobilizing Personal Resources (PR)
8) Identifying and Employing Emergency Resources (ER)

These steps should be part of every clinician's repertoire, as should a commitment to thoroughly documenting how they were implemented in the session.

The authors provide multiple examples of how to conduct "possibility-focused" interventions, demonstrating a clinical style that highlights the value of "empathic knowing" as a way to enter the world of their clients. They invite their clients to become curious and perform personal experiments, noting the variations in and exceptions to presenting problems. In this way, suicidal clients can change their relationship to their problems, recognizing patterns and undertaking small doable changes. The authors therapeutically "sprinkle implications of strength and possibility" into the assessment discourse and, in so doing, "establish a context for hope" (p. 68).

Effective psychotherapists are good storytellers, and Flemons and Gralnik are among the very best. Kudos!

—Donald Meichenbaum, Ph.D.

Donald Meichenbaum is Distinguished Professor Emeritus at the University of Waterloo in Ontario, Canada. He serves as the research director of the Melissa Institute for Violence Prevention in Miami, Florida (www.melissainstitute.org).

PREFACE

A family therapist and a psychiatrist walk into a clinic . . .

OUR COLLABORATION STARTED in 2004, when Douglas, a family therapist and director of a student counseling center, hired Len, a psychiatrist, as the center's medical director. We worked together as clinical colleagues for 6 years, during which time we, along with the center's professional staff, routinely assessed and provided therapeutic services for acutely and chronically suicidal students.

This book had its inception in the trainings we co-developed for our staff. Len drew on the research literature and his earlier experience working as a psychiatrist and medical director in a community mental health clinic to highlight the primary suicide risk factors to which the counselors should attend. He also outlined the procedures for conducting an effective psychiatry-informed evaluation with patients. Douglas, steeped in the relational and resource-based foundations of his field, as well as his experience as a therapist and supervisor, encouraged the counselors to balance their attention to risks with a curiosity about resources, and he stressed the importance of grasping the clients' experience within the context of their relationships with significant others.

Our staff told us that the approach to assessment emerging from the juxtaposition of our respective points of view gave them a depth and uniqueness of understanding unavailable when either was considered alone. We, too, recognized and appreciated the synergistic effects of our collaboration. As we continued conducting assessments and offering trainings together, we decided to shape our ideas into a manuscript, and now, 8 years later, we have refined a method that we think does justice to both perspectives.

One area where we couldn't find common ground was what to call the people who come to us for therapy and assessments. Clients? Patients? We

aren't entirely comfortable with either. The word *patient* doesn't offer enough
sense of agency and possibility to convey the resourcefulness of our clients,
and *client* overemphasizes the business transaction side of our therapeutic
work with patients. In the end, we decided that any term other than these
two traditional ones would sound too awkward, so we settled on *client* as the
more ubiquitously accepted term.

As clinical and medical directors, we were committed to assuring that our
staff felt prepared and resourceful when assessing for suicidality. We maintain
the same commitment as authors. We want you to be fluent with the research
literature, so you know which risks and resources are important to ask about
and why, and we want you to know how to juxtapose that professional knowledge with your empathically derived gut sense of the client's mindset. We
want you to know how to use empathy as a means of entering your clients'
worlds, giving you an insider's glimpse of their suffering and potential, and
giving them the experience of feeling heard and understood. We want you to
know how to pose questions so that the assessment can be as informative as
possible for you and as therapeutic as possible for your clients. We want you
to know how to deal with the inevitable, pervasive uncertainty that suffuses
all suicide assessments *and* arrive at a decision about the client's safety that
embodies your empathic appreciation for both danger and possibility. And
we want you to know how to collaborate with your clients on developing
safety plans that address all the critical issues you're figuring out together.

We've illustrated the ideas throughout the book with cases from our joint
time in the Student Counseling Center, as well as from our clinical work in
other settings. We've protected confidentiality by changing names, altering
identifying details, and, on occasion, combining aspects of more than one
case, perhaps from more than one clinic, into a single narrative or vignette.
Young adults are perhaps over-represented in the stories, but not in the literature we used to shape the structure and content of the Risk and Resource
Interview Guide (RRIG) in Chapter 3. The relational approach to suicide assessment that is sketched in the forthcoming pages is relevant for at-risk individuals of all ages, including those who belong to particularly at-risk groups,
such as military personnel and the lesbian–gay–bisexual–transgendered–
questioning (LGBTQ) community.

We hope the book provides you with the necessary ideas and tools to help
you confidently and compassionately conduct assessments with people desperately in search of relief. The work you do is profoundly difficult and vitally
important. Our thoughts and respect go out to you.

Douglas Flemons & Len Gralnik
Fort Lauderdale, Florida, June 2012

RELATIONAL
SUICIDE ASSESSMENT

1

FOUNDATIONS

SUICIDE ASSESSMENTS ARE relational conversations, interactive dialogues that trace back and forth across the sometimes too thin line separating death from life—back and forth between giving up and going on, between pulling away and reaching out, between hopeless certainties and faint-hope possibilities. It takes considerable patience and empathic curiosity to engage your clients in traversing these borders and to explore together the territories that lie on either side. As you undertake that challenge, you need to know how to make sense of what you're discovering and what to do with what you're coming to understand. The demands are great; the stakes are high.

If you were to fail to adequately pick up, say, on a young woman's airless desperation, her determination to end her suffering, her paranoia, or her drug-fueled impulsivity, you could incorrectly decide that she was not in imminent danger of dying when she actually was. It is sobering that many completed suicides take place soon after the individuals see a mental health or medical professional (Appleby et al., 1999).[1] Alternatively, if you were to overreact to the danger signs you noticed, say, in talking with an older man, and you took steps to involuntarily hospitalize him when his circumstances and state of mind didn't actually warrant such a disruptive intervention, you'd risk undermining his trust in you and in other helping professionals, increasing the likelihood that he wouldn't return to see you, or anyone else, if things were to get worse. The American Psychiatric Association wisely recommends that, in general, patients with suicidal thoughts, plans, or behaviors "should be treated in the setting that is least restrictive yet most likely to prove safe and effective" (American Psychiatric Association, 2003, p. 52).

No wonder, then, that reliable means for accurately assessing suicidality are so sought-after. Under the gun to be right and with the consequences of being wrong hanging in the balance, we all desire accuracy and certainty in our noticing and our knowing. Some degree of accuracy is certainly possible, but it is accurate to say that certainty is impossible. Social scientists can predict the tendencies of groups, but never the idiosyncratic behavior of an individual. As Gregory Bateson (1979) put it, *"The generic we can know, but the specific eludes us"* (p. 45, italics in original).

In an attempt to render the elusive less so, researchers and clinicians have developed a variety of strategies designed to assess suicidality, from general screening devices[2] and self-report inventories for individual clients[3] to clinician-administered rating scales,[4] semistructured clinical interviews,[5] practice guidelines,[6] and overarching evidence-based protocols.[7] Our approach—Relational Suicide Assessment (RSA)—shares attributes with, and differs in important respects from, each of these methods. In order to better clarify what we do and why we do it, we'd like to say a few words about five approaches that we have found particularly helpful: the Scale for Suicide Ideation (Beck, Kovacs, & Weissman, 1979); the Reasons for Living Inventory (Linehan, Goodstein, Nielsen, & Chiles, 1983); the Suicide Assessment Decision Tree (Joiner, Walker, Rudd, & Jobes, 1999); the Chronological Assessment of Suicide Events (Shea, 2002); and the Collaborative Assessment and Management of Suicidality (Jobes, 2006). We'll then discuss how *we* manage the challenges and complexities of conducting effective assessments.

Aaron Beck and colleagues' Scale for Suicide Ideation (SSI) (Beck et al., 1979) is considered a classic among clinician-administered suicide assessments (Range, 2005). Composed of 19 items, worded both positively (e.g., assessing the wish to live) and negatively (e.g., assessing the wish to die), the SSI is balanced and comprehensive. A self-report version has also been developed (the SSI-SR). The SSI follows Beck's earlier Hopelessness Scale (Beck, Weissman, Lester, & Trexler, 1974), which helped determine that suicide is more highly correlated with hopelessness than with depression. Beck's work sensitized us early on to the crucial importance of expectancy in assessing for suicidality.

In 1983, Marsha Linehan and her colleagues introduced the Reasons for Living Inventory, which presents 48 reasons for not acting on thoughts of suicide—for example, "I believe that I could cope with anything life has to offer"; "My religious beliefs forbid it"; and "It would not be fair to leave the children for others to take care of"—and asks respondents to rate, on a 6-point Likert scale, how important each would be in helping to protect them should they be suffering from suicidal ideation. We don't give our clients rating scales to complete; however, we appreciate these authors' recognition that it is possible to inquire about risks by asking questions framed in a positive manner. For example, you could apply Beck's recognition of the importance of hopelessness by asking a client directly, "How hopeless are you?"

Alternatively, you could access the same realm of experience by putting a "Linehanian" spin on the question: "This has been an exhausting and painful time for you. How much hope do you have that things will improve?" The therapeutic implications of such a questioning strategy are elaborated in Chapters 2 and 3.

Thomas Joiner and his colleagues have worked hard to "scientize and routinize" the process of assessing suicidal risk (Joiner et al., 1999). Drawing on both empirical and clinical research, they organize suicidality into three domains of experience: suicidal desire, suicidal capability, and suicidal intent. They advise the clinician to consider each of these three domains, both individually and in combination, as a means of determining the client's level of risk. They also highlight the importance of attending to buffers—for example, reasons for living, social support, and a collaborative relationship with a professional caregiver—that may be ameliorating the severity of the suicidality.

Like Joiner, we are committed to providing clinicians with an effective assessment framework, grounded in research findings and attuned to both risks and protective factors. We differ, however, in how we conceptualize the decision-making process. Rather than attempting to compress the complexity of the client's mindset and circumstances into a single point along a continuum of risk, we strive to retain the multidimensional richness of the information we gather in the process of making a decision about the client's safety. Our means for doing so are thoroughly explained in Chapter 4.

Recognizing that for an approach to suicide assessment to prove useful, it needs to be easily learned, remembered, and taught, Shawn Christopher Shea (2002) proposed a chronological structuring of assessment interviews. He advises clinicians to organize their questions into "four contiguous time frames[,] extending from the distant past to the present" (p. 152), in the following order:

1. The presenting suicidal ideation and behaviors.
2. Any recent suicidal ideation and behaviors (over the preceding 8 weeks).
3. Past suicidal ideation and behaviors.
4. Immediate suicidal ideation and future plans for its implementation.

We share Shea's commitment to defining a user-friendly method, as well as his sensitivity to the therapeutic possibilities of suicide assessments (p. 174) and his recognition that the validity of the information you gather depends on the quality and kinds of questions you pose (pp. 126–137).[8] We make the assumption that infusing a suicide assessment with a therapeutic sensibility alters it beneficially for everyone involved. When you engage empathically with your client, you are each less likely to feel alienated by the process, and when you bring your therapeutic curiosity into the equation, the tone and parameters of the assessment shift. You learn information that wouldn't otherwise have come into play, giving you and the client access to expanded potential response options.

Like David Jobes (2006), we recognize the importance of collaborating with clients. His Collaborative Assessment and Management of Suicidality (CAMS) approach stresses "the importance of seeing the world through the patient's eyes and forming a more viable therapeutic alliance" (p. 47). Jobes encourages collaboration by physically sitting next to his client, working with him or her to complete a Suicide Status Form, and then proceeding with the coauthoring of a treatment plan, including a "crisis response plan" (p. 27). We encourage it by inviting the client into an engaged conversation, a dialogue that twists and turns, touching on and delving into relevant issues, and, when appropriate, the interactive development and virtual testing of a safety plan. Our approach involves a semistructured interview, rather than a written assessment tool, but common to both CAMS and RSA is the recognition that the client, "who is the expert of his or her own experience" (Jobes, p. 41), needs to be "an active collaborator in clinical care" (p. 41).

RELATIONAL SUICIDE ASSESSMENT

Unlike self-report inventories, an RSA is not a paper-and-pencil instrument that can be completed by clients themselves. And although it is designed to help you determine, as thoroughly as possible, your clients' risk of suicide, it doesn't purport to measure a quantifiable amount of "suicidality." It is informed by sociological, epidemiological, and clinical research on risk and protective factors; however, the method doesn't lend itself to the generation of reliability and validity data, and it won't help you assign the equivalent of an objective "risk score" or "danger score" that you can use in your decision-making.

It could be argued that some form of quantitative measurement is an inherent part of any assessment process. After all, the word *assessment* originally referred to the judicial estimation of money a person or community owed in taxes—a sum arrived at, no doubt, by adding and subtracting amounts of assets and debts. However, clinicians deal not with quantities of capital but with patterns of relationship—interactions informing, comprising, and weaving together clients' thoughts, emotions, behaviors, urges, sensations, images, and social networks (Flemons, 2002). In this realm, in the informational world of mind (Bateson, 2000), there are no "things" to add and subtract, so no "bottom-line" conclusions about personal safety (or anything else) can be drawn with arithmetic simplicity and objective neutrality. "It is impossible, in principle, to explain any pattern by invoking a single quantity. . . . Quantity and pattern are of different logical type and do not readily fit together in the same thinking" (Bateson, 1979, p. 58). Thus, when conducting an RSA, we set our sights on deriving a gestalt appreciation for—a patterned sense of—the clients' current experience, woven from the threads of our conversation with them.

Eschewing quantitative thinking as much as possible in our work, we align our approach in accord not with the original use of the word *assessment*, but rather with its etymology, which derives from the Latin *assidēre*, "to sit by." We conduct our assessments by conversing with our clients, sitting, in effect, alongside them,[9] doing our best to enter their experiential worlds so as to get a sense of the logic and details of their lives from *their* perspectives. In this effort, we are influenced, in part, by the qualitative research tradition of ethnography. Rather than using surveys as a means of gleaning information from a broad spectrum of people, ethnographers use *themselves* as a research instrument, typically relying on participant observation (immersing themselves in the cultural practices of the people they are studying) and in-depth semistructured interviews as data-gathering techniques. As will become clear in Chapters 3 and 4, our participant observation is limited to the exercising of our empathic imaginations while talking with our clients (we don't go and live with them for a year, as a traditional ethnographer would, nor do we conduct home visits, as a traditional home-based family therapist would). However, our suicide assessments do share important commonalities with ethnographic semistructured interviews and, as we are conducting them, we endorse an ethnographic sensibility:

> Ethnographers adopt a particular stance toward people with whom they work. By word and by action, in subtle ways and direct statements, they say, "I want to understand the world from your point of view. I want to know what you know in the way you know it. I want to understand the meaning of your experience, to walk in your shoes, to feel things as you feel them, to explain things as you explain them. . . ." (Spradley, 1979, p. 34)

In the realm of therapy, this sensibility is termed *empathy*, and we embrace it not just as a way of connecting with clients, not just as a communication technique, but as a core component of the therapeutic process, a crucial means for getting a reliable sense of the complex layers of client circumstances and mindsets, as well as for making potentially life-and-death clinical decisions. Chapter 2 delves into the therapeutic principles informing our work, but, as a preliminary, we'd like to offer an overview of what we mean by the term *therapeutic* and how this perspective orients our assessments. We'll then provide a quick sketch of the details of the RSA process.

THERAPEUTIC CONVERSATIONS

The Greek root of the word *therapy* means "healing," which in turn derives from the Old Saxon word *hal*, meaning to "make whole." As Karl Tomm (1988) notes, therapists "always [assume] a special role in a conversation for healing. This role entails a commitment to be helpful with respect to the personal problems and interpersonal difficulties of the other" (p. 1). If an assessment is to be not only informative to the clinician but also therapeutically helpful to the client, it must be conducted with an appreciation for the potential of the conversation to begin the process of making whole, of healing. Such an appreciation is realized by striving for conversations that are collaborative, empathically grounded, and oriented towards discovering possibilities.

• *Collaborative conversations*: To complete an adequate suicide assessment, you necessarily need to ask multiple questions, many of which must be probing and direct. However, if you aren't careful, your client, subjected to an onslaught of queries, can end up feeling interrogated, assaulted by your laser-focused curiosity. We take seriously the Latin roots of the word *conversation*: *con-*, together/altogether, and *versare*, to turn—to "turn together." Rather than firing a unidirectional line of questions at our clients, we strive for the interview to feel as informal and fluid as possible. We intersperse empathic comments throughout the conversation, and we remain flexible about when and how we turn and return to the questions that need to be asked.

• *Empathically grounded conversations*: Given how anxiety-provoking it is to talk with a person who is seriously contemplating suicide, objective detachment can beckon as the most desirable stance for conducting an accurate evaluation and making a safe and valid clinical determination. We, however, head in the opposite direction, convinced that gaining empathic entry into a client's experience is best for acquiring reliable information and making wise safety decisions. Our goal is not to remain objectively removed but, rather, to become empathically connected. In keeping with Mary Catherine Bateson

(1994), we treat empathy as a "legitimate, conscious discipline, . . . a form of knowing, leading to effective action" (p. 141).

- *Possibility-focused conversations*: Questions not only make an ostensible request for information, they also define the parameters delimiting the client's search for answers. Thus, they are never merely a means of gathering data; they are also, always, interventions (Tomm, 1987). Recognizing this double nature of questions can help you construct your questions so that in the midst of gathering the information you need about the dangers the client is facing, you are simultaneously orienting him or her toward possibilities for change (O'Hanlon & Beadle, 1997). As Strong (2003) recognizes, "Our questions have the capacity to bring forth . . . new perspectives or meanings . . . [and] invite and mobilise client positions and actions" (p. 264). You can reinforce this capacity by interspersing direct questions about strengths throughout the interview:

- "You've found yourself thinking a lot lately about dying and some ways you might make that happen. In the midst of those thoughts, or at different times, do you ever drift into thinking about how to survive? Any ideas about how *that* might happen?"
- "When you hear that voice in your head telling you to hurt yourself, do you always obediently do what you're told, or do you sometimes get a kick out of giving it the finger or turning your back on it or just not taking it seriously?"

And you can also do it by posing questions that are *implicitly* resource-oriented:

- "What advice would you give a depressed friend who is terrified by what he thinks might be hallucinations?" (Implies that the client has helpful knowledge that could be used to help someone who is suffering.)
- "Who do you know who's able to look under the surface of your despair and recognize the determination it has taken to stay alive?" (Implies hidden strength that others may have missed.)

THE RSA PROCESS

When confronted with a client in crisis, you bear responsibility for assessing imminent danger of harm to self or others. However, you are equally responsible for assessing whether the person has the necessary resources available for safely and effectively dealing with the crisis (Jurich, 2001). We agree with

Simon (2011) that "it is important to assess protective factors against suicide to achieve a balanced assessment of suicide risk" (p. 21). This notion of a balanced assessment is in keeping with Jobes's CAMS approach, which highlights the "tremendous value in considering both" (Jobes, 2006, p. 21) a person's reasons for living (Linehan et al., 1983) and his or her reasons for dying "*simultaneously* in the same assessment" (Jobes, p. 21). However, our exploration of resources extends beyond inquiring about the client's reasons for living. As we discuss throughout the next three chapters, client resources include beliefs, stories of resilience, exceptions to prevailing problems, past successes and current skills, strategies for responding to internal and external stressors, and so on.

An unnecessarily pessimistic clinical impression can result from exclusively homing in on problems and risk factors, and an overly optimistic view from primarily attending to mediating factors and exceptions to problems. These are two types of potential tunnel vision that can problematically limit your inquiry; however, there is also a third. Given the isolating nature of suicidal ideation and actions, it is easy to become narrowly focused on the individual client. Of necessity, you are always attempting to determine the state of mind of the person in front of you. But to do this well, you need to attend carefully not only to the individual's unique experiences, but also to the interplay of these experiences with those of significant others (alive and deceased) in his or her social context (Jurich, 2001; Meichenbaum, 2010). As Jobes (2006) points out, "*Homo sapiens* are relational creatures; we live in family units, tribes, villages, and cities. . . . Most suicides can almost always be linked to interpersonal issues" (p. 84). Indeed, according to Joiner (2005), "thwarted belongingness (i.e., thwarted love, ruptured relationships) and perceived burdensomeness (assaulted self-image, fractured control, anger related to frustrated dominance)" together contribute significantly to suicidal desire (p. 96). We are constituted by our relationships with others, and when those relationships are disturbed or troubled, our relationship to life itself can be undermined. In contrast, positive relationships—those characterized by trust, respect, caring, and meaningful engagement—can serve as profound protections for those facing pain and suffering.

To avoid all forms of tunnel vision, an RSA involves three imbricated steps. First, you empathically explore both risks and resources, not only in the *intra*personal realm of the client's world, but also the *inter*personal. Second, you come to a decision about the potential for safety by juxtaposing all available information, allowing a sense of the whole to develop. And third, when warranted and possible, you and the client collaboratively develop a detailed safety plan.

1. Empathically Exploring Risks and Resources in the Client's World

Most clinicians embarking on a suicide assessment know the importance of inquiring about ideation, a concrete plan, and access to means. However, researchers have demonstrated the importance of many other risk factors as well. Joiner (2005) conducted a quick search of websites related to suicide and psychology and found over 75 risk factors or warning signs listed (p. 207). Some of the more commonly accepted risk factors include hopelessness[10]; previous threats and attempts[11]; mood and emotional problems and instability, including depression,[12] bipolar disorder,[13] posttraumatic stress disorder (PTSD),[14] panic,[15] and anxiety[16]; self-harming behaviors[17]; intensive psychiatric involvement[18] and psychiatric hospitalization[19]; substance abuse[20]; psychotic symptoms (including hallucinations and delusions)[21]; a family history of suicide attempts[22]; neuropsychological dysfunction[23]; access to firearms[24]; recent losses[25]; sleep disturbances, including nightmares[26]; a history of physical and/or sexual abuse[27]; sexual orientation[28]; chronic pain[29] and medical conditions[30]; unwanted pregnancy[31]; and stress related to school,[32] work,[33] and legal entanglements.[34]

Such research is important; indeed, as you'll see in Chapter 3, the results of these and many other studies have contributed to both the content and organization of our method. However, when you are sitting in front of a particular client, it is necessary to remember that the studies are epidemiological or sociological in nature—they can tell you a lot about *groups* of people, but they can't and don't translate directly to individuals. Smoking, for example, is a risk factor (Breslau, Schultz, Johnson, Peterson, & Davis, 2005), as is a history of moving frequently as a child (Qin, Mortensen, & Pederson, 2009), but that doesn't mean that your warning bells should start ringing loudly just because you have a pack-a-day smoker or former "military brat" sitting in front of you. Henden (2008) puts it this way: "It is not . . . simply an awareness of the main risk factors which is helpful, but also . . . an understanding of the uniqueness of the person presenting" (p. 36). Shea (2002) is even more forthright: "Not a single piece of research has shown that the presence of any collection of risk factors can accurately predict the imminent dangerousness of a client" (p. 70). We use research results to inform, but not dictate, our curiosity about each individual client.

In Chapter 3 we bring this broad brushstroke awareness into clinical relevance, distilling the results of risk- and protective-factor research (and our clinical experience) into 51 topics of inquiry, distributed within four broad categories of suicide-related experience—*disruptions and demands, suffering, troubling behaviors,* and *desperation.* The result is organized into what ethnographers call an *interview guide*—an organizing document that comprises "a listing of areas to be covered in the interview along with, for each area, a listing of topics or questions that together will suggest lines of inquiry. The guide functions for the interviewer as a prompter might for an actor" (Weiss, 1994, p. 48). In our clinically oriented guide, each topic is introduced with a brief discussion of the research findings and/or clinical cases that support its inclusion. We call it the *Risk and Resource Interview Guide* (RRIG).

Ethnographic interview guides typically offer qualitative researchers a series of "themes to be covered, as well as some suggested questions. Yet at the same time there is openness to changes of sequence and forms of questions in order to follow up the answers given and the stories told" (Kvale, 1996, p. 124). The RRIG similarly provides you with sample questions (along with an accompanying commentary) that illustrate how to bring each possible risk and resource into a clinically relevant dialogue with a client.

Researchers and clinicians alike devote themselves to ensuring the credibility of the information they collect. Quantitative researchers establish the reliability of their data by statistically estimating the degree to which the answers given by a group of respondents completing a questionnaire or survey today consistently line up—all other things being equal (including the sameness of the circumstances)—with the answers they would have given at an earlier or later time. Qualitative interviewers also establish the reliability of their data, but they don't do it statistically. Instead, they attend to it in the process of gathering the information, circling back to touch on the same issues at different times during the conversation. This qualitative approach gives researchers the ability to compare the consistency of the respondents' answers.

When you conduct an RSA, you may bring the client back to the most pertinent topics multiple times throughout the course of the conversation, approaching them from different angles and asking about them with different kinds of questions and/or with different emphases. This approach allows you to develop a sense of your client's consistency of response, but it also creates opportunities for the client to correct your misunderstandings, add new layers, elaborate on details, and reveal what had earlier remained unspoken. Thus, the process of the conversation itself helps you get a feel for how confident you can be in your observations.

This use of the process of the conversation as a means of validating your clinical impressions touches on another important aspect of an RSA. The information you gather is about various relationships in the client's world—those between the client and his or her experience (including thoughts, sensations, perceptions, emotions, images, behaviors, desires, and choices);

those between the client and his or her significant others; and those between the client and possibilities for safety and therapeutic change. By attending not only to all this content-based relationship information, but also to the *process* of the conversation you're having, you are able to also take into account the unfolding relationship between the client and *you* (Rudd, 2006). How is the client engaging with you? Is she forthcoming, or do you sense that she doesn't trust you? Is he making eye contact? Are your questions upsetting her or calming her down? Does he provide thoughtful, in-depth responses, or do you feel like a dentist trying to extract a tooth? Is she expressing an interest in getting some kind of help? The answers to such questions are critical in helping you develop a sense of the client's relationship to suicide.

In Chapter 5 we present an annotated transcript of a sample RSA. Among other things, it illustrates this aspect of conducting an effective interview— the process of connecting empathically and exploring relevant topics of inquiry in a relationally balanced way.

2. Coming to a Safety Decision

According to the American Psychiatric Association (2003), "the estimation of suicide risk, at the culmination of the suicide assessment, is the quintessential clinical judgment" (p. 24). From our perspective, clinical judgment is quintessentially a decision about the client's safety that takes shape, often gradually and seldom linearly, over the course of a suicide assessment, informed by an empathic grasp of the client's intra- and interpersonal risks *and* resources. In order to come to a decision about the client's potential for staying safe over the coming days, you must continually juxtapose different sources of information throughout the session:

- Your empathic grasp of the client's intrapersonal and interpersonal risks and resources.
- Your perceptions of the client's engagement with you in the assessment process, including his or her response to your empathic comments, to your questions, to your therapeutic suggestions (both direct and implicit), and to the development and possible implementation of the safety plan (see Step 3, below).
- Your insider (empathic) and outsider (professional) sense of whether the safety plan *feels* safe.

For reasons outlined earlier, we don't believe it makes sense to try to metaphorically "weigh" or quantify these data as a means for decision-making. Instead, we again turn to qualitative researchers for inspiration. They analyze their data by juxtaposing information from various sources, allowing under-standing to "emerge" from the ongoing comparisons. There is an appreciation in this process not only of analytical (outsider or professional) understanding, but also of body-based (empathy-informed) knowing and inductive reason-ing. As we elaborate in Chapter 4, understanding and decision-making syner-gistically coalesce through focused, absorbed juxtaposition of relevant data.

3. Collaboratively Developing a Detailed Safety Plan

Douglas once saw a client who thought about the benefits of suicide when nothing else would work to calm her down. By reminding herself that she had "an exit plan if things were to get too rough," she was able to "keep plugging along." When a person is overwhelmed and hopeless, death can seem like the only way out of an impossible predicament, the only way of achieving relief or peace. This third step of an RSA entails exploring with a client whether it is possible for him or her, with help perhaps from significant others, to safely negotiate the dangerous territory of suicidal ideation, desires, urges, plans, and access to means. If it does seem possible and appropriate, then you can collaborate on etching out a detailed (but not overly elaborate) plan that you can both endorse.

To be adequately comprehensive and protective, a safety plan needs to anticipate dangers, identify resources, specify action steps, account for worst-case scenarios, facilitate communication, and detail plans for follow-up. The guidelines below—which together comprise the Safety Plan Construction Guide (SPCG), presented in Chapter 4—offer ideas for the brainstorming and writing down of possibilities, options, alternatives, and choices:

   I. Identify significant others who could assist in implementing rele-vant details of the safety plan.
  II. Work out how to prevent and/or restrict access to means for mak-ing a suicide attempt.
 III. Explore reasonable alternatives to troubling behaviors for coping with distress.
  IV. Identify safe havens the client could, if necessary, access for a lim-ited time.
   V. Consider the possibility of the client's taking a leave of absence from work and/or school.
  VI. Determine if the client would consider initiating, resuming, or con-tinuing psychotherapeutic and/or medical treatment.

VII. Generate a list of personal resources the client could contact if necessary.

VIII. Identify emergency resources the client could access if necessary.

Chapter 4 describes, and Chapter 5 illustrates, how to develop a safety plan and how to gauge whether it is, indeed, safe and doable. In Chapter 4, we also clarify the important differences between safety plans and no-harm contracts and explain why our commitment to the former is matched by our avoidance of the latter.

As you will see in Chapter 3, the *content* of the RSA method—the specific risks and resources represented in the 51 topics of inquiry contained in the RRIG— was significantly informed by the research literature on suicide. However, the *design* of the method—the relational structure of the RRIG and the details of the interview process (how to gather information, come to a safety decision, and collaborate on the development of a safety plan)—owes much to the assumptions we hold about the relational nature of experience, language, and therapeutic change. Chapter 2 is devoted to delineating and illustrating principles derived from these assumptions.

NOTES

1 Appleby et al. (1999) reported in a large U.K. study that 50% of people who committed suicide had been in contact with mental health services in the week before death. At final contact, the clinicians had estimated immediate risk of suicide as absent in 30%, low in 54%, moderate in 13%, and high in 2% (pp. 1235–1239).

2 For example, Teen Screen (Shaffer et al., 2004); Paykel Suicide Items (Paykel, Myers, Lindenthal & Tanner, 1974); The Symptom Driven Diagnostic System for Primary Care (Broadhead et al., 1995); Suicidal Ideation Screening Questionnaire (SIS-Q; Cooper-Patrick, Crum, & Ford, 1994).

3 For example, The Beck Scale for Suicide Ideation (BSI; Beck & Steer, 1991); The Suicide Intention Probability Scale (SPS; Cull & Gill, 1982); The Suicide Probability Scale (Huth-Bocks, Kerr, Ivey, Kramer, & King, 2007).

4 For example, The Scale for Suicide Ideation (SSI; Beck, Kovacs, & Weissman, 1979); The Scale for Suicide Ideation-Worst (SSI-W; Beck, Brown, & Steer, 1997); and the Suicide Status Form-III (Jobes, 2006).

5 For example, Chronological Assessment of Suicide Events (CASE; Shea, 2002).

6 For example, *Practice Guideline for the Assessment and Treatment of Patients with Suicidal Behaviors* (American Psychiatric Association, 2003); *Recognizing and Responding to Suicide Risk: Essential Skills for Clinicians* (American Association of Suicidology, 2008).

7 For example, The Suicide Assessment Decision Tree (Joiner, Walker, Rudd, & Jobes, 1999).

8 The notion that an assessment could be therapeutic in intent and effect is not limited

to Shea's or our work or, for that matter, to the assessment of suicide. Stephen Finn and colleagues (e.g., Finn, 2007; Finn & Tonsager, 2002), guided by what they identify as core humanistic values—collaboration, humility, respect, compassion, and openness/curiosity (Finn, 2009)—have developed a therapeutic approach to conducting various psychological assessments (e.g., MMPI-2; Rorschach).

9 Whereas our suggestion to "sit alongside" clients is metaphorical (we *physically* sit across from them while *imagining* ourselves next to them, surveying their experience from their vantage), David Jobes (2006), as mentioned above, advocates actually sitting next to clients to facilitate the collaborative filling out of his Suicide Status Form.

10 Beck, Brown, Berchick, Stewart, & Steer, 1990; Beck, Kovacs, & Weissman, 1975; Beck, Steer, Kovacs, & Garrison, 1985; Beck, Weissman, Lester, & Trexler, 1974; Minkoff, Bergman, Beck, & Beck, 1993.

11 Beautrais, 2003; Ostama & Lönnqvist, 2001; Owens, Horrocks, & House, 2002.

12 Angst, Stassen, Clayton, & Angst, 2002; Høyer, Mortensen, & Olesen, 2000.

13 Isometsä, Henriksson, Aro, & Lönnqvist, 1994; Strakowski, McElroy, Keck, & West, 1996; Tondo, Isacsson, & Baldessarini, 2003.

14 *Archives of General Psychiatry*, 2009, 305–311.

15 Weissman, Klerman, Markowitz, & Ouellette, 1989.

16 Norton, Temple, & Pettit, 2008.

17 Stanley, Gameroff, Michalsen, & Mann, 2001.

18 Bostwick & Pankratz, 2000; Harris & Barraclough, 1997.

19 Pirkis, Burgess, & Jolley, 1999.

20 Adams & Overholser, 1992; Frances, Franklin, & Flavin, 1986; Petronis, Samuels, Moscicki, & Anthony, 1990.

21 Axelsson & Lagerkvist-Briggs, 1992; Hawton, Sutton, Haw, Sinclair, & Deeks, 2005; Pompili, Amador, et al., 2007; Radomsky, Haas, Mann, & Sweeney, 1999.

22 Brent & Mann, 2005; Brent et al., 2002; Mann et al., 2005.

23 Keilp et al., 2001.

24 Miller & Hemenway, 1999.

25 Hall, Platt, & Hall, 1999.

26 Bernert & Joiner, 2007.

27 Joiner et al., 2007; Tiet, Finney, & Moos, 2006.

28 Eisenberg & Resnick, 2006.

29 Walker et al., 2008.

30 Druss & Pincus, 2000; Pompili, Vanacore, et al., 2007; Waern et al., 2002.

31 Pompili, Ruberto, Girardi, & Tatarelli, 2005.

32 Csorba et al., 2001.

33 Stack, 2001.

34 Jobes, 2006.

2

THERAPEUTIC PRINCIPLES

IN THIS CHAPTER, we outline the therapeutic ideas and practices that inform our orientation to assessment. This is not to imply that you need to adopt our therapeutic approach before you can make use of the RSA method in assessing suicidality. Indeed, you can bring this method into any clinical practice, even incorporating it, if you wish, with other means of assessment that you're already comfortable using. Nevertheless, because our approach to assessment is significantly influenced by our understanding of experience and our approach to therapy, we consider it necessary to illuminate some of the philosophical, theoretical, and clinical tenets underpinning our RSA suggestions and recommendations.

Before we get started talking about ideas relevant to both therapy and assessment, though, we should clarify some of the ways the two activities differ. Therapy usually takes place in response to a client's request for help in effecting a change in some realm of his or her experience—freedom from an addiction; a decrease in anger or anxiety; an improvement in mood, sleep, or sex; resolution of an intrapersonal or interpersonal conflict; and so on. In contrast, a suicide assessment is typically undertaken in response to someone—a family member, another professional, or even the client him- or herself—wanting to determine whether the client is in imminent danger of taking his or her life. The ramifications of this shift in context can be felt throughout the assessment process.

Given the vulnerability experienced by clients while undertaking significant change, therapists are always taking safety into account when exploring options and possibilities. However, in a suicide assessment, the issue of staying safe moves front and center, eclipsing, for the time being, other considerations. It's not that the possibility of change isn't taken into account, but that it is now discussed within the context of finding, establishing, and maintaining possibilities for safety.

This gestalt shift in how safety is addressed, moving from background importance to foreground prominence, is accompanied by an adjustment in the collaborative nature of the therapeutic relationship—one that many therapists, including us, find challenging. In a regular therapy session, we encourage and celebrate our client's curiosity and ability to discover and choose, and we offer any suggestions tentatively, respectfully withdrawing or modifying them if the client rejects or is reluctant to embrace them. Primarily adopting what Anderson and Goolishian (1992) termed a "not-knowing" stance, we don't assume that we know what is best for the client, and we limit any claims of expertise to the realm of effecting change.[1] That is, we are willing to say that we are experts in helping clients respond differently to the intra- and interpersonal problems they face and to helping them discover satisfactory resolutions to those problems. But we are forthright in asserting that we are decidedly *not* experts in what clients should do with their lives or in what decisions they should make. Recognizing that therapeutic change often results when clients are comfortable making mistakes, we celebrate error-activated learning and are thus at pains not to tell them what we think they should do or to exclusively support any one side of a choice they are facing.

In a suicide assessment, however, when we are trying to figure out whether a person is in imminent danger of killing him- or herself, we sometimes act unilaterally to prevent what seems to us a too-high possibility of death. If that means arranging an involuntary evaluation at a hospital or taking some other action to secure safety, such as contacting a family member without the client's endorsement, then we take that step. We are willing, when necessary, to take away the client's immediate ability to choose as a means of preserving his or her freedom to make choices in the future. Recognizing that you can't learn from a mistake if the mistake was to kill yourself, we do what we deem necessary in the short term to save the client's life. But such a decision is never made lightly, and we remain exquisitely sensitive to the possibility that such efforts to help, however seemingly warranted, could potentially make matters worse.

Our approach to therapy is informed by how we understand the nature of experience. Inspired by Gregory Bateson's (1979, 2000) communicational theory of mental process and the recognition that mind is embodied (Lakoff & Johnson, 1999), we start with the assumption that sensations, thoughts, and emotions are best conceived of as relational processes, comprised of and contributing to patterns of communication within and between individuals. This relational conception of mind means that when a client comes to us, we are less interested in identifying a reified label to fit his or her suffering—an "anxiety disorder," say, or a "mood disorder," or a "substance-related disorder"—than we are in exploring the relational patterns constituting and contextualizing it.[2] "Problems do not exist as static entities. They are best considered as dynamic processes. If a problem is viewed as a dynamic process, it can be considered a sequence, even though it is perceived as a discrete event" (Zeig, 1994, p. 306).

Reification (from the Latin, rēs, a thing) is inevitable in speech and thought. Most of us can't get beyond a sentence or two without freeze-framing some relationship or process and attributing thing-like properties to the resulting abstraction. The result is what Alfred North Whitehead (1925/1953) termed the "fallacy of misplaced concreteness"—the "error of mistaking the abstract for the concrete" (p. 51). Such misplaced concreteness pervades the world of mental health assessment and treatment. When clinicians diagnose their client or patient, they are thereby inclined to consider the person's problem as an isolable entity, an encapsulated some*thing*, a condition that the client *has*. This assumption in turn tends to invite a particular class of interventions organized around the intention to limit or eliminate the concretized abstraction or condition. If undesirable physical objects can be contained or dispatched, it follows that clients and clinicians alike would approach metaphorical objects—abstract things such as DSM diagnoses or other categorizations—with an analogous approach to goal setting, seeking to control or cure them.[3]

There are obvious benefits that derive from reifying the experiential conundrums we call mental health problems. Without reification, effective psychiatric medications couldn't be researched and prescribed, and clinicians would lose a useful shorthand for communicating about and comparing client dilemmas. However, reification also limits possibilities for assessment and intervention. Clinicians devoted to investigating seemingly discrete, concretized entities (e.g., suicidality or a diagnosable mental illness), and/or to intervening with attempts to do something *to* these categories of experience, risk becoming overly focused on, and possibly exacerbating, the very "things" they are attempting to understand and ameliorate.

Our alternative to conceiving of problems as things is to approach them as *relationships*, as patterns of interaction, unfolding in time at both intra- and interpersonal levels of experience. Informed by Bateson's (1991) idea that we "live in a world that's only made of relationships" (p. 287), we don't attempt to isolate a defined problematic object; instead, we focus on identifying the relationships that compose problematic and resourceful patterns of intrapersonal and interpersonal interactions. This continual focus on relationships allows our curiosity to move freely across the boundaries typically perceived or imposed between the individual and the interpersonal context (the family and the system of helpers), and between the problem and internal and external possibilities for change.

At the intrapersonal level, we concern ourselves with how the strands of a troubling symptom—the component sensations, perceptions, thoughts, images, behaviors, emotions, dreams, assumptions, and/or choices—are weaving the client's distress. We explore, for example, what thoughts or images arise before and after a client's heart starts to pound and her chest begins to constrict; what another client does or avoids doing when the weight of the world is upon him; or what emotional stirring precedes and/or accompanies a third client's choice to pour her next drink. We also attend closely to any exceptions to the seeming inevitability of these patterns (cf. de Shazer, 1985). When has the heart, contrary to what the circumstances would suggest, kept beating normally? Or when has it sped up as usual but, curiously enough, hasn't been accompanied by thoughts and images of suicide? Any times when heavy feelings have felt easier to bear—or have, surprisingly, lifted on their own? Have there been occasions when the next drink doesn't get poured (cf. Berg & Miller, 1992)? How does that choice come about? How does that pattern unfold?

At the interpersonal level, we attend to the client's relationships to his or her significant others, exploring how these relationships contextualize (i.e., pattern) the client's experience, particularly variations in the experience of the problem. How, for example, do the people who matter respond when the client with the pounding heart communicates to them that she is too panicked to leave her house; when the weighted-down client lets slip that he lacks the desire to eat or to go to work; when the hard-drinking client, off on yet another spree, fails to come home? What have significant others done in the past to try to help? Are there actions they've taken or words they've not spoken that have made a significant difference? What was going on with them just before the client's most recent flare-up of the problem? And before that—what was happening with them when things were on a more even keel?

Our interpersonal curiosity also includes within its purview the client's relationship to the therapist and to the therapeutic context. Is the panicky client able to concentrate on the therapist's questions? What has been her response to previous suggestions for change? Does the not-getting-out-of-bed client hold out any hope that talking with a therapist could make a difference? Is the alcohol-bingeing client in our office voluntarily, or does she not believe that her drinking warrants so much worried attention and so is only coming as a half-hearted attempt to mollify a too-worried spouse or parent? Exploring a contextualizing pattern of interaction between the client and family or the client and therapist can contribute much to an appreciation of the patterns weaving the problem and/or to possible solutions.

Whether we are attending to patterns of *intra-* or *inter*personal experience, our focus is always *intrarelational*; that is, directed toward the *inside* of relationships, toward the dynamic patterns of interaction, rather than the points— the "things" or, as Bateson (2000) called them, the *relata*—at either end of them. This intrarelational orientation suffuses our assumptions about the nature of mental health problems and the difficulties and possibilities inherent in working to resolve them. Of course, it also provides the scaffolding for our process of assessing for suicidality, but we'll get to that later, in the next two chapters. Here, we're concerned with articulating the relational shifts that need to happen for the patterns composing the client's problem to unravel— or to change in some way that the client would recognize as "therapeutic."

The first needed shift is in the relationship between the therapist and his or her clients; the second, in one or more of the relationships constituting the problem (cf. Flemons, 2002; Flemons & Green, 2007).

SHIFTING THE RELATIONSHIP BETWEEN THERAPIST AND CLIENTS

Your clients come to you, a stranger, for help with a problem. Because you're not part of their social world, they can feel safe talking to you, and you can feel free to pose questions and offer suggestions that a friend or family member probably couldn't or wouldn't. Your therapeutic effectiveness and professional integrity depend in part on your maintaining your status with clients as a social outsider—just as you can't be your friends' therapist, you can't be your clients' friend. But if you are to be helpful, you must use the safety afforded by this social separation to help your clients risk an experiential connection. You remain a social outsider in order to become an experiential insider.

There are two methods for crossing the experiential boundary that separates you from your clients, two ways for you to gain entry into their world, to become an insider. The first is obvious—you ask questions that, if answered, will help you see their lives from their perspective. The second involves making empathic statements and offering empathic hunches. We'll discuss each in turn.

ASKING QUESTIONS

A 25-year-old woman seeks help because of the "crying jags" and lethargy she's experiencing, as well as the "constant need to make sure everything is in place." The therapist asks, "How long have you been struggling against the depression?"

"For about 3 years," she says.

"And how bad *is* your OCD [obsessive–compulsive disorder] at the moment?"

"It takes me quite a while to leave my apartment, what with all the checking. I used to wash my hands incessantly. They got pretty chapped."

The therapist asks a question, and the client answers it immediately. This is followed by a second question, and the client is again right there with an answer. Perhaps because of the client's lightning-fast response time, the "back-and-forthness" of the process appears simple, not unlike what happens at a fast-food joint: You order a burger, and the cashier grabs one for you, already wrapped and ready to go. You follow up with an order for fries, so he reaches for one of the stuffed-to-overflowing cardboard containers lined up under the heat lamp, and he adds it to your tray.

The seamlessness between the therapist's request for information and the client's retrieval and reporting of a response can leave both of them with the impression that her answer was almost prewrapped, simply being kept warm until the therapist's order for information arrived. But the transaction is more complex, more intricately interwoven, than that. Each of the questions posed to the client pointed her in a particular direction, so that the answers she came up with were in part determined by what the therapist was asking and how he asked it. And that's not all. Extrapolating from the memory research of Elizabeth Loftus, as well as research on expectancy (e.g., Kirsch, 1990), we would argue that the therapist's questions not only affected what the client was invited to think about, but also contributed to the fabric of her experience and her expectations regarding possible change.

Loftus, a research psychologist and distinguished professor at the University of California, Irvine, has devoted her career to investigating how memories can be altered and even created by virtue of how the search for them is instituted. She has conducted multiple studies that consistently demonstrate that the phrasing of a question about an event can influence how the event is interpreted and subsequently remembered. In one of her most famous investigations, Loftus asked 150 undergraduates to watch a short film that included a 4-second multiple-car accident (Loftus & Palmer, 1974). Following the viewing, the students were separated into three groups of 50 each and were asked to write answers to a series of questions about what they'd seen. The series was the same for all three groups, save for one critical question. The first group was asked, "About how fast were the cars going when they smashed into each other?" and the second group, "About how fast were the cars going when they hit each other?" The third (control) group was not asked about speed at all. When the results were analyzed, it was found that the *smashed* group reported a statistically significant faster speed than the *hit* group, which, the researchers suggested, is consistent with the relatively greater strength of the verb *smashed*.

A week later, the students were asked a set of 10 additional questions about the accident, including this one, embedded somewhere in the middle of the set: "Did you see any broken glass?" No glass had in fact broken in the accident, so none was seen in the film, but the "smashed" group answered "yes" to this question at a statistically higher rate than the other two groups. Loftus and Palmer (1974) concluded that the presupposition of greater intensity, contained in the verb *smashed*, primed that group to remember the accident as more severe than it actually was.

So how do presuppositions end up in questions? Well, if you're Elizabeth Loftus, you put them there on purpose so you can study their effects. And if you're a hypnotherapist as adept with implication as Milton Erickson was, you put them there on purpose as a means of inviting hypnotic phenomena to emerge.[4] But most people in conversation, even most therapists, don't purposefully insert presuppositions into their questions as a means of influencing the experience of their listeners. Rather, most presuppositions become insinuated into questions by virtue of the (often unexamined) assumptions held by the questioner.

An assumption is an orienting idea that calibrates or contextualizes a set of other ideas. For example, if a woman considers men inherently untrustworthy, this thought will pervade and thus influence any specific thoughts she has about the activities her husband engages in without her—his upcoming business trip, the night out with his buddies last weekend, the texts he was sending and receiving before leaving for work this morning, and so on. And when she questions him about what he is, has been, or will be doing, the presuppositions in the questions will implicate him with her assumption that her suspicion is warranted: "Why are you afraid to give me the password to your computer?" "Why did you refuse to answer my texts?" "Why are you so secretive about where you'll be staying?"

If the woman's husband strives to answer the questions without unknotting the presuppositions entangling them, he will find himself trying to justify or deny that he is afraid, that he refuses to communicate with her, and that he is secretive. Because presuppositions in questions operate at a contextual level, indirectly communicating assumptions, they contextualize the experience of the person responding to the questions, regardless of how he or she answers them. So unless the husband comments directly on the presence of the presuppositions and challenges their legitimacy, they can invisibly classify, and thus define, him and his behavior, shaping his experience of himself, his reputation within the relationship, and his expectations for himself in the future.[5]

Let's transport this understanding back into a clinical setting by taking a second look at the two questions posed by the therapist seeing the client with crying jags, lethargy, and a need for orderliness: "How long have you been struggling against the depression?" and "How bad *is* your OCD at the moment?" The first question reveals the following presuppositions:

- Crying + lethargy = depression.
- The depression has been going on for some period of time.
- Depression is "other," something separate from your sense of "self."
- This "self" has been engaged in a fight against this "other."

And the second question, these presuppositions:

- Needing everything to be in place = OCD.
- The OCD is "yours"—it is something you *have*.
- OCD is bad.
- There are levels of severity of OCD.
- The severity of OCD can worsen.

These presuppositions suggest, in turn, some presumed assumptions held by the therapist concerning mental health challenges and therapeutic change:

- It is useful to move from the level of experienced symptoms (e.g., crying, lethargy, need for orderliness) to the level of reified abstractions (e.g., diagnostic labels such as depression and OCD).
- It is useful to gather information about the length of time and level of severity of such reified categories.
- It is useful to demonstrate to clients the therapist's facility with diagnosis.

When the client responded to the therapist's two questions, she didn't challenge the presuppositions within them, which meant that they could influence, outside of her or the therapist's awareness, her orientation to her experience, including her expectations regarding the possibility of that orientation changing. The implications of this point are twofold.

First, it means that there is no such thing as a neutral question. "A question constrains the recipient to answer within a framework of presuppositions set by the question. In doing so, the answerer contributes to the perspective imposed by the question and accepts it as a shared perspective" (McGee, Del Vento, & Bavelas, 2005, p. 371). Sure, some questions are more laden with presuppositions than others, but all are posed by *someone* who is inquiring from *some* position and who holds *some* assumptions about what questions are important to ask and why. You must ask questions if you're going to cross the boundary separating you from your clients, but you can never explore their experiential world as a detached, objective visitor, popping in via some neutral queries to unobtrusively observe and jot some notes and then discreetly exit. The assumptions you hold about therapeutic change in general—and, more specifically, about your clients' capacity to change—find their way into the questions you pose, and the resulting presuppositions in those questions partly construct the very experience about which you are inquiring.

Second, researchers in different fields have been showing for some time that "the behavior of students may be affected by the expectancies of their teachers, the behavior of experimental subjects by the expectancies of experimenters, and the behavior of clients by the expectancies of their therapists" (Kirsch, 1990, p. 11). Indeed, "meta-analyses reveal that expectancy can account for at least half of the effectiveness of psychotherapy . . . [and] that expectancy effects can be substantial and long-lasting" (Kirsch, p. 50). Thus, it makes good sense to attend carefully to your assumptions about mental health problems, the nature of therapeutic change, and your clients' capacity to change (i.e., to your expectancy) so that you're aware of what you are communicating, via the presuppositions in your questions, to your clients. The questions you ask to learn about their experience are also contributing to their ability to change that experience.

COMMUNICATING EMPATHIC UNDERSTANDING

Despite the fact that empathic statements and hunches are at least as critical as asking questions for assisting you in becoming an experiential insider, empathy is too often neglected by clinicians, particularly those who think that all the sizzle of therapy is found in the particular classes of questions they pose. Questions transport you across the experiential boundary between you and your clients, but empathy is a transportation device that alters the perception of the boundary itself. According to Carl Rogers (1980),

> An empathic way of being . . . means entering the private perceptual world of the other and becoming thoroughly at home in it. It involves being sensitive, moment by moment, to the changing felt meanings which flow in this other person, to the fear or rage or tenderness or confusion or whatever that he or she is experiencing. It means temporarily living in the other's life, moving about in it delicately without making judgments; it means sensing meanings of which he or she is scarcely aware. . . . It includes communicating your sensings of the person's world as you look with fresh and

unfrightened eyes at elements of which he or she is fearful. It means frequently checking with the person as to the accuracy of your sensings, and being guided by the responses you receive. (p. 142)

To better understand the boundary-shifting effects of empathy, imagine yourself singing in a large choir where the director has you and the others all sustaining the same tone. As you sing, you hear the note you're producing via vibrations conducted through the bones of your skull, and you hear the same note produced by everyone around you via vibrations conducted through the air. A sense of "oneness" with the others envelops you. Why? With such precise matching of internally and externally generated sound, the boundary between "inside" and "outside" disappears, affecting your perception of the boundaries of your "self."

Empathy operates in an analogous, albeit more complex, way. When clients hear empathic statements and hunches from you that accurately reflect what they are conveying to you, they experience the same information being communicated both internally and externally. This allows their perception of the boundary between you and them to become less noteworthy, which shifts their experience of being isolated in pain—they get a sense of being "of one mind" with you (Flemons, 2002), of your being an experiential insider.

Whereas empathic statements give your clients a digested version of what they've been offering to you, empathic hunches make a small leap beyond what they have so far communicated directly. Empathic hunches are informed guesses, offered as tentative statements or questions, of what you imagine they *might be* thinking and/or feeling. Consider, for illustration, the following interchange between a therapist and a woman in her late 20s:

Client: I OD'd on coke last week and ended up in the ER. The doctor looked at my chart and said he couldn't believe I wasn't dead (*laughs*).

Therapist: Must have scared the crap out of you [empathic hunch].

Client: He did . . . it did! I don't want to die (*pause*), but I'm not sure I can quit.

Therapist: You beat the odds—you've been given another chance.

Client: Yes.

Therapist: And it sounds like you don't want to blow it (*pause*), as it were . . .

Client: (*laughs*)

Therapist: . . . because the next time I guess you could easily wake up dead [empathic statement].

Client: Exactly.

Therapist: (*pause*) High stakes [empathic statement].

Client: Crazy high.

Therapist: Yeah. Terrifyingly high [empathic hunch].

Client: (*nods*) Yeah.

Therapist: A safety net would be nice [empathic hunch] . . .

Client: Tell me about it!

Therapist: . . . because you're not yet sure you can quit [empathic statement].

Client: (*quietly*) No, I'm not.

Therapist: Not yet sure you *can* quit or *want to* quit [empathic hunch]?

Client: (*pause*) Both.

Through a series of empathic statements and hunches (and humor, but we'll leave that till the next chapter), the therapist demonstrated that he grasped the particularities and emotional complexities of the client's cocaine-fueled brush with death. As he did so, the client could hear, coming back from the therapist, a translated version of what she herself was expressing, so she was experiencing the same information on both sides of the boundary that separated the two of them. Not unlike a singer in a choir, the client could experience the result of this cross-boundary redundancy as a heightened sense of oneness—the recognition of being understood and a blurring of the experiential boundary that normally separates social strangers.

And a complementary process was going on with the therapist. He was obtaining information from the client and then communicating back to her his imagined sense of what it must be like to have narrowly escaped death, to want to live, and yet to not be sure, given the addictive pull of the cocaine, whether it would be possible to give up the drug before it was too late. Given the accuracy of his empathic hunches, it is clear that he, like the client, had the sense of a blurring of the experiential boundary between them, of their being "of one mind." Maintaining the social boundary that kept him professionally separate, he could use his imagination to create a communicated experiential connection, allowing him, with her assistance, to project himself inside the logic and details of her experience.

We think of this approach as "empathic knowing"—listening closely enough and imagining vividly enough to project ourselves across the self–other experiential boundary. The better we are at grasping and communicating our clients' experience from their perspective, the more our clients are able to trust that we "get" them, and the better our therapeutic alliance. After all, "if a person can be *understood*, he or she *belongs*" (Rogers, 1987, p. 181). More than an attitude, empathic knowing is a commitment to strive for an engaged understanding.

We've had students and supervisees who rolled their eyes or laughed dismissively when mentioning a client. When this has happened, or when someone is holding a client at arm's length in some other way—say, through negative labeling—then we shift the discussion from the "ridiculous" or "irritating" thing the client is doing to the therapist's relationship with the client. Opportunities for change open up when engagement becomes possible.

Soon after joining our staff, one of the counselors in our Student Counseling Center began a group supervision meeting by saying that he wanted to "get some input on how to work with a cutter." Douglas suggested that we could do that by way of exploring how figures of speech, such as the synecdoche he had just employed, influence our experience of clients and our ideas about change. He agreed, so Douglas reminded him and the rest of the staff of the definition they had learned in high school: A *synecdoche* uses a part of something to refer to the whole of it. In this instance, *cutter* places a salient feature in the woman's behavioral repertoire in the foreground and becomes her defining feature. We all do this, all the time, so the question is not how to avoid using synecdoches, but whether the ones you're using result in your feeling resourceful or creative as a therapist. Does anything shift for you, Douglas asked the counselor, if you were to think of this "cutter" as "a young woman who has been cutting"?

As the rest of the staff joined in the discussion, we tossed around the idea that if the client is a *cutter*, then there's nothing in this identity that suggests the possibility of change. That's who she *is*—it comprises all of her. If, instead, she were to be thought of as *a young woman who has been cutting*, then her age and gender individualize her somewhat—she's a step or two closer to being an actual person with a name and a history and whole complex life, and inside that complexity are openings into other possibilities. In addition, her cutting behavior, which of course is a concern, has now been characterized with a tense form[6] that captures what *has been happening*—with the unspoken implication *up until now*—but doesn't determine what might happen *next*. In our meeting and in the new counselor's head, the potential for change had entered the picture, and we hadn't even started exploring the particularities of the case.

Shifting your descriptions of your clients can help you stay open to possibilities, but in and of itself, this won't be enough. You not only have to speak of your clients' humanity, you have to believe it and, in a sense, embody it. If you remain an experiential outsider, your clients can easily appear fickle or irrational or inept—and if that's how you view your caseload, you'll get burned out pretty quickly (more on that below).

You can recognize an outsider mindset by noticing the times you find yourself beset by thoughts such as, "Why doesn't she just leave her abusive husband?!" or "If only he'd do something about his drinking, he could begin getting his life together!" or "Doesn't she see that she's just making it worse?!" In contrast, you'll know you're in insider mode when your clients' distress, choices, and ways of coping make sense to you, when you find yourself thinking, "Of course she hasn't been able to leave! How could she have left before now?" or "Of course he hasn't stopped drinking yet!" or "Of course she's continued trying to make things better, even though her efforts are making them worse!"

Once your clients' dilemmas make empathic sense to you, you're able to sidestep much of the so-called "client resistance" about which some of our colleagues complain. To the degree that your clients experience you as an insider, they won't have to dig in their heels to protect themselves from you, your questions, or your suggestions. But at those times when they do balk, you needn't view their reluctance to go along with you as a result of their hopelessness or intransigence. Greenleaf (1994) recognizes that "across the room from every resistant patient we may encounter a stubborn therapist" (p. 17). If you keep this in mind, then instead of pushing for compliance, you'll figure out the lack of fit between your clients and yourself and look for opportunities to adjust what you're doing and offering. For example, to help facilitate the shift to our being perceived as empathic insiders, we may match aspects of our clients' posture and/or qualities of speech (e.g., volume or intensity) to better grasp the felt realities of their way of being in the world (and to assist them in considering as mostly irrelevant the differences between them and us). If we're seeing a teenage girl who is disappearing into her chair, we don't lean forward in an attempt to engage her, and we don't dismiss her as uncommitted; rather, we reach out by slouching down, not making much eye contact, and making sure we don't sound too upbeat. Indeed, that's just what Douglas did with Rebecca, a 15-year-old high school sophomore.

Rebecca's concerned parents, Gabe and Sheila, joined their daughter in Douglas's office, hoping that if an expert would reiterate what they had been telling her, she might just listen to reason. They had found out a few days earlier that their daughter, who they'd always thought of as lonely and shy, had been performing oral sex on several of the high school football players. Appalled at what they viewed as blatant exploitation and afraid for her health and reputation, they had demanded that she immediately cease and desist, but Rebecca stubbornly refused. She had let them know that she enjoyed the sex, enjoyed her newfound popularity, and had no intention of stopping, regardless of the punishments they threatened to enforce.

Rebecca came to the session girded for an onslaught. It was clear that she wouldn't be listening to anything further her parents had to say, and if Douglas had been naïve enough to side with them against her, he no doubt would have encountered the same "resistance" they had. Instead, he sunk down in his chair, lowered his eyes and voice, and commented on how difficult and embarrassing it must have been to be dragged into see him. She agreed. Douglas made some other empathic comments, directed both to her and her parents, and then he asked Gabe a question that he figured would reassure Rebecca that he wasn't going to gang up against her: "If Rebecca were a guy—say, she was actually your 16-year-old son, Reb, rather than your daughter, Rebecca—and you found out that Reb was performing oral sex on the cheerleaders at the school, would you be in my office today?"

Gabe smiled but took the question seriously, deciding after a moment's hesitation that no, he probably wouldn't be concerned. In fact, he'd probably be proud of a son who was gaining sexual experience and demonstrating his willingness to be a generous lover. Douglas and the parents spoke at some length about the unfairness of our culture's differing expectations and demands for boys and girls, and at some point Rebecca joined the conversation as an equal participant. Later, they got onto the topic of respect and the importance for each of us, particularly around sex, to be able to make our own choices about our bodies and our partners. Rebecca cast a reproachful look at her parents and defiantly agreed with Douglas. She was with him, so he turned to her, this time looking in her eyes, and said, "Rebecca, I have a question for you. There's no need to tell *me* your answer, but I'm curious about something. Do you remember the last time you gave one of the football players a blowjob at a party on the weekend?" She nodded. "You enjoyed giving him that pleasurable experience and you could tell that he, too, was pleased, right?" She nodded again. "So when you saw him in the hall at school on Monday morning, what did you notice about him? Did his eyes seek you out and light up? Did he acknowledge you with a smile?" These were insider questions she could hear and ponder, questions she didn't have to protect herself against, suggestions she didn't have to resist. She looked thoughtful but didn't offer a verbal response.

Douglas continued seeing the family for a while, sometimes just the parents, sometimes just Rebecca, sometimes all three of them. Over the next few months, Rebecca decided on her own to stop associating with the football team, and she got involved with a guy whom both she and her parents liked.

In the process of acquiring our insider's grasp of what our clients are facing, we make a considerable effort to experience, as firsthand as possible, their hopelessness, frustration, or fear, and we don't rush to reassure or offer expert advice. Throughout, we maintain our therapeutic curiosity. We are continuously wondering what small shift here or there might provide an opening to other possibilities, but we find that such openings appear most easily and are accepted most readily when they *emerge* from our insider empathic collaboration with clients, rather than when they are imposed as the expert advice of an outsider.

Several years ago, Douglas met three times with a very bright 9-year-old boy, Gordie, and his divorced parents. A devoted reader of *Popular Mechanics* and *Popular Science*, Gordie was captivated by the invention and workings of machines; however, he wasn't interested at all in biology, including the workings of his own body. His parents brought him in because he defecated in his pants almost every day, and it never occurred to him to head to the bathroom until someone complained about the smell. The parents had tried everything they could think of, from rewards and punishment to pleading and encouragement, but nothing had made a difference. The most recent doctor they had consulted, a behaviorist, had instructed the parents to sit Gordie on the toilet for half an hour every evening, which they had been doing consistently. Gordie used the time to keep current with his magazines, but not much change had ensued. The occasional bowel movements that happened to occur while he was in the bathroom had only slightly diminished the number of accidents he had in his pants; he still hadn't proactively made his way to the bathroom in advance of pooping; and there had been no change at all in his habit of sitting in his poop until one of the parents explicitly told him to go clean himself up.

Gordie and his parents' responses to various empathic statements and hunches helped Douglas develop an imagined sense of being a 9-year-old aspiring engineer with a problematic pooping habit, a trail of failed doctors in his wake, and a couple of continually exasperated parents hovering over him. It was from that position—inside Gordie's experience—that Douglas was able to start wondering, as would any curious engineer, about the signals being sent and received throughout Gordie's body. Douglas asked him what he knew about how radio stations work, and he gave an adequate explanation, with some help from his dad, about radio waves and transmitters and antennas and receivers. Douglas then asked if he knew that various parts of the body, just like radio stations, are forever sending out signals, and other parts, just like radios, are forever receiving the signals, converting them, and passing them along. He hadn't thought about that before, but it made sense to him.

Douglas learned that Gordie had a good appetite and that he always peed in the toilet, so, he mused out loud, the signaling systems in Gordie's stomach and bladder must be in good working order, alerting him when it was time to eat and time to urinate. Given that such messages were successfully being sent, received, and acted upon, then, they agreed, most of the relays, capacitors, switches, and transformers in his body must be correctly calibrated. Clearly, then, there must simply be some glitch in the messaging system involving his rectum and surrounding areas. Maybe the signals weren't being sent, maybe the signals weren't being broadcast with enough juice, or maybe the signal-to-noise ratio was simply too low. Did he know what a signal-to-noise ratio was? Not really, he said. But his father, himself an engineer, did, and he perked up at the prospect of explaining it to his son on the way home from the session.

They explored the possibility of Gordie and his dad drawing up some blueprints of his broadcast-receiving system and locating possible sources of signal interruption or corruption. And then they talked about the benefits of obtaining some hard data by running a scientific experiment. Since Gordie never seemed to notice when he'd pooped in his pants, it was clear that he wasn't getting poop-relevant signals either before or after his bowel movements. If, during the time until the next appointment, Gordie only realized at some point that he had gone (rather than that he had to go), then before cleaning up, could he close his eyes and notice the various sensations that came to his attention? Douglas offered the tentative hypothesis that once Gordie started getting post-poop signals, the system could be activated and calibrated for his acting on "I-gotta-poop" signals. No doubt he would continue to have accidents for a while, but these would, at least, be helpful for the information gathering necessary for scientific advancement. The parents agreed that when he pooped in his pants, they would, before addressing the mess, help him tune into the various post-poop sensation-based signals (smell, consistency, volume, temperature) and the memory of pre-poop sensations (pressure, fullness, discomfort). They'd then see what effect, if any, this had on improving the signal-to-noise ratio or the amping up of the "I-gotta-poop" signals.

Within 2 weeks of the first appointment (and few days after the second), Gordie had his first successful bathroom experience in years. Playing on his own, he received a signal that he needed to poop, and he made it to the toilet in time without anyone telling him to go. He'd also had a few accidents, which had served their purpose for information gathering. By the third session, a week later, Gordie had had only one accident, and his parents were ready to stop therapy. Five months later, during a follow-up conversation, his mother reported "considerable improvement." There had been only a few accidents, and when they had happened, Gordie had been proactive in cleaning up the mess.

Some of our students and supervisees get nervous when we talk about empathic knowing, worried that developing significant experiential connections with their clients could put them—the clinicians—in danger of losing their therapeutic perspective, crossing an ethical line, or heightening their risk of emotional exhaustion and vicarious trauma. The concerns warrant individual attention.

MAINTAINING A THERAPEUTIC PERSPECTIVE

For those clinicians who assume that some degree of professional detachment is necessary for accurate diagnosing and effective intervening, empathic knowing could appear to be a threat, or at least a mistake. According to the *Oxford English Dictionary*, the word *diagnosis* comes from the Greek *diagignoskein*, to distinguish or discern, and the word *intervention* is formed by the combination of the Latin *inter*, between, and *venire*, to come: "to come between," as in to "come in as an extraneous factor or thing." If you're operating from the position of "outside expert," it's easy to get caught up with the idea that your interventions can come between clients and their problem, can help them stop, cure, or control their troublesome thoughts, emotions, or behaviors.

We find the discernment afforded by an insider perspective to be more fine-grained than discernment from a distance, and, as a result, our diagnosing doesn't give rise to *inter*ventions but rather to what are better thought of as *intra*ventions: possibilities and opportunities for change that come (*venire*) from within (*intra*) the logic of the clients' experience (for a further elaboration, see Flemons, 2002). As you saw with Rebecca and Gordie, the particularities of the intraventions were developed out of an empathic grasp of the intra- and interpersonal interactions interweaving their respective problems.[7]

Perhaps an analogy will help. Let's say you are a jazz pianist. If you go to a club to hear a band that's in town and you sit with the rest of the audience, you and they listen from a distance, and your influence on what unfolds is limited to clapping (or not) after the improvised solos and at the end of each of the pieces. The band members, attentive to the level (or lack) of everyone's enthusiasm, might alter the length of their solos or of a song or of the set, but that's about it. Clapping is a blunt instrument. But if the musicians recognize you and invite you to come up and join them for a number, your listening becomes *participatory* and your ability to invite change becomes intricate and nuanced. The way you accompany the sax player will influence the improvised line he or she produces, and your rhythmic and harmonic choices will shape the musical conversation that unfolds between you and each of the band members.

By assuming an insider position in the experiencing of the piece, you don't lose your expert knowledge; rather, you bring it into the flow of the extemporaneous interplay between you and the other musicians. Your listening informs the musical choices you make, which in turn affect what you're able to hear. In so doing, you trade detached diagnosis (assessing as an audience member) for interactive discernment (listening for openings and possibilities as a band member) and intervening from outside (clapping) for *intra*vening from inside—introducing melodic riffs for the others to improvise off of, making shifts in the rhythm to see how they will react, enriching the sonic palate through different chord voicings, and so on.

Okay, so back to the realm of therapy. Empathic immersion affords you the opportunity to collaborate with clients in extemporaneously constructing a fitting approach—an approach that fits for them and for resolving their problem. But jazz bands notwithstanding, is such an orientation to working a good fit for you? Is it safe? Does practicing empathic knowing increase your vulnerability to crossing an ethical boundary or suffering from emotional exhaustion and vicarious trauma? Of course professional boundaries are vital for staying sane and ethical. You can't take the risk of imagining yourself as the client if you're not feeling fully grounded in your professional identity and your own body of experience and if you're not fully committed to respecting and protecting the client's boundaries. And when the client walks out of the room, you need to be able to return fully to yourself, to ready yourself for traveling into the world of the next client or into your private life with friends and family. Let's talk about the logistics.

MAINTAINING ETHICAL BOUNDARIES

If you and your internist are both to feel comfortable and safe when you go for your yearly physical, he or she has to be able to look at and touch your unclothed body without the encounter feeling in any way sexual for either of you. The hard surfaces, the color of the walls, the bright fluorescent lighting, the doctor's white coat, and your paper gown all serve as implicit reminders that this is a context for professional examination, not personal excitation. And if your doctor is still uncomfortable, he or she can always fall back on a brisk bedside manner to create further emotional distance.

When you're in *your* office, seeing clients, you obviously don't need to manage the interpersonal challenges of examining unclothed bodies, but your clients *do* feel exposed in other ways. Since your office is probably more evocative of a home than a hospital, and since your clients wouldn't open up to you if you were to be emotionally distant, you can't rely on a sterile environment or a reserved persona to keep your relationship with clients feeling professional.

Douglas once saw a psychoanalyst as a client who revealed that he had, a year earlier, become sexually involved, for the first time in a long career, with one of his female patients. Having recently ended the affair (and earlier, the therapy) with her, he was now trying to come to grips with how the transgression had happened and whether he could or should continue working in the profession. He believed that loneliness and disappointment in his personal life had made him vulnerable, and he didn't think he would have become sexually involved with his client if she hadn't begun requesting a "reassuring hug" at the end of their sessions. The embraces gradually lengthened, and somewhere down that slippery slope, he said, a line was crossed.

The notion of a slippery slope implies that therapeutic and sexual intimacy are adjacent points (or, at least, not too many metro stops apart) along a continuum of closeness. We don't see it that way. Instead, we think of the two kinds of intimacy as defining entirely different domains of relationship. In a sexual relationship (at least one that's not exploitive), much of what happens unfolds as a symmetrical dance—one person feeling or doing something invites a mutual or reciprocal response from the other. Mutual desire gives rise to reciprocal touching, which in turn gives rise to mutual arousal and, if things go as hoped, maybe even mutual climax. For a relationship to be therapeutic, however, most of what happens must unfold as an *a*symmetrical dance, with each person's goals and participation fitting with, but remaining demonstrably different from, the other's. The client desires change; the therapist desires to help. When the client opens up with explicit details about his or her experiences and problem, the therapist doesn't reciprocate with analogous vulnerability; rather, he or she responds by delving further into what the client is saying. The client may seek advice from the therapist and may benefit from his or her positive regard, but the therapist isn't hoping to get anything similar back from the client—neither guidance nor warm feelings. Indeed, in an ethical therapeutic relationship, the therapist doesn't request anything in particular from the client, save for a fee. If the therapist ever starts looking to the client as a source for reassurance, respect, or companionship, or for the satisfaction of some feeling, desire, or need, then he or she should take this as a critically important sign, long before touch is involved, that something is

awry, that the essential asymmetrical complementarity of the therapeutic relationship is in jeopardy.

What all this means is that if you practice empathic knowing with an ethical commitment to an asymmetrical—*non*reciprocal—relationship, then your
therapeutic curiosity and your skill at becoming an experiential insider need
not put you in danger of slipping down some imaginary slope. The risk isn't
in "getting too close" to your clients but in getting close to them with the
hope for, or expectation of, some kind of mutuality or reciprocity.

You and the client both need to feel safe in the relationship, but the responsibilities for creating and maintaining that safety are not equally distributed. The client needs to be able to trust that your personal and professional
well-being and your involvement in the relationship is not dependent, in any
way, on what he or she does or doesn't say, feel, choose, or accomplish. And
you need to be able to trust that if you, at some point, don't feel comfortable
working with the client, you won't let that discomfort continue unexamined—you'll address the issue directly with him or her, seek supervision to
help you figure out what's going on, and/or make a responsible referral to another clinician.

We should add, though, that just because *you* are rock solid on the difference between therapeutic and personal intimacy doesn't mean that your clients will be. If you demonstrate excellent listening skills as you, with deep
curiosity and caring, explore their lives in a nonjudgmental way, then why
wouldn't some of them, at times, think you'd make a great partner? When
we've had clients who've intimated as much, we've been able, without blame,
to reassure them that the sanctity of the therapeutic relationship precludes
any such possibility. But we're guys and we're tall and we're approaching the
north end of middle age, so we can handle such situations without breaking a
sweat. Some of our students and trainees, however, particularly the young
women, have felt less sanguine about being, as they've put it, "hit on" or
"propositioned," and they haven't always felt comfortable bringing it up with
the client as a therapeutic issue. Worried that talking about the client's attraction directly "will only encourage him," they have sometimes, in therapy sessions, withdrawn into themselves. We don't think "less therapeutic closeness"
is ever the solution, so we have encouraged these young therapists to think in
terms of protecting the nonreciprocity inherent in the helping relationship,
to bring another therapist into the room with them, if necessary, to help them
find their voice, or to refer the client to another therapist without inferring
that the client had done anything wrong.[8]

Of course, Douglas's psychoanalyst client was his age, so getting older is
no guarantee of safety. However, if the client had scheduled his first appoint-

ment with Douglas or another therapist when the first stirrings of desired reciprocity were making themselves apparent, rather than after he had acted on them, he could have avoided his ethical transgression.

MAINTAINING THERAPEUTIC RESILIENCE

Douglas once saw a psychologist who said that she felt like she was absorbing her patients' symptoms. One evening after an intense session with a man suffering from panic attacks, she herself had a similar attack. Soon after, working with another patient who struggled with obsessive thinking, she found herself at night obsessively replaying her own troubled thoughts. As this continued, she, not surprisingly, concluded that it was dangerous for her to care about her patients—dangerous, indeed, to even talk with them about their symptoms. Prior to coming to Douglas, she had cut back on her practice and worried about going into work. Other therapists, rattled by the traumatic stories and deep suffering of their clients, develop what researchers call *vicarious trauma* (McCann & Pearlman, 1990; Pearlman & Saakvitne, 1995) or *compassion fatigue* (Figley, 1995), exhibiting the intrusive imagery, nightmares, flashbacks or invasive thoughts common to PTSD (Dutton & Rubinstein, 1995).

Given such dangers, we can understand why clinicians might be inclined to play it safe by limiting the degree to which they bring alive in their imagination the insider realities of their clients' lives. When Besman-Albinder (2006) interviewed resilient therapists, some cited emotional distance as a protective strategy. However, others specifically mentioned active listening and empathy, combined with good professional boundaries, as a means of staying safe, a means of not absorbing their clients' distress (p. 173). They also described the importance of taking care of themselves in their daily lives—exercising, meditating, actively engaging in meaningful activities with family and friends, consulting with colleagues or supervisors about cases, and having strategies for compartmentalizing their work (pp. 144–172). They engaged fully with the client they were seeing at the moment and then, when the session was over, they closed the door on that session before walking into the next, and closed the door on their day before heading home.

Because Douglas's psychologist client described herself as feeling "infected" by the symptoms of her patients, they talked about how medical doctors, by consistently washing their hands after each patient consultation, are able to keep from catching their patients' illnesses, even though they conduct physical examinations on dozens of people throughout the day. They decided that it made sense for her to create a short, circumscribed cleansing ritual at the end of each session and then again at the end of the day—a ritual to bring her back in touch with herself and the contributions she was making to her patients' lives. She instituted this strategy, and her feelings of vulnerability decreased significantly.[9]

Far from fearing that our efforts to become experiential insiders with our clients make us more vulnerable to vicarious trauma, we believe that they make us safer. Besman-Albinder's (2006) research participants indicated that their resilience owed much to their recognition that, for the most part, they were making positive contributions to their clients' lives (pp. 129–130), so they weren't simply inundated with stories of loss and pain. Although they worked with victims of abuse, they focused on their clients' positive attributes, strengths, and resourcefulness (p. 175), helping them move beyond what had happened and define a nonvictim identity. Our experience is similar—we don't absorb our clients' suffering as we empathically connect with them; we discover opportunities for change in the midst of their pain, and then, when the session is over, what stays with us the most is the memory of their resilience. And because our empathic knowing helps us grasp the contextual and personal logic of our clients' suffering, we don't feel bewildered or exasperated by their choices—they make sense to us, and this, too, helps protect us from burnout.

Certainly, when we're working with a suicidal client or someone dealing with domestic abuse, worrisome thoughts about him or her can extend beyond the end of the appointment. But once we have completed tasks that we consider clinically responsible—making sure the notes are up-to-date, making a follow-up phone call, contacting another treatment provider—we're usually able to file away the case, both physically and mentally, and open the door to our personal lives. This is made possible in part by our recognition that important changes often happen in response to handling crises and responding to pain. Sometimes at the end of sessions, clients will wish us a good week. We don't respond in kind. Instead, we typically wish them an intriguing or a productive week—one full of opportunities for learning and for discovering new ways of responding to the challenges they face.

Accepted by your clients as an experiential insider, you can tease out the organizing principles and assumptions, the vulnerabilities and strengths, the sensitivities and possibilities inherent in their relationships to significant others, themselves, and their problem. You're then positioned to invite therapeutic change, offering *intraventions* that introduce shifts in one or more of the relationships constituting their problem—the intrapersonal relationships among the component strands of the problem and between the client and the problem as a whole, and the interpersonal relationships between the client and his or her significant others.

SHIFTING RELATIONSHIPS THAT CONSTITUTE
THE PROBLEM

If you approach your clients' problem as a reified category to be controlled or cured (eradicated), then your job will be to join your clients in doing battle against it. But if you think of the problem in terms of the patterns of interaction that have been defining it and holding it in place, then the need for a battle disappears. Instead, you and your clients can devote your time and attention to introducing small changes into the unfolding of these patterns. Why *small*? Because people often try too hard to change and then suffer the consequences of their failure; because therapeutic change is typically nonvolitional in nature, so trying hard doesn't help; and because when you're dealing with patterns rather than things, a tiny shift in one part of it can ramify through the whole of it.[10] To illustrate this last point, let's return to the realm of music—that most pattern-based of all art forms.

Classical musicians know that in performing a complex piece of music, just one prominent unexpected note out of thousands can alter the pattern enough to unsettle their listeners' (and their own) experience. Something of this sort once happened to Franz Liszt, the 19th-century Hungarian composer and renowned pianist, when he was playing a high-profile concert. According to a member of the audience, Amy Fay (1891),

> he was rolling up the piano in arpeggios in a very grand manner indeed, when he struck a semi-tone short of the high note upon which he had intended to end. I caught my breath and wondered whether he was going to leave us like that, in mid-air, as it were, and the harmony unresolved. . . . [Instead,] he instantly went meandering down the piano in harmony with the false note he had struck, and then rolled deliberately up in a second grand sweep, *this* time striking true. (p. 243)

Because the audience was expecting to hear the particular final note Liszt intended, but failed, to play, he needed to come up with some pyrotechnics to repair his error and save his listeners from disappointment (and himself from their disapproval). According to at least one person in attendance, he was successful in all respects. Fay (1891) said that she

> never saw a more delicious piece of cleverness. It was so quick-witted and so exactly characteristic of Liszt. Instead of giving you a chance to say, "He has made a mistake," he forced you to say, "He has shown how to get out of a mistake." (p. 243)

Problems, like melodies, are composed of patterns and so are similarly capable of being dramatically altered when some unanticipated slight change shows up in their performance. However, whereas classical musicians are paid to assiduously avoid or creatively fix deviations from the patterns audience members know and love, therapists are paid to assiduously and creatively *introduce deviations* into the patterns that clients know and hate. Such deviations —variations, really—can be developed within three overlapping domains of the clients' experience:

- The relationships among the elemental strands that individually and together have been weaving or characterizing the pattern of the problem—sensations, perceptions, thoughts, images, behaviors, and emotions, but also time, meaning, focus, intensity, details, thresholds, feedback loops, and pattern
- The relationship between clients and their problem
- The relationship between clients and the people who matter to them (their significant others)

We'll discuss all three, but in reverse order.

The therapeutic variations introduced into clients' patterned problems, regardless of which domain, share two elements in common. First, all are facilitated by the clients' expectation that therapeutic change is possible and that you are in a position to assist in the process (see Kirsch, 1990). This means that you must think not only about shifting problem-related patterns but also about how your clients are orienting toward you and toward change. Second, all therapeutic variations in patterned problems involve some degree of relational freedom. That is, our goal is not to help clients fashion freedom *from* their problem but, rather, to help them find freedom *within* it or freedom *in relation to* it (Flemons, 2002). As alternate possibilities or choices open up, the problem may resolve, its meaning may shift, or it may move from foreground prominence to background irrelevance.

SHIFTING THE RELATIONSHIP BETWEEN CLIENTS AND SIGNIFICANT OTHERS

Working from inside our clients' frame of reference, we explore how the pattern of their problem has been fitting (woven) within and through the more encompassing ecology of their interpersonal context. How have significant others been making sense of the client's predicament? What, if anything, have they been trying to do to help? And has the client's problem been contributing something of a solution to someone else's problem?

TREATING INDIVIDUAL PROBLEMS AS CONTEXTUAL SOLUTIONS

A family came to see Douglas in late October many years ago. Alex, a bright, sensitive, and sometimes surly 11-year-old, was joined by Karen, his frazzled mother, and Sandra, his almost perfect younger sister.[11] The three of them had moved during the summer, several months after Karen had split from the dad, so the kids were new to their school. Sandra had adapted well, but Alex had made no friends and had developed what his mother described as a school phobia. Every weekday morning was greeted with a loud confrontation, with Karen alternating between demands and entreaties that Alex get ready and Alex vociferously refusing, screaming that he didn't want to go. On the days Karen was successful in overcoming her son's stonewalling, he would have a good morning in the classroom, but when he came home for lunch there would be another confrontation, and this one Alex was much more likely to win. At night, faced with doing homework, he would throw yet another fit.

Sandra presented no such challenges with school, but ever since her parents' separation 9 months earlier, she had felt afraid at night, so again and again she found her way into her mother's bed. Karen had tried everything she could think of to entice Sandra to head back to her own room, but nothing worked. Still, in the grand scheme of things, Karen wasn't all that concerned. She longed for privacy, but Sandra was such a good companion to her, sharing a bed didn't feel like too much of a hardship.

Despite the family's struggles, Karen probably wouldn't have made an appointment had Alex not, a few days earlier, told her that he no longer wanted to live. She took his comment seriously. She herself had taken an overdose of sleeping pills less than a year earlier, when she first discovered that her husband was cheating on her. She knew that her soon-to-be ex-husband had told the children of her suicide attempt when she was still in the hospital, and she was worried that this put Alex more at risk.

Family friends and extended family had told Alex that with his father out of the picture, he now needed to be the man of the house. Karen dismissed that message, saying that he was only 11 and didn't need to be thinking that way, but she wouldn't have minded *some* help. Far from shouldering the family responsibilities, she said, he was heaping more stress on her. In addition to the fighting, he nagged her continually about her smoking and complained about how ineptly she was running things.

Karen appeared exhausted and wound tight as she expressed her deep frustration with her son. Having been unable to find a job since moving in the summer, she was collecting unemployment insurance and checking the want ads, but she knew she couldn't seriously look for something until Alex got sorted out. She requested that Douglas help Alex calm down about school, learn to obey her, and make some friends. Fixing these problems seemed to her to be the necessary first steps to her getting back into the workforce. How could she enforce his going to school in the morning and again at noon if she was employed?

As Douglas made his way inside the logic of their interrelationships, it became obvious that both kids were deeply worried about their despairing mother's well-being. Alex, along with Sandra, had been helping to keep tabs on her. What initially appeared to be a problem to be solved—Alex's seeming school phobia—could now be contextually understood as a resourceful solution to be maintained until it was no longer necessary. Douglas told the family that he suspected Alex had taken the admonition to "be the man of the house" to heart and was doing his best, in the only way he, as an 11-year-old, could, to make sure that his mother wasn't facing her challenges alone. True, his refusals to go to school were taking their toll on his mother, and Sandra's bedtime fears meant that her mother didn't get the privacy she craved. But how else could they be providing almost 24/7 monitoring, with Alex taking the day shift and Sandra handling nights? Douglas speculated that once Alex was convinced that his mother was okay and it was thus safe for him not to be around during the day, school wouldn't seem like such a big deal, and he might be comfortable making some friends and maybe even going over to their houses sometimes. And once Sandra knew her mother could safely handle lonely nights, she'd probably find herself wanting the comfort of her own bed. In the meantime, it seemed they were all doing an outstanding job of putting safety first, and over the next few appointments, Douglas and the clients explored the possibilities of freeing up alternate ways they could continue to do that—ways that didn't necessitate huge fights and lots of tears.

One morning a few days after their third appointment, Karen received a letter from the government informing her that they had been mistaken in granting her unemployment benefits. She hadn't done anything wrong, but she would need to pay back everything she had collected to date, and no further checks would be forthcoming. Desperation overwhelmed her, and once again the thought of suicide presented itself as her only option. However, Alex hadn't gone to school that morning, so he happened to be there with her. She wasn't alone. Instead of taking her life, she took action, calling former business associates to let them know that she had moved and was committed to finding immediate employment in a new position. Within 4 hours she had secured a job, which she started the next day. Within 2 weeks Alex was going to school without a fuss, and he had made some friends. He started whistling around the house. A few weeks after that, Sandra was sleeping in her own bed. Within a few months, Karen had started seeing a new man. Everyone felt safe.

FINDING CONTEXTUAL SOLUTIONS TO INDIVIDUAL PROBLEMS

When you approach client conundrums with contextual sensitivity, you will find that the resolution of an individual's problem can happen as a result of a shift in his or her interpersonal relationships. Alex's school fears and Sandra's night fears both dissipated once Karen kicked into action and got a job. And a similar change happened with the Wilson family. Marie, the mother, called originally to ask whether Douglas could recommend a good military school for her out-of-control 12-year-old son, Jeffrey. Douglas told her he didn't know of any, but if she wanted to bring the family in, he'd explore alternatives with them. She agreed, and 10 days later Douglas met with Marie and Jeffrey, as well as the father, Pete, and Jeffrey's 14-year-old sister, Ronnie.

Following the advice of Jeffrey's individual therapist, Pete and Marie were looking for a school that could teach Jeffrey the discipline and respect that 18 months of counseling had failed to instill. The parents had closely followed the therapist's recommendations regarding "logical consequences," removing, over time, every possible privilege from Jeffrey's life and everything but the bed from his room. But to their dismay, he continued acting "like the Tasmanian Devil," spinning trouble and chaos everywhere. Sometimes too "physically aggressive" with Ronnie and verbally abusive toward his parents, Jeffrey often angered and irked them. The decision to send him off to military school was born of their deep frustration and the sinking feeling that their son was too far gone to be helped by concerned family members or a once-a-week therapist. Jeffrey seemed worse now than ever, despite everything they had tried.

Despite everything? Or *because* of it? Sometimes a problem is exacerbated by ineffective attempts at solutions, and sometimes the attempts themselves become the problem (Watzlawick, Weakland, & Fisch, 1974). Pete and Marie had punished Jeffrey consistently, just as they had been advised, but, in the process, they had become less like parents than guards, and he less like a son than a convict. His bedroom, empty of possessions and comfort, contributed to the impression. Given the logic of their escalating interaction, military school or some kind of locked facility was the obvious next step. But what if, instead, they challenged this logic? Douglas was curious about whether they ever experienced Jeffrey as something other than a prisoner-in-training. In fact, they did.

When he wasn't driving them crazy, Jeffrey was quite capable of enthralling his parents with his "magical imagination," and, when he was in a "soft mood," he was loving and engaging. Pete described how much he had enjoyed his son during a recent weeklong "guy-trip," occasioned by the death and funeral of a family member in another state. Jeffrey had been sensitive and cooperative, and Pete, relaxed and absent of anger. Indeed, they had been off on that trip when Marie made her original call to book the first appointment.

While he and Jeffrey were away, Pete had given himself a vacation from meting out rewards and punishments. And it hadn't really been necessary anyway, because his son seemed "like a different kid," having himself taken a vacation from his "usual impossible self." What if these two changes were connected? Pete and Marie had shrugged off Jeffrey's temporary improvements as merely the result of there being no demands, no schedule, no school hassles. But what if the change on the trip held the key to possible changes at home? Douglas and the parents explored what might happen if they held firm to their goals for their son but fired themselves as prison guards.

As Douglas and the parents continued to meet over the next few months, that "different kid" was much more in evidence, and, 2 years later, when they came in for a tune-up, the change was holding steady, with no military school on the horizon. The parents held Jeffrey accountable, but they did so within an ongoing commitment to preserving a warm relationship with him. Correction still happened, but within a context of connection.

SHIFTING THE RELATIONSHIP BETWEEN CLIENTS AND THEIR PROBLEM

Aggravated by and/or afraid of their problem, clients typically come to a therapist feeling helpless and hopeless, victimized by something that seems to have a mind of its own, and a malevolent one at that. Looking for relief, they desire to have better control over the problem or, once and for all, to successfully rid themselves of it. Both of these goals pit the clients in opposition to something they consider to be *Other*. But, of course, as long as there is an intrapersonal component to the problem—whether panic attacks, abuse of alcohol, nightmares, or some other form of suffering—it is part of *them*, so "othering" it and trying to avoid or distance themselves from it serve only to further divide them from themselves.

Therapeutic change becomes possible when clients are freed up from attempting to contain, negate, or otherwise separate from an alienated chunk of their own experience. We help them head in the opposite direction, facilitating their connecting to their problem in such a way that they can respond to it resourcefully, creating opportunities for choice and change. Below, we discuss four interrelated ways of creating expectancy for, and development of, therapeutic change through the facilitation of a resourceful connection between clients and their problem. We do this by encouraging the following:

- Curiosity and learning
- Coordination with (rather than control of) the problem
- The introduction and preservation of choice
- Relational freedom

CURIOSITY AND LEARNING

When you're curious about something—when you want to learn more about it—you tend to lean toward or into it, both physically and attitudinally. This shift, from separation to connection, from frightened withdrawal to fascinated engagement, is sometimes all it takes to occasion a significant change in the problem itself.

At a party populated by adults and young children, a man was regaling Douglas with a captivating tale when the man's almost-3-year-old daughter appeared at his side. She tried to get her father's attention, but he, caught up in his story, hardly registered her presence. Aiming to rectify this state of affairs, the girl became more insistent in her entreaties. The volume of her voice escalated, as did the strength of the tugs on his pant leg. Luckily for all concerned, the dad at some point realized that he needed to acknowledge her presence. Breaking off his conversation with Douglas, he knelt down and, in a soft and inquisitive voice, sought to find out what his daughter had come to tell him. The effect of his shift was instantaneous. The volume of the girl's voice dropped, her body relaxed, and her upset tone evaporated. She told him her news and headed on her way.

A problem will sometimes similarly calm down and wander along when the person dealing with it gives up trying to ignore it and, instead, turns to it with curiosity. A client came in who was close to losing her job as a result of frequent displays of anger, and her partner and children were fed up with her tirades. Most people she knew were scared of her, and she herself was unnerved and mystified by the speed and intensity of her temper. At the end of the first session, Douglas asked her to devote a week to tracking her experience. What did she notice when she felt an episode of anger coming on?

What sorts of information from others could trigger an angry response? What did the other need to say or do before she would start feeling furious? What was the first sign that she was about to start yelling? Did she feel anything in her body? Where? Was it always the same, or were there variations? How long after that first sensation till she felt out of control? What did she notice in the face of the other person as she was losing it? What occasioned the end of the episode—a signal of some kind from the other person, or something internal? A thought? A feeling? An image? And then what did she notice once the storm had passed? And so on.

When she came back for the second appointment, the client said that she'd gone in search of the information Douglas had requested, but on the several occasions when she did, she found herself crying rather than yelling. This had unnerved but also intrigued her. As a result of her curiosity, the anger seemed to have turned into deep sadness. Douglas suggested, then, that until their next appointment 2 weeks hence, she devote herself to tracking her sadness in the same way she had tried to follow the pathways of her anger. She did so, and when she returned, she reported that the anger had continued to be a *non*problem, and, in fact, the sadness had also transformed. She hadn't been crying as much, but had become increasingly reflective, which she found weird but calming. Others in her life had noticed the change, and she was recognizing that she had some tough questions to ask herself and tough choices to make. Douglas told her he'd be happy to help her figure that out, should she decide she needed input other than her own reflections.

In search of the information Douglas had asked her to gather, the client shifted, in essence, from a helpless victim of an uncontrollable and frightening emotion to an active researcher in pursuit of knowledge. With such a change in orientation, the object of her curiosity—a problem that was, after all, part of *her*—could itself begin to change. In the relational world of experience, a change in a relationship occasions change in the *relata* at either end of it.

COORDINATION

To enhance the potential for curiosity-induced change, we invite clients to change their relationship with their problem. Rather than attempting to control it, can they *coordinate with* it? What happens to their symptoms if they concentrate their efforts on getting in sync with their problem, rather than dispensing with it?

During an initial telephone contact to set up a first appointment, Inez had described feeling hopelessly depressed, so Douglas was surprised by the firmness of her handshake and the forthrightness of her manner when he greeted her in the waiting room. But it soon made sense. Afraid that her despair would take her down, she was determined to keep it in check, which she did by organizing herself with military-like discipline. Every night without fail she composed on sticky notes as many as 20 new positive affirmations about herself and her accomplishments, positioning them all over her bathroom mirror so she would see them first thing in the morning. This and other strategies had been keeping her afloat, but she had become so exhausted by the required relentlessness of her protective efforts that she recognized the necessity of an alternative approach.

Douglas told her about an elite woman athlete he'd seen who was struggling to scramble out of a slump and regain mastery over her performance. Strength of will and precision of effort had been vital to her earlier success, so she had naturally assumed that she could bootstrap herself out of her black hole by working at it long and hard and with more and more conscious focus. But this approach only seemed to make matters worse. By the time she arrived for her first appointment, she was frustrated and discouraged. She came to discover that what was needed wasn't better conscious control, but rather better mind–body *coordination*. When she left off trying to micromanage her body and started, instead, trusting herself to become more absorbed in the flow of her performance, she was able to get back into the zone.

Later in the session, Douglas told the story of a young California surfer he'd once seen who explained how he was able to keep surfing the whole day, long after his friends, completely spent, had gone home. He said that when his friends fell off their boards and the wave they'd been riding came down on top of them, they would use up their strength swimming against the force of the water to get to the surface. He, in contrast, had figured out that if, after falling, he swam *down with* the direction of the water, rather than *up against* it, then the natural circular flow of the post-break wave would soon deliver him to the surface, with his having expended only a minimum of effort. All this strategy required was a counterintuitive 180° change in direction—to stay safe by swimming down, rather than up.

Inez and Douglas explored the possibility of her adopting a surfer strategy with her desperation. Would she feel safe coordinating with the thoughtfulness of her body-based experiences (particularly her emotions), rather than consciously fighting against them? She was willing to try, so they experimented with her letting go of the positive affirmations and protecting time to purposefully swim down into her fear and depression. Within a few weeks, a positive sense of herself was emerging from inside, rather than being imposed from outside, and, no longer afraid of her sadness, she was relaxing her grip on her life (and on Douglas's hand!).

CHOICE

After bingeing and purging regularly for over 20 years, Silvie wanted to stop. She wasn't sure she could, given her previous failed attempts to do so and her current level of stress in her job and her marriage. But she was exhausted by the effort and subterfuge it took to keep her behavior a secret from her husband, friends, and coworkers, and she was worried about the effects it was having on her physical health.

Douglas initiated a conversation about two kinds of trains—milk-run and bullet. Milk-run trains stop at every station along their route, able to take advantage of all the junctions on the line to divert to multiple possible destinations. Bullet trains never alter course once they've left the station, and because they're relentlessly zooming toward a singular, fixed destination, the junctions on the line are irrelevant—they don't even register. A choice not considered is not a choice.

Douglas said that he was most interested in her experience while she engaged in procuring binge-able food, readying it for consumption, eating it, and then making her way to the bathroom. At what point did it seem as if she had boarded a bullet train and couldn't get off until arriving at the vomit station—until she was seeing, hearing, feeling, tasting, and smelling partially digested food rising in her throat and splashing into the toilet? For how much of the trip was she, in fact, on a milk run, a line that had available multiple opportunities for a switch in tracks—points at which she might find herself heading somewhere else? Did she find any junctions on the way to the grocery store? In the store? At the checkout? On the way home? While putting away her purchases? Unwrapping them? Preparing them? After the first bite? After the second or tenth or twentieth bite? As she made her way down the hall to the bathroom? As she locked the door behind her? As she lifted the lid of the toilet?

Silvie's previous attempts to stop her habit had prominently featured will-power as the primary strategy for change—essentially attempting to compel herself not to feel compelled. In contrast, the approach she and Douglas were exploring stressed the importance of *preserving choice*, and the junctions could only serve as choice points if vomiting was still available as a possible destination; otherwise, she'd only be trading one optionless experience ("I have to throw up") for another ("I have to *not* throw up"). Junctions can't be injunctions.

Silvie's train-route inquiry resulted in a change of habit that was still in place a few years later when she consulted Douglas again for help with a different issue. She told him upon her return that essential to her earlier change was her discovery that the bingeing and purging was, contrary to her previous belief, a milk-run phenomenon that included any number of junctions, each one offering a possible change in course *and* the option of continuing on to vomiting. She found it reassuring and motivating to realize that she *could* keep heading in the direction of the toilet but didn't have to do so.[12]

RELATIONAL FREEDOM

Clients come in wanting freedom *from* their problem, but such a goal inspires efforts to negate and banish, which, as we explained earlier, tend to exacerbate, rather than dissipate, the problem. So, instead, we offer opportunities for freedom *in relation to* their problem. For example, over the years, Douglas has seen several clients who, concerned about or threatened by a voice in their head, wanted him to help them permanently silence it: A young boy who would answer his mother out loud when he heard her voice during class, giving rise to the derision of his peers and concern of his teachers; a creative young college student who was driven to distraction by various insistent voices whenever he tried to write; a mother who became anxious and lost self-confidence when, in her head, her mother railed against her each time any of her children got sick; and a woman terrified of heights who heard an unidentified voice urging her to jump. Rather than try to get any of these disembodied voices to shut up, Douglas assisted his clients in becoming more resourceful in experiencing and responding to them.

The young boy learned how to keep listening to his mother's excellent advice (particularly during tests and in-class assignments), but to hear it being whispered, rather than spoken. This made it easier for him to lower his voice in return. The whispering became so quiet that he didn't even need to bother moving his lips, which meant that those around him became unaware of whether he and his mother were conversing.

The college student had a background in experimental theater, a tenet of which is that, when playing an improvised scene, you never negate or dismiss something another character has introduced into the dialogue. Utilizing this same principle with the voices, he was soon able to use them as inspired contributors to his creative writing.

The anxious mother discovered that she could turn the volume of her mother's voice down low enough to hear herself think, which helped her use the ideas articulated by the voice whenever it had something useful to contribute and to discover that she herself knew a lot more than she realized about protecting her children from harm.

The terrified-of-heights woman recalled that as a teenager, she quite commonly failed to pay attention to the advice, demands, and admonishments of parents, teachers, and other authorities. She brought this same spirited defiance to encountering the dangerous voice in her head and found it delightfully liberating to not bother giving it the time of day. Heights once again became safely accessible.

In all of these cases, when the clients left off trying to keep the voice(s) in their head in check, the voice(s) left off being so insistent, fading in significance and even perceptual presence. The symptom shifted significantly when the clients freed up their relationship *to* it, rather than trying to liberate themselves *from* it. Such is the case in most instances of therapeutic change—when clients move from feeling imprisoned or bullied by their problem to discovering freedom in responding to it, both relationship and *relata* become resourceful and/or a *non*issue.

SHIFTING THE RELATIONSHIPS AMONG EXPERIENTIAL STRANDS OF THE PROBLEM

If you approach problems not as things, but as patterns unfolding through time, then you can invite change in the whole of a problem by introducing a shift in one or more of the experiential strands that have been constituting it. To do this, you take a client's problem and track the thoughts, emotions, behaviors, sensations, perceptions, assumptions, dreams/images, and/or communicational interactions that comprise and/or contextualize it. And then you look at how attributes of each of these strands could be varied in ways that might ramify in an experientially significant way. Is it possible to adjust the time frame or predictability of an emotional expression or communicational interaction? To suggest a shift in the meaning of a dream, perception, or behavior? To speculate out loud on how the details of an image or assumption might begin to transform? To help alter the threshold, intensity, or rhythmic quality of a sensation? Or the reflexivity of a thought? The possibilities are varied and many; let's look at a few examples to give you a sense of how you might proceed.

SHIFTING THE TIME FRAME AND INTENSITY OF EMOTIONAL EXPRESSION

Douglas once consulted on a case with a woman who had lost her adult son in an accident several weeks earlier and, since then, hadn't been able to stem her tears. Her remaining children had been understanding and supportive for what seemed to them a reasonable length of time, but they had recently been advising her to pull herself together and get on with her life. And her doctor had warned her, with considerable urgency, that because her nonstop crying was causing a lot of swelling in and around her eyes, her optic nerve could be compromised, jeopardizing her sight. Given that such advice hadn't produced the desired effect, the therapist knew that if she were to urge the client to stop or even control the crying, it wouldn't help and could even make matters worse; however, she saw no alternative, so she was in search of a different approach.

Douglas suggested that the therapist talk to the woman about the importance of mourning fully and deeply. Her crying was an understandable response to a tragic loss, a fitting way to express the scale of her despair. Yes, it was dangerous to cry, but how could she not? Rather than follow others' advice, why not listen to her body? She felt the need to wail, so she should. Perhaps she could cry more thoroughly than she had so far, allowing her tears, whatever the danger to her sight, to express more purely the agony she felt. The best way for this to happen, Douglas said to the therapist, would be for the client to *protect time*, perhaps an hour a day, to concentrate and intensify her grief. During this hour, she could let the tears flow freely, could *encourage* them to flow plentifully, knowing that this was a necessary, if dangerous, part of her honoring the memory of her son.

Soon after this idea was conveyed to the client, her crying abated considerably (except for the designated hour), the swelling went down, and her sight was saved. By protecting time to cry, she was able to fully enter her grief, which allowed her emotional expression to begin changing.

We often suggest such time protection strategies to clients when their emotions ambush them, erupting spontaneously at inopportune times. A top executive at a large company was terrified of getting fired because he kept "breaking down" in front of his bosses, colleagues, and staff. Recently abandoned by his wife, he was beside himself with shock, anger, regret, and despair. When Douglas found out that the man could lock his office door and unplug his phone, he encouraged him to schedule 20-minute appointments with himself twice a day, and a 45-minute time in the evening, when he could relax his efforts at "keeping himself together." Almost immediately, the man stopped "losing it" in front of people at work and soon after began making concrete plans for dealing with his impending divorce.

SHIFTING THE MEANING OF EMOTIONAL EXPRESSION

At the funeral for one of his close friends, a psychiatrist went up to the deceased's 30-year-old daughter and, after offering his condolences, pressed two prescriptions into her palm, one for sleeping pills, the other for an antidepressant. He told her that the medications would help her through the difficult weeks and months ahead, and he urged her to find a therapist for her inevitable depression. She didn't immediately fill the prescriptions, but, following the psychiatrist's advice regarding therapy, she called Douglas for an appointment. At the beginning of the first session, she said she anticipated needing weekly appointments for 6–9 months. Asked how she had come up with this time frame, she explained that this was how long she imagined she'd be feeling depressed.

They talked about her grief over her mother's death, but also about the rest of her life—her career, close friends, activities, and so on. She seemed to be responding amazingly well, given the circumstances, so Douglas asked how she thought he could be helpful. She looked at him quizzically and said, "You're the professional—don't you know?" He told her that in contrast to her mother's friend, he differentiated between depression and grief, and he didn't assume that deep sadness necessarily requires medication and professional involvement. "My expertise," he said, "doesn't reside in knowing what's best for you, but, rather, in helping you discover what you already know and are able to learn. I help people who are stuck, but I don't get the sense that you are. You're grieving, but I don't assume that this means there's something wrong with you. How could you feel otherwise?"

By the end of the session, the woman decided that perhaps she didn't need to schedule a series of appointments. Douglas saw her, at her request, a few weeks later and once again a month or so after that. She deeply mourned her mother's death, withdrawing for a while from some aspects of her busy life, but she never found it necessary to rely on the medication, and she decided that she didn't require a professional to guide her through her grieving.

SHIFTING DETAILS AND THE PREDICTABILITY OF IMAGES/DREAMS AND INTERACTIONS

A therapist, Sean, consulted Douglas about a 7-year-old girl named Isadora whose nightmares scared her so much that she was afraid to go to bed. She couldn't fall asleep without a light on, and when she'd jolt awake in the middle of one of the dreams, it often took her parents up to an hour to help her calm down. Douglas reasoned that because her nightmares probably wouldn't be so vivid if she didn't possess a remarkable imagination, it only made sense for Sean to assess the artistic range of this imagination. He suggested that Sean, with the parents' permission, ask Isadora to close her eyes and, with his help, to create and change the color, size, and shape of various suggested objects. He did so, and after Isadora had successfully completed several imagination exercises in the session, he sent the family off to buy her a box of crayons and drawing paper. He asked them to give her 10–20 minutes alone every evening before bed to draw and color the nightmare she expected to have. If the exercise began to go stale, the parents could stimulate her imagination by shutting off her light, leaving the room for 60 seconds, coming back, turning the light on again, and then giving Isadora time alone to bring the necessary vitality to her artwork. If, on subsequent nights, Isadora were to again feel uninspired, her parents should increase the duration of darkness, 60 seconds at a time.

The family returned 2 weeks later, apologetic that Isadora had managed to complete only a handful of sketches. They explained that on the third night, Isadora had felt bored, so they switched off her light as planned. This had had the intended effect on her imagination that night and the next, but on the fifth night, when they returned to her room to switch her light back on, she'd fallen asleep. Hating to disturb her, they took the art supplies off her bed and tucked her in. The same thing happened the next few nights, and, after that, they could no longer convince Isadora to bother with the drawings, particularly since her nightmares had stopped.

THRESHOLDS OF PERCEPTION AND REFLEXIVITY OF THOUGHTS AND EMOTIONAL EXPRESSION

Deirdre, a young, fair-complexioned English woman who blushed easily, couldn't keep herself from noticing unintended double entendres. During conversations, she would automatically latch onto words that could be interpreted—usually out of context—as oblique references to something sexual. The thought produced a blush and then, afraid that the other person would guess what had triggered her reaction (and conclude she had "a filthy mind"), she'd redden still more.

Deirdre had what she described as a healthy, open attitude about sex, so she couldn't understand why she automatically found sexual significance in "innocent" words and why her body responded to them so dramatically. A previous therapist had introduced thought-stopping (and other) techniques, but nothing had worked. "By the time I'd reach over to snap the elastic on my wrist," Deirdre explained, "the blush had already started." She'd tried her best to keep her thinking process in check, but, predictably, this effort had only exacerbated the situation. Her efforts to this point in time had all been directed toward getting herself to blush less or not at all.

Douglas agreed that if her blushing only happened in response to obvious sexual puns, others might potentially connect cause and effect. But if she *in-*

creased the sensitivity of her double-entendre radar (decreasing the threshold at which it was triggered), then she could hear (and blush at) double meanings discernible (but only to her) in even the most mundane words. This would effectively erase the potential for pattern recognition on the part of the people with whom she was conversing, so no one would catch the sexual overtones of her thinking. If, for example, she could redden at hearing *lips* or *head*, why not at *but*? All she needed to do was add an automatic *t* to the end of it when she heard it, and she'd be on her way. And this wasn't the only word with promising automatic titillation possibilities. Douglas suggested she let her quick-witted mind supply a letter or a word here and there in order to produce an *orgy* of meaning in almost every sentence.

Two months after they finished working together, Douglas followed up with Deirdre on the phone, and she told him things were better. Whenever she anticipated hearing double entendres, she said, she'd "destroy the pattern" by trying to blush as much and as often as possible. As a result, her blushing hadn't "been that bad" and, when it did happen, she "simply accepted" it as part of who she was. Instead of thought stopping, she was pattern shifting.

Common to all four of these examples is the Ericksonian recognition that introducing a small, seemingly insignificant change somewhere in the midst of the experience of a problem makes it possible for the pattern as a whole to change in significant ways (Cade & O'Hanlon, 1993). The opportunities for intravention are limited only by your imagination and what fits with your clients' sensibility and their willingness and ability to experiment.

As you continue reading, you'll see the therapeutic principles outlined in this chapter reflected through the rest of the book. In our approach to assessment, you'll find a commitment to empathic knowing as a way of encountering and grasping the experiential complexities of clients. You'll notice an appreciation of historical and social contexts as a means for making sense of clients' predicaments and possibilities. You'll recognize how our intrarelational focus informs how we attend not only to the patterns weaving our clients' suicidality, but also to their, and their significant others', *relationship to* their suicidality. And, finally, you'll see that we don't recommend going in search of a detached, rational, objective position from which to judge. Rather, we suggest developing an engaged, relational, intersubjective positioning within which to assess and evolve a decision regarding safety.

NOTES

1 We differ somewhat in this. As a psychiatrist, Len is comfortable in offering expert opinions about medications and accepting responsibility for medical decisions. As a family

therapist, Douglas is more likely than Len to take a "one-down" position (Fisch, Weakland, & Segal, 1982) with clients.

2 A diagnosis becomes essential if Len is conducting a psychiatric evaluation or prescribing medication, or if either of us is billing an insurance company.

3 See Lakoff and Johnson (1980) for an exploration of how metaphors embedded in our language shape our experience and choices.

4 Erickson would ask, for example, "Would you like to go into hypnosis with your eyes open or your eyes closed?" The client would attend to the choice being offered and, in so doing, not notice the presupposition that either way, he or she would be going into trance (Erickson & Rossi, 1980).

5 For example, the presuppositions in his wife's questions could find their way into the questions he asks himself, further substantiating their legitimacy: "Am I really afraid?" "Why *am* I so slow in responding to her texts? What's up with that?" "Is she right? Am I really a secretive person?"

6 Present perfect continuous tense.

7 Although Milton Erickson never used the term *intravention*, his therapeutic approach, more than anyone's, exemplified this "insider" sensibility.

8 To accomplish this, the therapist would need to acknowledge that he or she had noticed the client's feeling attracted to the therapist, and to talk about how, though such an attraction was an understandable response to a helping relationship, it precluded their continuing to work together.

9 From an Ericksonian perspective, Douglas was therapeutically *utilizing* her symptom (Erickson, 1980).

10 Milton Erickson explained to Jay Haley (1993) that "if you want a large change you should ask for a small one" (p. 57).

11 A more complete description of the case can be found in Flemons (1991).

12 See Wilk (1985) for a brief discussion of helping clients to find choice points.

3

RISKS AND RESOURCES

WILL THIS DESPERATE person sitting in front of me make an attempt on his or her life in the next 2 or 3 days? This question hovers over everything you ask, observe, and think during a suicide assessment, and for you to have any degree of confidence in the answer you eventually arrive at, you need to know what information is most relevant to gather and how to best go about gathering it. In this chapter, we provide such a schema; in the next, we offer guidelines for how to make use of this information in coming to a safety decision and how, when possible, to collaborate with your client in creating a safety plan.

INFORMATION TO GATHER

Over the course of developing this book, we have distilled an extensive research literature on risk factors for suicide into 21 risk descriptors—classifications that detail the sorts of stressors, events, relationships, moods, emotions, symptoms, thoughts, urges, behaviors, or choices that contribute to and/or express an individual's suicidality. We treat each descriptor—for example, "Overwhelming expectations/obligations"; "Anxiety/Anger/Obsessive thinking"; "Substance abuse/Disordered eating"; or "Intention/Plan to act on suicidal thoughts"—as a "topic of inquiry," a specific realm of experience for you to explore, if relevant, at some point during an assessment.

To help you develop your understanding and facilitate your memory of these topics during the assessment process, we have organized them under four broad categories of suicidal experience:

1. *Disruptions and Demands* covers the range of stressors that can provoke a sense of overwhelmed helplessness.

54

2. *Suffering* includes the significant mental health and physical symptoms that can contribute to or exacerbate desperation.
3. *Troubling Behaviors* encompasses the urges, actions, and choices that can intensify the unpredictability of the situation.
4. *Desperation* groups together the mindset, willingness to act, and circumstances that converge at the height of suicidality.

All relevant problems and exacerbating complications must be taken into consideration during an assessment, but, as we pointed out in Chapter 1, you will only get part of the story if you focus on them exclusively. To get a sense of the potential imminent lethality of the suicidality, you must consider these risks in relation to the person's resources for dealing with them. Thus, in addition to the 21 risk descriptors mentioned earlier, we have identified 12 resource descriptors to help organize your exploration of the individual's abilities to stay safe.

We should clarify that for us, resources are not, for the most part, simply synonymous with the "protective factors" that quantitative researchers, studying the characteristics of populations of less-at-risk people, have identified. Hope is a protective factor, as is faith, resiliency, being married, or being a young African American woman. When conducting a suicide assessment, we use many such abstract attributes and categories of experience to inform our questions, but we primarily focus our curiosity at the level of the individual in front of us. How has this person been coping with the challenges and danger that he or she has been facing? Has there been any variability in symptoms, thoughts, emotions, or behaviors? How, up to this point, has he or she been able to negotiate a pathway through the danger? Or find safety somehow inside it? Or define an identity outside it?

Finding variations and possibilities within problematic experiences becomes easier if, as we explained in Chapter 2, you conceive of problems as intra- and interpersonal patterns of interaction, unfolding through time. This positions you to explore periods or brief durations when, say, suicidal thinking has been less pronounced or absent; when encountering suicidal thoughts in a different way has allowed them to dissipate; when the desperate desire for relief has given rise to thoughts other than dying; or when reaching out for help has actually made a difference. We cast a broad net when listening for individual characteristics that could prove critical in establishing or protecting safety. What are the person's particular skills, choices, beliefs, desires, talents, attitudes, commitments, abilities, realizations, orientations, experiential discoveries, or relationships that are possessed or accessible, especially at times of danger? Concrete examples of resources include a young man's re-solve, developed back when he was playing college football, to keep moving forward, even while suffering great pain. Or a woman's realization that her thoughts about dying actually vary in intensity and sometimes fade into the background for periods of time. Or a college student's demonstrated willing-ness to call her university's student counseling crisis line in the middle of the night, even though she, in the past, has worried about burdening others with her negativity.

Your search for resources can also be aided by associational thinking. If a teenage girl has cultivated the skill of tuning out her parents' voices, has she ever experimented with tuning out the thought that she should hurt herself? A decent chess player knows how to imagine his opponent's branching po-tential responses to this or that next move; has he ever brought that ability to bear on dealing with desperate situations? If a dancer were to choreograph her life-and-death struggle with her desperation, who or what would need to join her on the wooden floor? How would she solve the aesthetic problems the dance presented to her?

A suicide assessment is not a therapy session; nevertheless, your job, in part, is to determine whether your client has the resources to safely navigate incredibly dangerous waters. Discovering and uncovering these resources is different from inquiring about risks, in part because clients often don't ini-tially recognize their resources, and thus aren't able to immediately identify them for you. They also might discount them if you were to ask directly about strengths: "What do you most value in yourself?" "What would you say are your best qualities?" "What do you do well?" Most depressed or discour-aged people would respond to such queries with a silent shake of the head, a dismissive grunt or comment, or perhaps an irritated clarification that they possess no positive attributes whatsoever. Thus, we mostly search for and es-tablish resources by inquiring about them indirectly and intermittently, and we remain casual and low key when we make note of them.

Therapist: And so at those times, when you're not feeling as bad or anxious as you do when you first wake up, you can breathe a little easier?

Client: Yeah, I guess.

Therapist: And is that sense of relief fleeting, or does it sometimes stick around for a while?

Client: Never long enough.

Therapist: No, I'm sure. Never long enough. Does that respite from the des-peration make it possible for you to do anything you wouldn't otherwise?

Client: What do you mean?

Therapist: I don't know. Get outside. Read for a while. Make a phone call.

Client: Sometimes I go to the park down the street.

Therapist: Do you know if the relief comes before you leave for the park, or after you head out to walk there?

Client: I don't know. I haven't noticed.

Therapist: Helps to get outside.

Client: It feels oppressive in my apartment.

Therapist: And do you ever call anyone?

Client: My mother.

Therapist: Does it help?

Client: Sometimes. Sometimes she starts in on me, and I can't take it.

Therapist: How do you end the call?

Client: I tell her I gotta go.

Therapist: You gotta take care of yourself.

Client: Exactly.

Therapist: Anyone else? Ever call anyone else?

Through this interaction, the therapist establishes that the client's anxiety and despair, which are high first thing in the morning, sometimes diminish for a period of time later in the day; that she gets out of her apartment; that she seeks social connections; and that she takes action to protect herself (e.g., ending a phone call) when what she tried isn't helping. Such variations are not unusual and all are potentially significant resources that can be returned to and elaborated on later in the interview.

In addition to assessing *intra*personal risks and resources, it is necessary as well to attend to the *inter*personal risks and resources contributed by the client's significant others. This contextual sensitivity can be found in the detailing of 10 topics of inquiry having to do with the risks contributed by significant others and another 8 that cover the resources of significant others.[1] All are arrayed in 2 × 2 panels under the four broad categories of experience mentioned earlier: *Disruptions and Demands, Suffering, Troubling Behaviors,* and *Desperation.*

To assist you in distinguishing (and us in referencing) the content of the separate quadrants in the panels, we have adopted a different numbering system within each. The intrapersonal risks of the client are itemized with uppercase letters (A, B, C, etc.); the client's resources, with Arabic numbers (1,

2, 3, etc.); the risks to the client contributed by his or her significant others, with lowercase letters (a, b, c, etc.); and the resources that the significant others bring to the table, with Greek numerals (i, ii, iii, etc.). Here are all 51 topics of inquiry, distributed throughout the four panels:

1. DISRUPTIONS AND DEMANDS

		Client		**Client's Significant Others**
Risks	A) B) C) D) E)	Loss/Failure of relationship Overwhelming expecta- tions/obligations Loss of social position/ financial status Legal/Disciplinary troubles Abuse/Bullying/Peril	a) b) c)	Distressing expectations/demands of the client Abandoning the client Abuse/Bullying of the client
Resources	1) 2)	Effective problem solving Positive personal/spiritual connections	i) ii)	Reasonable expectations/encour- agement of the client Helping the client meet obligations

2. SUFFERING

		Client		**Client's Significant Others**
Risks	F) G) H) I) J) K)	Depressed/Manic mood Anxiety/Anger/Obsessive thinking Conflicted identity/Shame/ Burdensomeness Hallucinations/Delusions Insomnia/Nightmares Pain/Illness/Injury	d) e)	Viewing the client as flawed/a burden Limited awareness of/Unhelpful re- sponse to the client's suffering
Resources	3) 4) 5)	Engagement in medical/ mental health treatment Variability in psychologi- cal/physical symptoms Effective response to suffer- ing	iii) iv)	Empathic response to the client's suffering Supporting the client's medical/ mental health treatment

3. TROUBLING BEHAVIORS

	Client	**Client's Significant Others**
Risks	L) Withdrawing from activities/relationships M) Substance abuse/Disordered eating N) Impulsive/Compulsive behaviors O) Harming self/others	f) Participating in the client's troubling behaviors g) Unhelpful attempts to regulate the client's troubling behaviors
Resources	6) Engaging in activities/relationships 7) Participating in therapy/rehab 8) Finding alternative behaviors	v) Reaching out to the client vi) Facilitating recovery/safety

4. DESPERATION

	Client	**Client's Significant Others**
Risks	P) Hopelessness Q) Intense desire for relief R) Intention/Plan to act on suicidal thoughts S) Communicating about suicidality T) Having/Gaining access to means U) Preparing for/Attempting suicide	h) Suicidality i) Ignorance/Denial of the client's suicidality j) Dismissive response to the client's suicidality
Resources	9) Hope/Reasons for living 10) Variability in suicidality 11) Willingness not to conceal suicidality 12) Active participation in developing and implementing a safety plan	vii) Compassionate response to the client's suicidality viii) Active participation in a safety plan

Combined, these four panels constitute what we call the *Risk and Resource Interview Guide* (RRIG), a template for conducting semistructured assessment interviews. Of necessity, no suicide assessment will ever be as comprehensive as the guide itself. You will never find yourself exploring all topics in a single interview, as only a subset of them will be relevant to a particular person's unique circumstances and experience. Indeed, if the client is clear and forthright about his or her intent to die, then your assessment will most likely be limited in scope, focused primarily on the topics under the fourth category of experience, *Desperation*. However, if the person's degree of suicidality is not clearly evident or consistently expressed, then your interview will probably touch on many of the topics arrayed throughout the four categories of experience.

Below, we discuss each topic of inquiry separately, acquainting you with some of the relevant research studies and/or the clinical ideas informing our decision to include it in the RRIG. For each topic we also provide sample questions (and some empathic statements) that illustrate how to broach and delve into relevant circumstances and experiences. Throughout these questions we've interspersed comments that provide a rationale for what is asked and how the query is posed.

We are challenged to demonstrate for you how to construct illustrative questions, given that, for any particular query to be effective, it needs to empathically reflect the idiosyncratic details of an individual client's life. To partially solve this problem, we are providing, prior to our discussion of the topics of inquiry, a comprehensive case study to which all the sample questions refer. This approach still leaves us a step or two away from capturing the interactive unfolding of an actual interview, where the statement being made or question being asked at a particular moment is informed by the client's responses to previous queries. We get closer to this in Chapter 5, where we present an annotated transcript derived from an RSA we did in our center. But back to the present chapter. Before we describe the case, itself based on another RSA we carried out with one of our clients,[2] we'd like to talk about the *process* of conducting the interview—about how to use the RRIG to organize your assessment conversations with your clients.

THE PROCESS OF THE INTERVIEW

The arrangement of the topics of inquiry listed in the RRIG is somewhat arbitrary. Those under "client risks" in the *Desperation* category—Hopelessness; Intense desire for relief; Intention/Plan to act on suicidal thoughts; Communicating about suicidality; Having/Gaining access to means; Preparing for/ Attempting suicide—are organized in ascending order of danger, and a similar order of intensification can be found in a few of the panels devoted to the risks related to significant others. Nevertheless, for the most part, the order of topics within the four categories of experience does not carry any particular importance.

The arrangement of the categories themselves—*Disruptions and Demands, Suffering, Troubling Behaviors,* and *Desperation*—is designed to facilitate easy recall. They are sequenced so as to accord with the way a conversation might naturally unfold with a desperate client. To help you remember them, then, you might imagine a person coming in and describing *disruptions and demands* that feel overwhelming—events that have torn the fabric of relationships and/or detoured the flow of his or her life (e.g., losses, expectations and obligations, financial or legal headaches, traumas). The person goes on to detail *suffering* that has resulted from or contributed to feeling overwhelmed—insomnia, anxiety, depression, obsessive thinking; physical or emotional pain; feeling existentially conflicted or victimized or shameful responsibility for an impossible predicament. He or she subsequently reveals *troubling behaviors* that sometimes temporarily provide some relief but also tend to intensify the sense of being out of control—withdrawing, self-medicating with substances or food, acting impulsively, self-harming. And then there's the *desperation*—frantic for relief, for escape, the person sees no way out, other than suicide.

In actual practice, an RSA, like an ethnographer's semistructured interview with a research participant, can start anywhere and go anywhere. Our goal is to use empathic reflections and questions to enter the world of our clients and to adapt, as much as possible, to their pace and style of filling us in on the details of their story. Your curiosity needs to be organized by the relevant topics of the interview guide, but we recommend creating smooth transitions between these topics so that clients, instead of feeling interrogated, experience the conversation as unfolding naturally.

Similarly to a qualitative research interview guide, the RRIG works best when you use it to prepare in advance for an assessment, holding a sense of it, the gist of it, in memory. By all means bring the RSA Backpocket version of the guide (located in the Appendix) with you into the interview, but leave it at your side, available to be consulted if necessary. Consider it an aid for remembering, not a script to be followed. This suggestion is in keeping with how qualitative researchers make use of *their* interview guides:

> If the interviewer is fully in control of the interview topics, the guide itself can remain unused. But if the interviewer begins to be uncertain about . . . whether an area or a topic has been skipped, the guide is there to be consulted. The interview guide may also be consulted at the very end of an interview as a last check that everything has been asked. . . . Focusing closely on the guide, at the cost of attention to the respondent and the flow of the interview, is always a mistake. (Weiss, 1994, p. 48)

With the RRIG as background support, rather than foreground checklist, you can focus your attention on conducting a comprehensive therapeutic assessment that both flows *and* yields critical information—empathically connecting with the person in front of you; managing your anxiety throughout the process; understanding what the client tells you within the context of his or her interpersonal relationships; broaching, delving into, and segueing between relevant topics; sprinkling in possibilities for therapeutic change; attending to the nature of the client's engagement with you; and knowing when to stop.

EMPATHICALLY CONNECTING

A strong therapeutic alliance is as essential for a reliable suicide assessment as it is for effective therapy (Meichenbaum, 2010; Rudd, 2006). The development and maintenance of empathic rapport allow you to cross the experiential boundary separating you from your clients, giving you an interior perspective of their pain and possibilities.[3] And such efforts also provide your clients with information about *you*. When you make an empathic statement, one that captures both the content and emotional character of what they've been telling you, you put your current grasp of their experience on display. This allows them to determine whether your understanding aligns with their own sense of themselves. If they judge you to be a sensitive and accurate listener, they may feel safe enough to continue telling you about the thoughts, feelings, and circumstances that have been plaguing them.

The questions we ask during an RSA are probably equaled or surpassed in number by the empathic statements we make. Such a balance helps ensure that clients don't end up feeling interrogated. If your assessment were to consist primarily of questions, you would risk your clients' retreating into themselves as a means of preserving privacy and integrity, overwhelmed by the machine-gun rhythm of your relentless curiosity. However, by frequently interspersing your questions with empathic statements, you change the pattern of the interaction.

We consider all of our contributions during an RSA—both questions and statements—to be *empathic inquiries*. Our questions are empathically steeped in and informed by the specificities of what our clients have been telling us, and our empathic statements, as in the following examples, provide opportunities for information gathering.

- "It sounds like the thoughts have been both terrifying and, in some confusing kind of way, a means of also achieving a semblance of relief."

- "How exhausted you must be, unable to sleep and unable to stop worrying about the foreclosure."

When we offer such empathic reflections, we pay close attention to what our clients say in response, as this helps, often as much as answers to our questions, to guide our developing understanding and to steer the course of the interview.

When clients find our empathic statements to be valid reflections of their experience,[4] they may feel somewhat less isolated in their suffering and desperation—which, in turn, can allow them to feel safe enough to further elaborate on what they've been experiencing. Such demonstrated trust provides us with important confirmation that we are developing an accurate insider's sensibility.

Not all of our empathic statements are accurate, however. When we're wrong and our clients take the trouble to correct our impressions, we're given the opportunity to refine our understanding, listen more carefully, and try again. The effective communication of empathy is thus the foundation for all information gathering throughout the assessment.

MANAGING ANXIETY

With a distraught person sitting across from you, the urgent need for reliable information staring you in the face, and the ramifications of making a mistake hanging over your head, you're necessarily going to feel anxious as you conduct a suicide assessment. Contributing to this unsettling feeling is the sobering realization that you're not yet sure what to make of the information you're gathering. How seriously should you take the intimations of desperation? The reassurances? The suggestions of impulsivity?

It won't help to try to keep your anxiety at bay or to admonish yourself that it's somehow unprofessional to feel this way, nor to try to short-circuit your anxiety by rushing to a sense of certainty about what your decision needs to be. Rather than attempting to contain or eliminate your anxiety, you'll find it much more helpful to *use* it. We have four suggestions for how you can do this.

- First, recognize the legitimacy of your body's anxious response to the situation by acknowledging its presence and welcoming it along for the ride. If you accept the likelihood that you'll remain at least somewhat anxious throughout the interview and you respect that the adrenaline in your veins will help keep you alert to the dangers and complexities of the situation, then you might be less inclined to try to rid yourself of it. Such an orientation to anxiety will help you avoid inadvertently creating more of it by getting caught in the reflexive, escalating spiral of feeling anxious about feeling anxious.

• Second, use your adrenaline-inspired discomfort as an empathic stepping-stone into the subjective experience of the client. Except in rare cases, the person in front of you will be much more anxious than you. If you tune into what's going on with your body, you'll have a head start on getting a sense of what it must be like to be inside his or her hell. Anxiety typically prompts a recoiling from whatever it is that you're anxious about. If, instead of heading in that direction, you allow it to take you *forward*, into rapport with your client, you will find most of it dissipating as you absorb yourself in the task at hand. So rather than concerning yourself with what you're feeling and then trying to get control or get rid of it so you can concentrate on your assessment, *use your emotional response to sensitize your involvement and fine-tune your discernment.*

• Third, accept that uncertainty will accompany you through most of your suicide assessments. You aren't alone in not being able to predict what your client will and won't do after leaving your office. You can arrive at a sense of what seems possible, likely, or unlikely, but specificities elude all of us. By recognizing how normal anxiety is, given the stakes involved, you may find it easier to stay relatively comfortable with not being sure, perhaps for much of the assessment, just what to make of what the client is (and isn't) telling you. Allow your uncertainty to fuel your curiosity, which can then prompt further information gathering.

At some point, of course, this information gathering will come to an end as you make a safety decision (see Chapter 4). If you find yourself still significantly unsettled at this point, listen to your discomfort and consider taking a second look at your decision and/or the safety plan. We'll address this possibility in greater depth in the next chapter.

• Fourth, let the anxiety you experienced in your most recent suicide assessment inspire you to more thoroughly prepare for the next one. Review all facets of the RSA method, focusing on the particularities of the RRIG and on the process of making a safety decision and co-creating a safety plan. The more familiar you are with the structure and topics of the assessment, the more comfortable you will be with the process of conducting the interview.

ATTENDING TO CONTEXT

It was mid-November, and a distraught and depressed young woman, a client in our center, was looking forward, she said, to going home for Thanksgiving. Overwhelmed with school and work demands and having flirted for the past few months with the thought of taking her life, she became animated when telling her therapist about her plans to relax, sleep, and cook and bake with her mother. The therapist endorsed the idea of her taking such a nurturing break, and they made an appointment for the week after she was to get back.

At the beginning of the next session, the client, looking more shaken than she had before her trip home, told her therapist that the vacation hadn't turned out as she'd hoped. It seems that her mother, out of earshot of the rest of the family, had proposed a joint suicide pact—a commitment to kill themselves together. Thankfully, the client had turned her down, perhaps more out of anger and a sense of betrayal than a desire to live. However, through her tears and sense of free-floating loss, she articulated a redoubled commitment to regaining a sense of balance, which now involved avoiding trips home and limiting the frequency and length of phone calls with her mother.

To fully appreciate your clients' risks and potential for safety, you need to understand what they're experiencing within the context of their interpersonal network of significant others. Most often, stable family and friends contribute much to your clients' ability to weather the storms of desperation (Brent & Melhem, 2008); however, sometimes clients feel diminished, marginalized, and even humiliated by the accomplishments and stability of their siblings or peers. Some clients, as in the case just described, are galvanized to "pull it together" in response to a desperate significant other, but, more commonly, their struggles are exacerbated by the struggles of those who mean the most to them. Teasing out such interpersonal complexities is a necessary part of determining possibilities for safety. Thus, if you are interviewing an individual client, allow your curiosity to extend beyond the person in front of you, down the invisible lines of relationship to relevant people in his or her life. You will find it helpful to ask questions not only about local family members, friends, roommates, classmates, fellow employees, spiritual leaders, teachers, and bosses, but also about those with whom the client is in contact only via phone or computer.

If you are fortunate enough to be able to invite one or more of the client's significant others into your assessment, you will benefit greatly from the stereoscopic depth of understanding afforded by the added perspective(s). However, be sure to reserve time to also speak with the suicidal person alone, as he or she may, during the conjoint portion of the interview, temper or intensify his or her comments in an effort to protect, alert, or scare the other(s).

BROACHING, DELVING INTO, AND TRANSITIONING BETWEEN TOPICS

Because the RRIG is designed to organize semistructured interviews, it provides the parameters for the conversation, but it leaves the process and the particular details of conducting it up to you. The choice of which topic to start with, where to go to from there, and how to broach, delve into, and segue between relevant subjects is determined extemporaneously, based on the circumstances of the client and the nature of the interaction the two of you are having at the moment.

A sensitivity to *how* and *when* questions are posed, and an interlacing of questions and empathic reflections, protects clients from feeling "grilled" and helps you to recognize options and possibilities that may have been escaping their notice. As part of our commitment to connect empathically with our clients, we do our best to match their language choices and level of comfort when broaching vital topics. If they are quick to describe their state of mind and are forthright in what they say, then we accelerate quickly to get up to speed:

Therapist: How have you been dealing with everything that's going on?

Client: I just want to blow my brains out.

Therapist: Feels like there's a gun to your head?

Client: You don't know the half of it.

Therapist: There are just too many demands.

Client: I can't take it anymore. It has to stop.

Therapist: So when you're feeling this way, do you get an urge to reach for an actual gun?

However, if clients are circumspect in what they are sharing, then we broach subjects less directly:

Therapist: How have you been dealing with everything that's going on?

Client: I haven't, really.

Therapist: Overwhelmed?

Client: Yeah.

Therapist: When people get totally stressed out, they sometimes have trouble sleeping.

Client: Yeah?

Therapist: How's your sleep been?

Client: Not so good.

Therapist: When you can't sleep, everything is so much harder to deal with.

Client: Too hard.

Therapist: Yeah, way too hard. . . . Can leave you feeling pretty desperate.

Client: Yup.

Therapist: So how desperate have you been feeling? Where do your thoughts take you?

If you don't get too far ahead of your clients, they will feel invited to explore issues with you, rather than feeling like they need to protect themselves from you and your questions.

One way to broach important topics is to normalize your clients' experience. The therapist did this in the second example, above, by making reference to what happens when "people get totally stressed out." We also normalize by telling our clients stories about other clients (changing details, of course, to disguise identities). This approach provides a means not only of broaching an issue, but of delving further into it.

Therapist: So how desperate have you been feeling? Where do your thoughts take you?

Client: I don't like thinking about it.

Therapist: Scary, huh?

Client: Yeah.

Therapist: I had a client once who was feeling so anxious and distraught, night after night he couldn't sleep. It got to where he was basically having dreams while he was awake, and it scared the hell out of him—made him even more anxious. He thought he was going crazy, and he started having these thoughts about hurting himself.

Client: I hate feeling this way. I keep getting this image . . .

Therapist: A scary image?

Client: . . . of jumping off my balcony.

Therapist: Must be frightening to go home.

Client: I hate being there.

Therapist: Of course.

Client: I'm afraid of what might happen.

When you conduct semistructured interviews with your clients, you keep track of what you've explored and what you have yet to delve into, but you don't concern yourself with the order in which you make your inquiries. If, in delving into a topic or even just in broaching it, you sense that your clients are becoming too anxious or are feeling like you're being too intrusive, you can always segue to some other topic and come back to the issue at hand at a later point.

Therapist: You're worried that you might actually do what you see in the image?

Client: I don't know.

Therapist: It's scary to think about.

Client: Yeah.

Therapist: Have you been able to talk about it to anyone? A friend? Someone in your family?

Client: God, no.

Therapist: They couldn't handle it?

Client: I don't want them to think I'm crazy.

Therapist: You don't want them to worry?

Client: I don't want to have to put up with them freaking out.

Therapist: Who would be the least reactive?

Inquiring about the availability and resourcefulness (or lack thereof) of the client's significant others will help the therapist develop a better contextual understanding of the client's situation, but it also shifts attention away, for a while, from the fear-inducing image of jumping off the balcony. It will be possible to come back to the details of the thought and image once more rapport and trust have been established. A semistructured interview approach means that you will be influenced as much by what the client has just said as you are by what you still need to cover from the topics in the four panels.

SPRINKLING IN POSSIBILITIES FOR HOPE AND CHANGE

If you try to convince clients that they should feel hopeful—or at least not so hopeless—or if you attempt to reassure them that their situation or their tunnel vision is only temporary and will no doubt improve, your well-meaning but blunt efforts to help will most likely have the opposite effect. When people feel that something is being forced down their throats, they fight against it so as not to choke. But if you sprinkle implications of strength and possibility into your conversations with them, then you can indirectly establish a context for hope without their finding it necessary to dismiss your suggestions as untenable.

Assessments are not an occasion for therapy, but nevertheless they *can be* therapeutic. In the process of empathically gathering information, you can give clients an experience of feeling deeply understood. This sense of connection, of not being alone in their agony, can have a beneficial effect, in and of itself. But the therapeutic potential of assessments doesn't stop there. Because of the experience-shaping effects of language, the way you gather information *from* your clients also implicitly communicates something *to* them.

As we discussed in Chapters 1 and 2, neutral questions do not exist. You can't make a determination of your clients' state of mind without simultaneously framing their experience. This means that every question you pose is not only a tool for collecting data, but also a tool for *intervening* (or, as we prefer, *intravening*)[5]—for contextualizing and orienting not only the clients' ways of relating to themselves and what they are facing, but also the relationship between their current circumstances and a possible future.

Below is an example of how, with a male college student, a therapist communicates curiosity about the client's means of coping and about variations in, or exceptions to, his problems. In so doing, the therapist manages to gently probe for resources without imposing naïve hopefulness.

Therapist: So you've been really down?

Client: Yes.

Therapist: How'd you even make it to the appointment?

The question establishes, through implication, that the client was able to take action to help himself, despite his mood.

Client: My mom drove me.

Therapist: You can count on her in a pinch?

Client: Yes.

Therapist: Did you have to remind her about our session, or did she remember on her own?

If the client reminded his mother, he took initiative; if she remembered on her own, she is reliable—either way, the question ensures that there's a resource in play. Note that the therapist didn't ask, ". . . or did she have to remind you?" Nothing helpful would come out of characterizing the client as lethargic or incompetent.

Client: I called her and told her I needed a ride.

Therapist: Sometimes the best way for us to get help from others is to help them help us.

By offering this as a universal statement of fact, the therapist makes it easier for the client to accept the proposition that he was acting proactively. Making sure not to irritate the client by dwelling on this point, the therapist next turns to asking about variations in mood.

Client: I guess.

Therapist: Are there particular times when you feel worse?

If there are worse times, then there are also, by implication, better times. Asking first about something positive, however, might be met with resignation or suspicion.

Client: When I wake up. I've been having disturbing dreams.

Therapist: And it probably takes awhile before the dream begins to fade and you find yourself not feeling as bad as you did when you woke up.

A depressed person would generally find it easier to endorse this description than something like this: "And it probably takes awhile before you start feeling better."

Client: Yeah. An hour at least.

Therapist: Over the course of an hour, the dream fades and your mood shifts?

Client: More or less, yeah.

Therapist: You told me last time that you had been having thoughts about ending your life.

Client: Yeah.

Therapist: Have you noticed any change in them in the last week?

Client: What do you mean?

Therapist: I don't know . . . maybe the thoughts have been stronger, or have been sticking around longer, or have been coming more often. Or maybe they are weaker, are lasting a shorter amount of time, or are coming less frequently. . . .

The therapist is curious about variations in the experience of the thoughts, particularly in variations that provide some relief. However, this interest is not pursued as an imposed agenda. You wouldn't want the client thinking that there was a correct answer, and if you make clear that you're only interested in hearing positive stuff, your ability to gather reliable information will suffer significantly. Nevertheless, curiosity about change can indirectly invite expectancy of change, which can inspire therapeutic movement.

Possibilities for hope and change can also be sprinkled by way of the tense forms you choose. When exploring the possible worsening of the client's suicidal thoughts, the therapist uses what grammarians call *present perfect* and *present perfect continuous* tenses: "Maybe the thoughts *have been* stronger, or *have been sticking* around longer, or *have been coming* more often." However, when speculating that the thoughts could possibly be improving, the therapist uses *present* and *present continuous* tenses: "Maybe they *are weaker, are lasting* a shorter amount of time, or *are coming* less frequently. . . ."

Verbs in past, present, and future tenses (as well as in past continuous, present continuous, and future continuous tenses) establish or underscore the stable state or ongoing existence of whatever is being described. They are thus useful when you wish to convey the possibility that something resourceful was, is, or can be an established fact or a continuing state: "He *had* thoughts about staying safe"; "He *was having* thoughts about staying safe"; "He *has* thoughts about staying safe"; "He *is having* thoughts about staying safe"; "He *will have* thoughts about staying safe"; "He *will be having* thoughts about staying safe."

Perfect tense forms establish the fact or ongoing existence of something only *up until the moment in time being specified*, after which nothing is certain or determined. So when the therapist wonders if the suicidal thoughts *have been* stronger, *have been sticking around* longer, or *have been coming* more often, he is offering appropriate acknowledgment that there may have been an increase in the severity of the situation. However, concomitantly, nothing in the verb forms he uses suggests that this state of affairs will necessarily continue into the future. The thoughts may *have been* stronger, *have been* more persistent, or *have been* more frequent, but this description of them doesn't assume or imply that they *will be* remaining so. Such indeterminacy keeps the door to change ajar.

Client: I don't think I've noticed any change.
Therapist: Okay, so they haven't gotten any worse, but you haven't yet noticed any improvement, either.
Client: Right.

The therapist's last statement accomplishes something similar to his previous one—it both acknowledges the client's current experience *and* introduces the possibility of some sort of shift. As before, the tense form of the verb assists in this double duty. The therapist says " . . . you *haven't* . . . *noticed* any improvement," rather than "you *don't notice*" or "you *aren't noticing* any improvement." The use of perfect tense establishes that what has been true up until this moment in time (no indication of improvement) may not continue to be true. However, this implication of future development is then intensified through the therapist's insertion of the word *yet*, a most helpful term for introducing the implication of anticipated change: "You *haven't yet noticed* any improvement."

We want to underscore that in approaching assessments in this way, we are not attempting to promote "positive thinking," and we are not turning a blind eye to danger and threat. We don't encourage our clients to lighten their spirits or to "look on the bright side" of anything, and when we are highly concerned about danger, we take relevant risks and resources into account and act accordingly. Nevertheless, we are continually looking for opportunities to sprinkle in implications that change could happen or has already begun. We view this time of high crisis as an opportunity for beginning to build a foundation for safety, as this is the best insurance policy against current and future despair.

ATTENDING TO CLIENTS' ENGAGEMENT

The RRIG itself is content-based—it provides you with an array of essential *topics* to explore with your clients. But while you're busy asking *about* this or that area of importance, you also need to focus on your clients' involvement in the *process* of your interaction. Here is a list of questions to *silently ask yourself* as the interview unfolds. For ease of presentation, we'll assume that the client is a woman, but the essence of the questions would remain the same if you were speaking with a man.

- How does she look? Clothes? Hair? Does she appear to have been taking care of her appearance?
- How do her eyes look? Does she appear to be under the influence of any drugs or alcohol?
- Does she appear grounded in the reality of the current circumstances?
- Is she speaking clearly, or is she mumbling or slurring?
- Does she appear lethargic? Agitated?
- What's the nature of her speech? Comfortably measured? Slow? Pressured?
- Is she focused in her responses to my questions, or does she often digress?
- Are her responses to my questions complete? Exceedingly terse? Exceedingly elaborate?
- As I continue talking with her, is she becoming less guarded? More?
- Is she making and maintaining eye contact?
- Is she answering my questions forthrightly, or does she appear to be constructing responses designed to alleviate my concern?
- If she is angry about, or frightened by, talking with me, to what degree does this make good contextual sense? That is, is she sitting here with me now because someone else has given her no choice in the matter?
- Returning to a topic that I broached earlier and asking about it a different way, is her answer consistent with what she said earlier?
- How is she responding to my voiced commitment to ensuring her

safety? Is she reassured or dismissive? If the latter, does her assertion that I don't need to be concerned match my impression of her well-being?

- How is she responding to my empathic statements? Is she letting me know when my reflections are accurate?

- How is she responding to my resource-based questions and to the therapeutic framing of my questions? Am I getting the sense that she could benefit from a professional relationship with a therapist?

Your answers to these self-posed questions will help you make sense of the content-based information you gather from your clients. In the next chapter, we'll talk about what to do with this contextualized understanding—that is, with the impressions your answers to the questions help you to form.

KNOWING WHEN TO STOP

Picasso once said that one of the most important skills for a painter to possess is knowing when to stop. Qualitative researchers know it is time to stop interviewing their research participants when the information they are gathering is not adding anything new to the understanding they have developed to that point. An analogous sensibility can inform your work, as well. The length of your interview shouldn't be determined by how loquacious your client happens to be or how curious you are. Rather, you should bring your conversation to a close when you become aware that, in the last little while, nothing the client has said in response to your questions, nothing about your emotional response to the interview, and nothing you're noticing about his or her involvement in the process is different enough from what you've already heard, felt, or seen to add anything new to your empathic grasp of the client's world.

THE RRIG

We now turn to a presentation and clinical illustration of the 51 topics of inquiry that together compose the RRIG—our template for conducting semi-structured suicide assessments. For each topic, we discuss the relevant research findings and clinical experiences that informed our decision to include it. Then, drawing on the case description we're about to provide, we list and discuss possible questions and empathic comments that could be used to broach or delve into that particular realm of the client's experience.

CASE DESCRIPTION OF LESLIE

Leslie, an only child and accomplished violinist, moved into the area 18
months ago to accept a position with the local symphony. A graduate from
a prestigious music school, she, at 24, has been struggling on and off for 5
years with significant depression and manic episodes. Over her parents'
objections, a psychiatrist in her home city originally prescribed an antidepressant and mood stabilizer for her. Leslie tried them for a while, but
not convinced they were helping and hating the side effects, she took
them inconsistently. When she moved here, the responsibility for prescribing and monitoring these medications fell to her primary care physician, who also prescribed an opiate to help control back pain stemming
from a car accident 3 years ago. Concerned about Leslie's well-being, the
physician referred her to you a few months back. Leslie has consistently
attended her sessions with you, but more, it seems, out of a desire to fulfill
a scheduled obligation than with any hope of making a significant change.
     Leslie began second-guessing her decision to join the symphony almost
as soon as she started with it. Intimidated by the conductor yet critical of
the caliber of the other musicians, she also struggles with the physical pain
that results from sitting and playing for long periods of time. She describes
rehearsals as "tedious," and although she has always loved performing, she
has, to her chagrin, begun to experience, in her words, "a weird strain of
subclinical stage fright" during concerts. Discouraged and unnerved, she
feels like "time is running out" and asks herself whether she will be able to
"win a permanent gig with a major orchestra" before her "musical integrity
disintegrates beyond repair." The conductor and the orchestra's general
manager have set up a meeting with her next week to discuss her contract.
     Four weeks ago, Leslie's 37-year-old boyfriend, Jeremy, a first-chair cel-
list in the symphony, informed her that he "needed some emotional space"
from her, which meant that she needed to move out of the second-floor
apartment in his house that she'd been renting from him, at a reduced rate,
for the better part of a year. She found another apartment a few blocks
away. The new landlord allowed her to keep her border collie, Mahler, but
he doubled the damage deposit, and the rent is significantly more than
what she was paying Jeremy. Small windows and dark walls create a space
she finds "dreary and depressing," and her neighbors complain if she practices. She describes herself as feeling "boxed in and musically silenced."
     Leslie's insomnia and headaches have recently worsened, and she is eat-
ing even less than usual. Her opiate medication, she says, has become necessary not only for her physical pain, but also for her emotional pain, so
she is taking more than her prescribed dose and is thus having to find
other sources to supply her heightened need. When she recently revealed

this to her parents, they apparently reacted with dismay and dismissive anger, demanding that she check herself into a rehab facility. She told them she'd "rather die than have a bunch of shrinks poking and prodding me like a junkie."

Unable to stop thinking about Jeremy, Leslie has been texting him multiple times per day, alternating between vicious attacks and plaintive entreaties, and she feels compelled to "more or less continually monitor his status on Facebook." He was, she says, her "first love." Her one previous serious relationship, when she was in college, was with an "insanely jealous," controlling, and, at times, physically abusive fellow freshman she met at orientation. In contrast, Jeremy is "ever the gentleman," a man "in possession of the aesthetic rigor and refined taste" necessary to understand her, but also, unfortunately, "lacking the requisite emotional depth, and musical and sexual courage" to appreciate what he has lost. Still, she fantasizes about his suddenly realizing what a mistake he has made, but "too late to do anything about it." She plans, as a parting gift, to have delivered to him a valuable "original musical manuscript in the composer's hand" that she inherited from her grandfather when he died earlier this year.

In a recent text, Leslie told Jeremy that she is going to "resign from the symphony," putting an end to "musical dreams that have become discordant nightmares." She thinks that "ultimately, Jeremy will be better off" without her and mentions in passing her belief that her parents, too, though they would never admit it, would be "deeply relieved" if she "were no longer here."

This description gives you some background information on the dangers entangling and defining Leslie's circumstances and mind-set. If you were responsible for conducting her suicide assessment, making a safety decision, and co-creating a safety plan with her, you would want a better appreciation of her intra- and interpersonal risks, as well as the degree to which her intra- and interpersonal resources offer tangible protection. The possible questions provided under the topics of inquiry, below, offer an opportunity for developing such understanding. You can consider each a unique entry point into the logic and details of the impossibilities Leslie is experiencing and the possibilities she has available to her.

Keep in mind that what follows is a template to help you organize your safety curiosity during a semistructured interview. When you use the template to inform an actual assessment, the total number and particular order of topics you address will be determined by what's happening in the unfolding conversation, not by what appears next in the structure of the interview guide.

DISRUPTIONS AND DEMANDS

	Client	**Client's Significant Others**
Risks	A) Loss/Failure of relationship B) Overwhelming expecta- tions/obligations C) Loss of social position/ financial status D) Legal/Disciplinary troubles E) Abuse/Bullying/Peril	a) Distressing expectations/demands of the client b) Abandoning the client c) Abuse/Bullying of the client
Resources	1) Effective problem solving 2) Positive personal/spiritual connections	i) Reasonable expectations/encour- agement of the client ii) Helping the client meet obligations

CLIENT RISKS

A) Loss/Failure of Relationship

In studies of suicidal people, researchers have noted that rejection within or loss of a relationship (e.g., a separation or divorce) is a critical factor in triggering thoughts of death, self-harm, suicide attempts, or completed suicides (Fanous, Prescott, & Kendler, 2004; Frances, Franklin, & Flavin, 1986; Stack & Wasserman, 2007). One study presented results suggesting that the risk of a suicide attempt can be as much as 6 times greater for those who are separated or divorced, rather than currently married or unmarried (Petronis, Samuels, Moscicki, & Anthony, 1990), and multiple losses are perhaps the most stressful (Stack & Wasserman, 2007). Luoma and Pearson (2002) reported that, in their study, the risk of suicide increased 17-fold among young (ages 20–34), widowed European American men and 9-fold among young, widowed African American men, in comparison to their married counterparts.

Conventional wisdom has it that if a significant other dies by suicide, it increases risk more than if the person died by some other means, perhaps because it lends credibility to the choice; however, the research to date has not borne out this assumption. Nevertheless, indirect support comes from research on complicated grief, which tends to be defined in terms of its PTSD-like symptoms, including intrusive thoughts about the deceased, avoidance of reminders of the deceased, feelings of bitterness and shock over the death, and survivor guilt (Prigerson et al., 1995). One study (Mitchell, Kim, Priger-son, & Mortimer-Stephens, 2004) of 60 adult survivors of the suicide of a family member or significant other reported significant levels of complicated grief in the survivors. And another demonstrated that elderly bereaved individuals with high measures of complicated grief were significantly more likely to develop suicidal ideation than were those with low measures (Szanto, Prigerson, Houck, Ehrenpreis, & Reynolds, 1997). Given that one of the symptoms of complicated grief is "identification symptoms or harmful behaviors resembling those suffered by the deceased" (Mitchell et al., p. 14), it might be expected that if the deceased took his or her own life, a surviving significant other with complicated grief might be at higher risk to engage in suicidal behavior.

Possible Questions
Leslie has lost one person to death (her grandfather) and another (Jeremy) in a quasi-divorce; both losses are worth exploring. The more Leslie's relationship with Jeremy had felt permanent, the more its demise could be affecting her:

- "If Jeremy hadn't ended the relationship, would it have continued? Were you expecting the two of you to stay together?"

Sometimes, ongoing contact with an ex heightens the intensity of the loss:

- "It must be painful to have to see him at rehearsals and concerts."

You would also want to gauge the effect of the death of significant others and know something, perhaps, about how they died:

- "Your grandfather left you a valuable gift when he died. How close were you? How did he die?"
- "Have you lost any other important people in your life? How did they die?"

B) Overwhelming Expectations and/or Obligations

People can become overwhelmed and depressed when needing to respond to multiple competing demands, whether placed by significant others or themselves. Kendler, Karkowski, and Prescott (1998) found that multiple stressful life events within a single month significantly increased the risk of the onset of depression. Other researchers have revealed associations between dimensions of perfectionism—the placing of overwhelming expectations on oneself—and perceived stress, depression, and hopelessness (Rice, Leever, Christopher, & Porter, 2006). Similarly, Sterud, Hem, Lau, and Ekeberg (2008) made a link between job-related emotional exhaustion (feelings of being over-extended and depleted of resources) and serious suicidal ideation.

Possible Questions

Save for needing to look after her dog, Mahler, Leslie doesn't have any personal obligations—no children or elderly parents for whom she feels responsible—so the curiosity would best focus on the expectations she has for herself and those she faces as a result of being a professional musician.

- "You've been putting a lot of pressure on yourself. You're here, but you had expected that by this point you'd already be in a major orchestra. In what other ways have you been setting the bar high for yourself?"
- "How are you handling the inability to practice as much as you would wish? Are you able to learn the music you're performing with the orchestra? Are you playing it with the precision and absorption that they and you demand?"

The following questions explore how the necessity of caring for a pet, which could itself be a protective factor, might possibly be increasing Leslie's stress level. However, notice the resource-based wording. The first question attributes the cause of the possible stress to the high-strung nature of the dog, not to some problem of Leslie's, and the second sprinkles the therapeutic idea that she is *managing*.

- "Does Mahler fit or defy the border collie stereotype for being smart and high strung?"
- "With all that's going on, how are you managing to care for Mahler?"

If she's reasonably satisfied with how she's caring for Mahler, you could find out if she is setting and meeting similarly reasonable expectations elsewhere.

- "In what other areas of your life are you giving yourself permission to do a 'good enough' job, given the circumstances?"

C) Loss of Social Position/Financial Status

In a study investigating thoughts of death or self-harm in female twins, recent job loss and financial problems were found to correlate significantly with thoughts of death or self-harm (Fanous et al., 2004). Other studies have noted increases in suicide risk being accompanied by the anticipated loss of a home or car, shortfalls in income, and the loss of employment (Stack & Wasserman, 2007). Low social class and chronic poverty are *not* predictive of suicide, but a recent negative change in financial status, whether through job loss or retirement, *is* predictive (Lewis & Sloggett, 1998; Turvey, Stromquist, Kelly, Zwerling, & Merchant, 2002).

Possible Questions
Leslie lost status, at least in her own eyes, when she took a job with this orchestra.

- "You're performing in an orchestra that you feel is beneath you. How difficult is it for you to be playing with musicians you don't respect?"

This job status could be looked upon as a chronic disappointment, rather than an acute loss; however, further loss, both social and financial, will occur if the conductor and general manager terminate her contract in their scheduled upcoming meeting.

- "Are you concerned about next week's meeting with the conductor and general manager? What are you thinking might be the reason for their calling the meeting?"

Also to be considered: Given that Leslie doesn't respect the other musicians in the orchestra, she may not have enjoyed any status from dating the first chair cellist, but it is possible that a public breakup is proving humiliating for her.

- "Did the other members of the orchestra know about your and Jeremy's relationship? Do they know about the breakup?"

Even if Leslie's contract isn't terminated at the upcoming meeting, it is possible that she has expenses, such as student loans, that will overwhelm her financial stability now that she has had to seek more expensive housing.

- "How's your money holding out now that you've had to get a more expensive apartment? How are you managing to make ends meet?"

D) Legal/Disciplinary Troubles

In addition to cataloging financial stressors as contributors to suicidality, Stack and Wasserman (2007) determined that involvement in the criminal justice system was also a predictor. Beautrais, Joyce, and Mulder (1997) found legal difficulties to be among the most common precipitants of serious suicide attempts among adolescents and young adults, and other researchers have found both legal and disciplinary problems to be predictive of completed suicide among adolescents (Brent, Perper, Moritz, & Baugher, 1993; Marttunen, Aro, & Lönnqvist, 1993). We have seen many clients over the years who were caught up in legal nightmares or were college or graduate students being investigated by their schools for plagiarism or some other serious infraction. Several of them saw suicide as the only way to escape from what they perceived to be an attenuated future and a life of shame.

Possible Questions
Leslie is no longer a student, so you would have no need to ask about any disciplinary actions against her, and nothing you've learned about her so far would suggest that she's had any run-ins with the law. Given this knowledge, if you *were* to ask her about any possible legal difficulties, you'd want to address the topic in an indirect way.

- "When you were dealing with your first boyfriend's abuse or the aftermath of your car accident, did you have to get lawyers or the police involved? Have you had any subsequent dealings with the legal system?"

E) Abuse/Bullying/Peril

Abused or bullied people experience a violation of their physical, emotional, sexual, or social well-being. Soldiers imperiled on the battlefield and civilian victims of violent events undergo a similar existential shattering of their sense of safety. Tearing the protective fabric of people's lives, traumatic experience can give rise to feelings of profound vulnerability, helplessness, and terror. Indeed, "up to 50% of psychiatric patients have a history of victimization" (Meichenbaum, 2006, p. 335).

Distress over an abusive past, as well as the symptoms of PTSD that may ensue from various kinds of trauma, have been shown to be associated with an increased risk of suicide (Anderson, Tiro, Price, Bender, & Kaslow, 2002; Andover, Zlotnick, & Miller, 2007; Oquendo et al., 2003; Tiet, Finney, & Moos, 2006). Boys with a current high level of distress about past sexual abuse were found to be 15 times more likely to make a suicide attempt than boys without an abuse history (Martin, Bergen, Richardson, Roeger, & Allison, 2004), and young adults who developed PTSD symptoms after a traumatic event were reported to have an almost threefold increased risk of suicide over those without such trauma (Wilcox, Storr, & Breslau, 2009). Researchers studying victims of crimes and accidents found similar increases. People attending a clinic devoted to PTSD treatment exhibited 3 times the level of suicidal ideation and twice the level of plans and attempts than the general population (Tarrier & Gregg, 2004).

Involvement in bullying, whether as a victim or perpetrator, also increases risk, particularly among special populations, such as children with learning disabilities or adolescents who are lesbian, gay, or bisexual (Kim & Leventhal, 2008). In a study of jail inmates in the Netherlands (Blaauw, Winkel, & Kerkhof, 2001), researchers found that at least 34% of suicide victims had also been the victims of bullying.

Risk of suicidality can extend far beyond the time of the original trauma, and, not surprisingly, the greater the intensity or duration of the traumatic events, the higher the risk. Tiet et al. (2006) identified both recent and lifetime histories of abuse as independent risk factors for recent suicide attempts among men seeking treatment, and Anderson et al. found that women who had experienced three forms of abuse in childhood were almost 8 times as likely to make an attempt as women who experienced no abuse as children. Researchers have recognized that veterans who are repeatedly wounded and/ or have more serious wounds are at greater risk of suicide than veterans with less intense tours (Bullman & Kang, 1996), and those with more severe PTSD symptoms are at increased risk of making a suicide attempt (Hendin & Haas, 1991). According to a recent report, "almost one-third of the troops returning from Iraq or Afghanistan have experienced a traumatic brain injury or meet criteria for major depression or PTSD" (Kuehn, 2009, p. 1111). Meanwhile, the suicide rate "among active-duty soldiers in the US army reached a 28-year high in 2008" (Kuehn, p. 1111).

Possible Questions
The abuse Leslie was subjected to by her first boyfriend happened a few years back, but the aftereffects could still be contributing to her distress. You might explore this possibility through curiosity about her resilience.

- "Your college boyfriend was incredibly jealous, right? Must have been suffocating. How did you survive?"
- "Somehow you were able to get out of that relationship and get on with your life. What made that possible?"

Such questions imply that it is possible to survive and move beyond something that is suffocating (which is broadly relevant to her needing to survive other kinds of suffocating circumstances now). The first question also gently introduces the idea of jealousy. Does her success in contending with her old boyfriend's jealousy provide her with any help in dealing with her own?

Leslie's car accident may also have had a traumatic effect on her.

- "The car accident has caused you a lot of physical pain. What kind of effect did it have on you emotionally?"

Depending on her response, you might follow up with inquiries about PTSD symptoms.

CLIENT RESOURCES

1) Effective Problem Solving

Because deficits in problem-solving skills have been identified in suicidal individuals (McAuliffe, Corcoran, Keeley, & Perry, 2003; Pollock & Williams, 1998; Schotte & Clum, 1987), researchers have explored whether improving problem solving lowers suicidality. Salkovskis, Atha, and Storer (1990), using a problem-solving cognitive–behavioral approach with 20 patients at high risk for repeated suicidal behavior, noted a reduction in distress and in repeat suicide attempts. Joiner, Voelz, and Rudd (2001) studied problem-solving treatment compared to treatment as usual for suicidal young adults with depression and anxiety disorders. The problem-solving approach—an intensive, structured, time-limited outpatient group psychotherapy, targeting interpersonal skill development and adaptive coping—was somewhat more effective overall and was particularly effective for patients with comorbid major depressive disorder and anxiety. In another study, patients hospitalized for a suicide attempt demonstrated decreased suicidal ideation after participating in therapy devoted to problem solving (Patsiokas & Clum, 1985).

Possible Questions

We don't attempt to teach problem-solving skills to our clients, but we do scope out the abilities they possess and can possibly access.

- "It has to be frustrating not to be able to play your violin in your apartment. What progress have you made in finding a place to practice?"
- "You've got so much to figure out right now. What helps you make decisions you can live with?"

2) *Positive Personal/Spiritual Connections*

In a study based on findings from the National Longitudinal Study on Adolescent Health, Resnick et al. (1997) concluded that the risk of suicidal thoughts and behaviors was significantly reduced by parent–family connectedness (e.g., "feelings of warmth, love, and caring from parents" [p. 830]) and by perceived school connectedness (e.g., "perceived caring from teachers and high expectations of student performance" [p. 831]). Spiritual connections, and the resulting religious community bonds that accompany them, also appear to increase safety. Dervic et al. (2004) found that depressed inpatients who reported a religious affiliation had a history of significantly fewer suicide attempts than those patients with no such affiliation. Marion and Range (2003) attributed lower rates of suicidal ideation in female African American college students (compared to other students) to their religiosity and social support from family. And Gibbs (1997), trying to make sense of the lower suicide rates among African Americans (compared to European Americans), speculated that religiosity was perhaps their most important protective factor; however, she also made note of extended family cohesion and the respect and dignity afforded elders.

Possible Questions
We routinely scan for the availability of social resources.

- "Is anyone offering you decent advice for how to handle the situation with the orchestra or with Jeremy? What's their take?"
- "Have you shared anything with any of the other musicians in the orchestra? Have they been helpful?"

It's not uncommon following a breakup for clients to request or even demand emotional reassurance or some other kind of assistance from their ex—the very person they deem responsible for their loss and isolation. Any response on the part of the ex to such painful and emotionally complicated communications can significantly increase the clients' distress. Kindness can hurt as much as or more than cold dismissals.

- "Sometimes when people lose a relationship, they feel compelled to reach out for some kind of support—emotional, financial, logistical, whatever—from the person who left them. Have you found yourself reaching out to Jeremy in this way?"

We will also ask directly about whether the client has a belief system or religious community that contributes to wellbeing.

- "Are you a spiritual person? Do your beliefs or your religious community offer you any comfort or support?"

SIGNIFICANT-OTHER RISKS

a) Distressing Expectations/Demands of the Client

When someone matters to you a great deal and that person expects or demands too much of you, the emotional pressure can feel overwhelming. The client featured in Chapter 5 is a good example of a person in such a predicament. Like many of the students we saw in our university clinic, he had a successful father who was critical of his motivation and dismissive of his intelligence. Failing not only in school, but also in his father's eyes, our client felt unbearably distraught.

Another client of ours, a suicidal young woman who was unemployed, profoundly anxious, and homeless, couldn't rely on her family for any kind of support. Her only friend offered a place to stay, but in return was making multiple demands that our client felt incapable of meeting. Thus, the one significant other who was protecting her from suicide was simultaneously contributing to her suicidality.

Possible Questions
It is possible that no one has as high expectations of Leslie as Leslie herself, but it would be good to check out. Are her parents attempting to lower the stakes, or are they, too, thinking that she is underachieving?

- "Who will be most disappointed if you don't get into a major orchestra?"
- "You have very high standards for yourself. Are you the most demanding, or are there others who expect even more of you than you do?"

b) Abandoning the Client

For individuals who struggle with unstable relationships, self-image, and affect, a decision to attempt suicide can be precipitated by real or perceived abandonment. Brodsky, Groves, Oquendo, Mann, and Stanley (2006) concluded that for individuals diagnosed with borderline personality disorder (BPD), "interpersonal conflicts and disappointments need to be taken as seriously as the seemingly more serious or 'valid' triggers of suicide attempts" (p. 320).

We have seen several clients over the years, not all of whom would have been diagnosed with BPD, who became suicidal after a parent refused to prevent financial ruin, a partner left them for someone else, or a loved one disappeared when the client received a life-threatening medical diagnosis. One of our clients drank bleach when her husband told her he no longer loved her and wanted a divorce; another became suicidal when her wealthy parents refused to step in and protect her from losing her house in a foreclosure.

Possible Questions

Without a clear opening from a client, we probably wouldn't ask directly about abandonment—for example, "In addition to feeling abandoned by Jeremy, do you also feel abandoned by your parents or anyone else?"—but we *would* listen for it and pose questions that would allow the client to bring it up.

- "Moving to a new city can leave you feeling isolated. Has anyone from your past—your parents, other relatives, old friends—found ways of supporting you from a distance?"

c) Abuse/Bullying of the Client

A young woman being seen in our clinic expressed ongoing suicidality. She made many calls to our crisis line, and, in addition to regularly scheduled appointments, she came in for several crisis sessions. At first she talked only of feeling overwhelmed by her demanding academic program, carrying significant debt, and worrying whether she would graduate. She cut herself as a way of coping, and the therapist worked with her to find alternative methods that would more safely relieve her of some of her stress.

Coming into a session shortly after returning from a visit home, she appeared much more distressed than before she had left, so the therapist explored what had happened during her time with her parents. It was then that the client revealed that her father had sexually abused her several times during her stay, continuing a habitual violation that had been going on for years. Brezo et al. (2008), investigating the effect of childhood abuse on suicidality, determined that individuals sexually abused by a member of their immediate family were at highest risk of making an attempt. Meichenbaum (2006) underscored the importance of ensuring that "patients are *safe* from the risk of further victimization and that any immediate disturbing symptoms . . . are addressed" (pp. 340–341).

Our client was terrified of the potential consequences of standing up to her father and revealing what was going on to her mother and/or to the authorities. She was afraid that he would withdraw the financial support she required to finish school, and she was worried about his capacity to take revenge in other ways. Despite the impossibility of her situation, the therapist was able to help her to find the ability to say *no*. Sometimes she refused to go home at breaks; at other times she went back but stayed with a friend, rather than at home, and thus was able to preclude her father's nighttime visits. As she found her voice, her suicidality decreased significantly, and she eventually graduated *and* managed to put a permanent stop to the abuse.

If, during a suicide assessment, you discover that the client is contending with ongoing bullying or abuse from a significant other, you will need to determine whether it is possible to limit the bully or abuser's access to the client and whether other significant others, who may or may not know of the situation, can be trusted to protect the client and take seriously the detrimental effects the behavior has caused. If they can't be trusted in this way, you won't want to rely on them to be part of a safety plan. If the client is under 18, you will need to breach confidentiality and report abuse to state authorities. If a child is contending with bullying, you may be able to successfully intervene, with the family's permission, with his or her school.

Possible Questions
Since Leslie has already credited Jeremy with not being abusive, it wouldn't be necessary to ask about their relationship in terms of the effects of violence, but it is possible that others, in addition to her first boyfriend, have been abusive in the past and that this history is contributing to her risk.

- "That first boyfriend of yours was incredibly controlling, emotionally, but also physically. Was that the first time you found yourself dealing with someone abusing you? And since then?"

SIGNIFICANT-OTHER RESOURCES

i) Reasonable Expectations/Encouragement of the Client

Sometimes parents, other family members, friends, or caseworkers are able to grasp, or can be helped to grasp, the client's despair and the danger of his or her situation. When they are able to adjust their expectations so as to be encouraging but not demanding, they can be relied upon to contribute to the safety of the client. When working with a suicidal client who is struggling to meet the demands of significant others, we have found it helpful to set up a conjoint meeting to explore possible flexibility in their expectations.

A medical student whose academic career was crumbling around him came into our center with unrelenting suicidal thoughts and desire. Despite being unable to study, he was desperately holding on to the belief that his only option in life was to follow in his father's footsteps—to graduate and go on to become a surgeon. With his permission, we invited his parents to fly in as soon as possible for an extended family session. They arrived a few days later, and though our client, anticipating their disappointment, was very nervous, we were able to meet with all of them.

Much to our client's surprise and to our relief, the parents discussed different options with him for future careers, making it clear that although they had indeed been proud of him for entering medical school, they by no means were committed to his continuing. They were, they said, concerned only about his safety and, down the road, his happiness. Following this appointment, our client withdrew from the university, ending his involvement at our clinic. Through follow-up contact, we learned that he continued to be understandably agonized about his failed efforts in medical school, but he was also relieved, and his suicidality appeared to be markedly decreased.

Possible Questions
Even though Leslie doesn't respect her orchestra colleagues and may be dismissive of others who consider her employment with them an accomplishment, it doesn't mean that she doesn't benefit from the positive regard and encouragement of others.

- "Who is proudest of your position in this particular orchestra?"
- "Is there anybody in your life who isn't pushing you to accomplish more than you're already doing?
- "Your dog, Mahler, thinks the world of you. Who else appreciates you for who you are?"

ii) Helping the Client Meet Obligations

A client with chronic pain had finally found a physician who treated her with respect, viewing her as legitimately in need of help, rather than as a drug-seeking addict, but she couldn't get to her appointments with him because her car was in worse shape than she was. No one was available to drive her to her appointments, and she couldn't walk to the bus stop because of her pain. The impossibility of her situation infuriated her and left her feeling profoundly suicidal. At a time when she seemed most hopeless, her church came through with a mechanic who volunteered to come to her house and fix her car, charging her only for the parts. This act of kindness not only solved her transportation issue, allowing her to get to her pain doctor, but it also up-ended her cynicism. Her suicidal ideation disappeared.

Possible Questions
If there are people available to offer help, has Leslie been accessing them? If not, could she? Would she? Could their assistance be expanded or reoriented?

- "Who helps you look after Mahler when you're away or you're tied up with rehearsals or performances?"
- "If your family were to kick in and help, would they do that only after you convinced them that they needed to, or do they ever offer assistance before you ask?"

SUFFERING

	Client	**Client's Significant Others**
Risks	F) Depressed/Manic mood G) Anxiety/Anger/Obsessive thinking H) Conflicted identity/Shame/ Burdensomeness I) Hallucinations/Delusions J) Insomnia/Nightmares K) Pain/Illness/Injury	d) Viewing the client as flawed/a burden e) Limited awareness of/Unhelpful response to the client's suffering
Resources	3) Engagement in medical/ mental health treatment 4) Variability in psychological/physical symptoms 5) Effective response to suffering	iii) Empathic response to the client's suffering iv) Supporting the client's medical/ mental health treatment

CLIENT RISKS

F) Depressed and/or Manic Mood

Numerous research studies from diverse countries have established that people diagnosed with mood disorders have a greatly elevated risk of suicide (Angst, Stassen, Clayton, & Angst, 2002; Guze & Robins, 1970; Harris & Barraclough, 1997; Ösby, Brandt, Correia, Ekbom, & Sparén, 2001). One study (Ösby et al.) concluded that people diagnosed with depression are more than 20 times as likely to die by suicide as those in the general population. Another, which looked at 100 hospital patients who had attempted suicide with either a drug overdose or poisoning, determined that 63% suffered from a combination of depressive and manic symptoms, 90% of whom displayed irritability, distractibility, and psychomotor agitation (Balázs et al., 2006). Some researchers have suggested that people who have been previously hospitalized for a mood disorder and/or a suicide attempt are the most at risk (e.g., Bostwick & Pankratz, 2000).

Possible Questions
We typically make several inquiries that touch on depression and possible manic symptoms.

- "It sounds like when you're this down, it takes everything you've got just to keep moving."
- "It must feel like such a relief when your energy comes back. How gradual is that process, usually? And when your energy does come back—does it level off, or does it just keep coming?"
- "Does your energy ever feel uncomfortably high at the same time your mood is low?"

G) Anxiety/Anger/Obsessive Thinking

Mandrusiak et al. (2006) noted that severe anxiety or agitation are among "only a few warning signs [that] have received some form of empirical support for their effectiveness in predicting risk of suicide over 12-month time periods" (p. 270). A landmark study by Weisman, Klerman, Markowitz, and Ouellette (1989) found that subjects diagnosed with panic disorder or panic attacks were at a demonstrably increased risk for suicidal ideation and suicide attempts, even in the absence of other diagnosed psychiatric disorders. Sareen et al. (2005) more recently found, in a large population-based longitudinal study in the Netherlands, that any anxiety disorder (social phobia, simple phobia, generalized anxiety disorder, panic disorder, agoraphobia, OCD) is an independent risk factor for both suicidal ideation and suicide attempts. And in a still more recent study of undergraduate students, Norton, Temple, and Pettit (2008) offered strong evidence that among their subjects, anxiety elevated the risk of suicidality. Even greater risk resulted when individuals suffered from both anxiety and depression. This conclusion is supported by a review of the literature conducted by Hill, Castellanos, and Pettit (2011).

The authors located research demonstrating a significant link between anxiety and suicidal ideation and suicide attempts among children and adolescents, but they located no studies identifying a significant correlation between anxiety and suicide completion.

Suicide risk has been found to be positively correlated with anger and impulsivity (Kotler, Iancu, Efroni, & Amir, 2001), and anger expressed as violence has been noted as a "potent risk factor for suicide" (Conner et al., 2001, p. 1704), particularly among women and younger individuals who demonstrated violent behavior in their last year of life. Apter et al. (1991) discovered a highly significant correlation between anger and risk of suicide in violent patients in a maximum security hospital, but the correlation was not significant among nonviolent patients in a large general hospital.

The literature is not conclusive about obsessive thinking as a risk factor. Morrison and O'Connor (2008), in a systematic review of the international literature on rumination and suicidality, found an overall dearth of research; however, they did identify 10 studies that reported an association between increased rumination and increased suicidality. We ourselves have recognized how frightened and agitated clients can become when they can't stop thinking about suicide. Barraged by the relentless repetition of the same notion, they become increasingly desperate and overwhelmed.

Possible Questions
Leslie mentioned that she had recently started feeling anxious before performances. We would want to know to what extent this is different from the past, how long it has been noticeable as a problem, and how it compares to what she's experiencing at other times during the day or night.

- "Just before a concert begins, you've been feeling 'miserably anxious,' I think you said. Is this new? What are the sensations and thoughts you notice that tell you that you're anxious? How do these compare to what you've been experiencing at night when you're not sleeping?"
- "When the anxiety arrives, does it gradually build or come all at once? How about when it dissipates? Do you start feeling calmer slowly or relatively quickly?"

Leslie is clearly angry, both with Jeremy and in response to her overall situation. We would want to get a sense of whether the anger is fueling any desire to act violently, either against Jeremy or herself. However, we don't want to be in the position of inadvertently suggesting a violent path. By making empathic statements and offering case vignettes, it is often possible to obtain information without directly asking for it.

- "You've been pissed at Jeremy for ending your relationship, and you've been pissed at yourself for taking this job and getting bogged down. Sounds exhausting."
- "I had a client once who was completely devastated and furious. She had just gotten dumped by her boyfriend, and, at first, the only way she had of getting any relief was to fantasize about hurting him or hurting herself."

So far we know that Leslie experiences obsessive thinking about Jeremy and that she is persistent in tracking and contacting him. We would want to know more about how this pattern of thinking and acting operates and whether it extends elsewhere.

- "What thought or urge has been taking you to Jeremy's Facebook page? When you go there, what effect does it have on you?"
- "What's been going on for you just before you send Jeremy a text? How soon after composing it do you send it? Do you ever write one and then decide *not* to send it? How do you make that decision?"
- "It must be maddening sometimes not to be able to get thoughts of Jeremy out of your head. Any other thoughts that at times just won't quit?"

H) Conflicted Identity/Shame/Burdensomeness

People feel conflicted about their identity when they are questioning or can't accept their sexual orientation or when they are questioning foundational assumptions about their faith or belief system. However, even when people feel certain about and are accepting of their own sexual or religious identity, they may still experience profound identity conflict in response to the conviction that those who love or matter to them will reject them for who they are.

Several studies have established a link between sexual orientation and suicidality among adolescents (Bagley & Tremblay, 2000; D'Augelli et al., 2005; Remafedi, French, Story, Resnick, & Blum, 1998). In their population-based research, Remafedi et al. (1998) compared suicidal ideation, intent, and self-reported history of suicide attempts between homosexual/bisexual youth and age-matched, straight controls. The data indicated a sevenfold increase in risk for bisexual or homosexual adolescent boys, but no increase for adolescent girls. However, Bagley and Tremblay (2000) showed that lesbian adolescent girls were also at risk. Among the teenagers in their study, the gay, lesbian, and bisexual youth were 4 times more likely than heterosexual youth to make a serious suicide attempt. One third of the adolescents in D'Augelli et al.'s study reported a history of suicide attempts, half of which were judged as related to sexual orientation. High levels of early psychological abuse by parents, parental discouragement of childhood gender-atypical behavior, and increased levels of lifetime gay-related verbal abuse were characteristic of attempters. These interpersonal factors suggest that elevated risk has some-thing, and perhaps much, to do with shame. We wonder what the risks would be, if any, for lesbian, gay, bisexual, transgendered, and questioning (LGBTQ) youth if families, our society, and our religious institutions were welcoming and accepting of their identities.

Lester (1997) offered cultural and historical examples of the important role of shame in suicide, and Hastings, Northman, and Tangney (2002) discussed diverse psychological and sociological theories that suggest "a special link be-tween feelings of shame and suicidal thought and behavior" (p. 71). In a study of college students, Lester (1998) found that shame predicted suicidality, which was in keeping with Breed's (1972) finding that as many as a third of the suicide victims he studied had been experiencing shame at the time of their death (as cited in Lester, 1997). Hastings et al. conducted two studies with a nonclinical sample of undergraduates and similarly found that "a dispo-sitional tendency to experience shame across a range of situations was reli-ably linked to suicidal ideation" (p. 73). Mandrusiak et al. (2006) identified precipitating events, often involving loss or shame, as an empirically sup-ported predictor of suicide over a period of 12 months.

Thomas Joiner has highlighted the critical importance of perceived bur-densomeness and failed belongingness in the development of suicidal think-ing and behaviors. Working with colleagues (Joiner et al., 2002), he compared suicide notes left by suicide completers with those written by suicide attempt-ers. The researchers determined that a feeling of burdensomeness ("loved ones will be better off when I'm gone") characterized people who completed suicide and was associated with the use of lethal means. More recently, Joiner (2005) drew on Shneidman's (1998) notion of *psychache*, defining it as "a gen-eralized form of perceived burdensomeness and failed belongingness" (p. 38), to bring theoretical focus and a new level of nuance to Beck's early recogni-tion (Minkoff, Bergman, Beck, & Beck, 1973) that many suicidal people feel hopeless:

> An emphasis on hopelessness cannot tell the whole story. What in particu-lar are suicidal people hopeless about? If hopelessness is key, why then do relatively few hopeless people die by suicide? In my view, the reply to the first question is burdensomeness and failed belongingness, and the reply to the second is that hopelessness is not sufficient; hopelessness about belong-

ingness and burdensomeness is required, together with the acquired capability for serious self-harm. (Joiner, 2005, p. 39)

Possible Questions

Leslie has said nothing overtly about her sexual orientation, but it is possible that her disappointment with Jeremy as a lover is informed by her having a more complex sexual identity than he was able to know or accept. If she were to be attributing his rejection of her to that, she may be struggling not only with loss, but also with shame or humiliation.

- "As much as you miss Jeremy, you recognize that he didn't have the necessary sexual courage to truly appreciate you. That can be so difficult—to find a partner with sexual courage."
- "Who do you imagine *would* have the kind of sexual fearlessness that would make them a suitable partner?"

The wording of these queries carefully avoids heterosexist bias, so, if her sexual identity is in flux or is other than straight, she may feel it is safe to talk about.

Leslie believes that her fellow musicians are not of her caliber. If her contract gets terminated in the upcoming meeting, she would be getting fired from an orchestra she doesn't respect: a double humiliation.

- "Many lesser musicians would be thrilled to be in this orchestra, but you have been rather less than thrilled."

The text she sent to Jeremy, telling him that she was going to resign from the symphony, may have been sent with the hope that he would try to dissuade her. Alternatively, she may have been making public her intention to leave so that she can preempt anticipated shame by getting a step ahead of what she expects the conductor and general manager have in mind.

- "You told Jeremy that you'll be leaving the orchestra; how do you envision that happening?"
- "What do you know so far about the meeting scheduled with the conductor and manager? Are you imagining best-case and worst-case scenarios?"
- "How emotionally difficult would it be for you if you were to leave this orchestra before securing a position with another one?"

Leslie has made some troubling comments about being a burden to both Jeremy and her parents. We would want to know more about what she's thinking, what's informing her conviction, and how pervasive it is.

- "You've been thinking that Jeremy and your parents will be better off without you? How so?"
- "Have you been feeling like you're a burden to anyone else?"
- "Are there times when you aren't burdened by this thought of being a burden? Times when you don't feel so responsible for your parents' or Jeremy's well-being?"

I) Hallucinations/Delusions

Hallucinations and delusions are primary symptoms of psychosis, experienced, for example, by people diagnosed with schizophrenia or schizoaffective disorder, or with a mood disorder with psychotic features. Researchers conducting a meta-analysis estimated that 4.9% of patients with schizophrenia complete suicide during their lifetimes, usually near the time of the initial diagnosis (Palmer, Pankratz, & Bostwick, 2005). In one study, researchers found that depressed patients experiencing psychosis had "significantly higher current suicidal ideation severity, as well as over four times greater odds of having a past suicide attempt" (Gaudiano, Dalrymple, & Zimmerman, 2009, p. 61), than depressed patients without psychosis. However, another research team's meta-analysis data indicated that hallucinations were actually associated with *reduced* risk (Hawton, Sutton, Haw, Sinclair, & Deeks, 2005).

Our concern when assessing people experiencing hallucinations and delusions is that a voice, a vision, or a false belief could impel them to harm themselves. We've had clients who became suicidal in response to paranoia or who heard a voice berating them or commanding them to "go ahead and do it."

Possible Questions
Nothing we've heard so far provides a strong indication that Leslie is dealing with paranoia or hallucinations, but given her history of not always taking the mood stabilizer prescribed for bipolar disorder, it is possible that she is experiencing symptoms that she hasn't yet revealed. Below are three different ways of entering this territory.

- "Jeremy has betrayed your trust. Are there others you can't trust? How do you determine that they are untrustworthy? Is there anybody whom you *can* trust?"
- "You said that since Jeremy broke off with you, you can tell that the people in the orchestra are whispering behind your back. How can you tell? What kinds of things are they saying?"
- "Sometimes when people are under a great deal of stress, they see

or hear things that other people don't. Has that ever happened to you?"

J) Insomnia/Nightmares

Analyzing data from a random sample of over 5,000 people, Wojnar et al. (2009) reported that people with two or more types of sleep problems (e.g., falling asleep, staying asleep, or early morning awakening) were "about 2.6 times more likely to report a suicide attempt than those without any insomnia complaints" (p. 528). Goldstein, Bridge, and Brent (2008), in a study of sleep disturbance and suicidality in adolescents, similarly noted a clear relationship between sleep difficulties and completed suicide, thus supporting a declaration of the American Association of Suicidology that insomnia is a warning sign of impending suicide (p. 88).

Sjöström and colleagues (Sjöström, Waern, & Hetta, 2007; Sjöström, Hetta, & Waern, 2009) were able to show that nightmares, independent of sleep disturbance, account for a fivefold increase in suicide risk (Sjöström, Waern, & Hetta, 2007). And based on data drawn from the general population of Finland, Tanskanen et al. (2001) concluded that the risk of suicide among people with frequent nightmares was over 100% greater than those with no nightmares at all.

Possible Questions
We typically explore issues of sleep disturbance separately from asking about nightmares.

- "When a person is contending with as much as you are, it's pretty common to have disturbed sleep. How has your sleep been lately?"
- "When you wake up in the night, are you aware that you've been dreaming? What have your dreams been like lately? Any nightmares?"
- "If you do have a nightmare, how long does it take for you to realize that you're safe in your bed?"
- "Can you predict before you go to sleep that this will be a night when you aren't going to have a nightmare?"

In keeping with our earlier discussion about sprinkling in possibilities and hope, notice the use of perfect tense for questions about problems ("How *has* your sleep *been*?"; "What *have* your dreams *been* like?") and regular tense for delving into resources or safety ("How long *does* it *take* for you to *realize* that you *are* safe?"; "Can you predict that this *will be* a night when you *aren't* going to *have* a nightmare?").

K) Pain/Illness/Injury

Researchers have established links between chronic pain and suicidality (Ilgen, Zivin, McCammon, & Valenstein, 2008), between chronic pain and completed suicide (Tang & Crane, 2006), and between general medical conditions and suicidal ideation and attempts (Druss & Pincus, 2000). Cancer appears to increase risk (Druss & Pincus; Walker et al., 2008), whether the patients are young (Druss & Pincus) or elderly (Waern et al., 2002).

Correlations have also been established between hopelessness and epilepsy (Pompili, Vanacore, et al., 2007); between suicidality and asthma (Druss & Pincus); and, among the elderly, between completed suicide and visual impairment, neurological disorders, or illness in any organ system (Waern et al.).

Injuries can also increase risk of suicide. Grossman, Soderberg, and Rivara (1993) found that young people (ages 16–35) hospitalized for any injury were 12 times more likely to end their life by suicide than nonhospitalized individuals, and those hospitalized for assault injuries or motor vehicle accidents were, respectively, 4–5 times more likely and almost 3 times more likely to eventually die by suicide. Injuries involving trauma to the brain appear to be particularly problematic. Teasdale and Engberg (2001) found increased rates of suicide after traumatic brain injury (TBI), with the highest rates seen in the more severely injured patients. Following TBI patients for 5 years post injury, Simpson and Tate (2002) discovered that over 17% made a suicide attempt. Silver, Kramer, Greenwald, and Weissman (2001) extended the time frame of their examination of TBI patients, concluding that there is an elevated *lifetime* risk of suicide attempts.

Possible Questions
Leslie's chronic pain may be heightening the stress she feels, and vice versa.

- "I know you've been dealing with physical pain ever since the car accident; how has it been in the last few weeks?"

Even if you took a medical history when Leslie first came to see you, it would be a good idea to see if there have been any recent developments or changes in her medical condition.

- "How's your health in general? Are you taking medications for any other medical conditions?"

Although the car accident happened 3 years ago, a concussion then could still be a contributing factor in her suicidality now.

- "When you had the car accident, did you hit your head? Did you lose consciousness?"

CLIENT RESOURCES

3) Engagement in Medical/Mental Health Treatment

Suicidal individuals often don't get the help they need. In one study, researchers determined that "the majority of suicide attempters with major depression failed to receive adequate treatment for depression—both before and . . . after the attempt" (Suominen, Isometsä, Henriksson, Ostamo, & Lönnqvist, 1998, p. 1780). And Möller (1989) expressed concern that "non-compliance for outpatient aftercare is very high in patients who have attempted suicide" (p. 647).

Clients who do receive good medical and/or mental health treatment lower their risk of suicide. For example, Angst et al. (2002) noted that patients in their research treated for unipolar depression or bipolar disorder were considerably (or as they said about the treated patients with bipolar disorder, "spectacularly") less likely to complete suicide (p. 174). This finding was in keeping with the meta-analysis of Tondo, Hennen, and Baldessarini (2001), who showed that suicide among patients with bipolar disorder was 82% less frequent when they were receiving lithium treatment, as well as a study by Isacsson, Bergman, and Rich (1996), who reported that suicide risk among untreated patients with depression was 1.8 times higher than those taking antidepressants. Rucci et al. (2002) showed that suicide attempts can be markedly reduced in patients with Bipolar I disorder by a combination of pharmacotherapy (primarily with lithium) and intensive adjunctive psychotherapy (defined as regular visits with an empathic clinician and help in organizing daily routines).

Helpful treatment may include either or both medical and psychotherapeutic interventions. Cooper, Lezotte, Jacobellis, and DiGuiseppi (2006) looked at subsequent suicidal behavior after a suicide attempt in individuals in Colorado. They found that residing in a county that offered adequate mental health services significantly reduced the rate of subsequent suicidal behavior in these individuals.

Possible Questions

Even though Leslie's consistency in coming for appointments hasn't been matched by a commitment to implementing changes, her participation is worth noting and using as a stepping-stone to other possibilities.

- "Despite feeling so overwhelmed, you come to see me regularly. What else are you doing to take care of yourself?"

Given the dangers Leslie is currently facing and the complexity of her psychiatric needs, it would be advisable for you to get a psychiatrist involved in her case.

- "If you were to find a psychiatrist you respected, would you consider having him or her oversee your psychiatric medications?"

Notice the use of the subjunctive in introducing this idea: "If you *were to find*. . . ." The tentativeness afforded by this linguistic mood can help you broach, in a nonthreatening way, the possibility of Leslie's becoming less averse to seeing a psychiatrist. The subjunctive is also used in the next question ("If you *were to be* . . ."), as she has also been reluctant to take her medications.

- "If you were to be prescribed medications with fewer side effects, do you think you'd be more inclined to take them regularly?"

4) *Variability in Psychological/Physical Symptoms*

As we discussed in Chapter 2, symptoms are best understood and responded to not as abstract entities but as relational patterns. Identifying the patterned unfolding of a symptom inclines both you and your client to be curious about and to discover variations in its manifestation. What time of day does the person typically feel the worst? How frequently do problematic thoughts visit, and how long do they stick around? What and where in the body are the physical sensations that the person experiences as "anxiety"? What does the client do and think when he or she first notices a wave of emotion? From where does the pain radiate and how and when does it shift in quality and intensity? Such questions help establish an expectancy for change, which, if nothing else, can initiate a degree of optimism. They also encourage the recognition that it is often possible to *do* something in response to the suffering.

A client came to our center, struggling with severe chronic back pain, depression, and suicidal thoughts. We became curious about variations in all of these, and she started discovering that not only were her symptoms not constant, but they also were responsive to her initiatives to do something about them. She began an extensive daily regimen of stretching exercises to reduce her pain to a manageable level, and the results gave her hope that she could accomplish something analogous with her emotional pain. Over time, she saw progress as a result of therapy, medication, relaxation techniques, and recreational activities.

Possible Questions

Leslie's suffering feels encompassing and unrelenting to her; however, if you were to approach it as a patterned phenomenon and you were detailed in your curiosity, you and she could together discover times when her physical and/or emotional pain are of greater or lesser intensity, or when there are shifts in the quality or location or expression of her distress. Identifying these variations could be an important step in similarly identifying possible resources, particularly if the transient improvements were connected to times when she is doing something different.

- "What's the longest you've gone without feeling the urge to check Jeremy's Facebook? Were you making an effort to keep the urge in check, or did you just find yourself interested in other things?"
- "Sometimes the pain in your back is incredibly intense, and so is your despair. When do you find one or the other feeling somewhat less horrible than usual? Does that ever happen without medication?"
- "What happens to your pain or your sadness when you're playing a piece of music that moves you emotionally?"

5) *Effective Response to Suffering*

Strategies for coping effectively with suffering can be divided into two main categories. Some clients find a way to *alter their response* to their suffering, whether through meditation, prayer, or some other analogous activity. In so doing, they lessen their reactivity to it, becoming less angry, less uptight, less angst-ridden. Other clients discover various means of *altering the suffering itself.* Ineffective strategies involve some form of self-medicating or self-injury, but effective strategies achieve similar results without the negative consequences. These include distraction techniques (e.g., video games, music, hobbies, exercise) and means of connecting with, and nonvolitionally changing, the suffering (e.g., self-hypnosis, stretching, yoga).

Possible Questions

Sometimes people are able to assist others even when they see no way out for themselves. Asking Leslie about how she would help someone else who is depressed is a way to indirectly access ideas and resources that then might be applicable to her own predicament.

- "What advice would you give a depressed friend who doesn't see a way out of his or her situation?"

Another way of getting outside the tunnel vision of current despair is to look into possible futures:

- "When you look back on this time at some point in the future—6 months, a year—what will you be able to recognize then that you can't yet see now?"

The creative expression of an emotion can sometimes alter the experience of it:

- "When you're feeling down, do you ever use your violin to supply the mood music?"
- "In what ways other than playing the violin do you give voice to your artistic nature? Do you maintain a journal or sketchbook?"

SIGNIFICANT-OTHER RISKS

d) Viewing the Client as Flawed/a Burden

A life coach who had devoted his career to motivating clients was disappointed and dismayed by his teenage son, who was depressed and exhibiting suicidal ideation. Unable to cajole the boy out of his despair, he brought him to a therapist, making it clear in a joint first session that he saw his son as fundamentally defective. Throughout the meeting, the father implicitly communicated that his son's inability to "pull out of it" was a personal affront and a professional liability. The therapist inferred that the father, both embarrassed and insulted by his son's current state, was worried that if the boy were to actually take his life, it would seriously undermine the father's status in the community as a prominent life coach.

Recognizing that the father's negative beliefs were exacerbating the son's suicidality, the therapist attempted to arrange separate meetings with the father and his wife, but they refused. After three appointments, during which little progress was made with the son, the father, confirmed in his conviction that the son was a lost cause, had him admitted to a residential treatment facility.

Possible Questions

If you don't have the opportunity to speak directly to the client's significant others, your ability to learn about their perspective necessarily depends on the client, whose view may or may not be accurate.

- "You said that you thought your parents would be deeply relieved if you were no longer around. What have they said to give you that impression?"

Does the client consider his or her burdensomeness to be generally true or idiosyncratically linked to a particular person or circumstance?

- "You think Jeremy thought that you were too high-maintenance? Is that view unique to him?"

e) Limited Awareness of/Unhelpful Response to the Client's Suffering

A client who is withdrawn or alienated from significant others is unlikely to inform them of his or her suffering or to ask for help. The significant others' resulting ignorance can then, in recursive action, confirm for the client that they just don't care, resulting in more painful withdrawal.

Other clients may have positive relationships with significant others, but, for whatever reason, they work hard to keep their suffering to themselves. A husband once came to see us after his wife ended her life with rat poison. Despite their close relationship, her death had been a complete surprise. He knew that she had been getting depressed, but he saw no indication that she was suffering to the degree she must have been to take her life. Ignorant of her distress, he was unable to intervene to protect her.

In a study of factors predictive of future suicidal acts in adolescents, Groholt, Ekeberg, and Haldorsen (2006) found that having parents who were both less caring and more controlling predicted a higher rate of repeat suicide attempts. This effect was most significant for fathers, but adolescents who repeated suicide attempts perceived both parents as less caring than nonrepeaters.

Not all unhelpful responses from significant others are the result of a lack of caring. Indeed, the very opposite may be the case, as Watzlawick et al. (1974), explained:

> What could seem more reasonable to relatives and friends than to try to cheer up a depressed person? But in all likelihood the depressed person not only does not benefit from this, but sinks deeper into gloom. This then prompts the others to increase their efforts to make him see the silver lining in every cloud. Guided by "reason" and "common sense," they are unable to see (and the patient is unable to say) that what their help amounts to is a demand that the patient have certain feelings (joy, optimism, etc.) and not others (sadness, pessimism, etc.). As a result, what for the patient might originally only have been a temporary sadness now becomes infused with feelings of failure, badness, and ingratitude toward those who love him so much and are trying so hard to help him. *This* then is the depression—not the original sadness. (p. 34)

Possible Questions

With Leslie's parents living in a different city, they may be unaware of the extent of her suffering, and it isn't clear whether any others might be keeping tabs on her.

- "To what extent have you been working to protect your parents and your friends from worrying about you? How effective have you been?"
- "Who is most worried about you? Who is least concerned? What does each of them see that the other doesn't?"
- "Do your folks know about the breakup with Jeremy? What did they say?"

We know that the parents were against Leslie's taking psychiatric medication for depression and mood stabilization. This could stem from their not taking seriously her diagnosis of bipolar disorder.

- "I was once seeing a depressed client whose parents thought she should 'just snap out of it.' When she couldn't, they took it as a moral failing and got angry."
- "What's your parents' take on your physical pain? Your emotional pain? What do they consider a legitimate means of coping with each of them?"

SIGNIFICANT-OTHER RESOURCES

iii) Empathic Response to the Client's Suffering

In a study of adolescents at risk for attempting suicide, De Wilde, Kienhorst, Diekstra, and Wolters (1994) found that the highest-risk group reported less perceived support and understanding from caretakers and siblings in the family, when compared to normal controls. The researchers' measure of "perceived understanding" included a component commensurate with the reflective nature of empathy. The study thus lends credence to the idea that significant others' empathic understanding of the client's suffering may reduce the risk of suicide. Empirical support for this position can be found in a review article of factors associated with suicidal ideation in adolescents (Evans, Hawton, & Rodham, 2004). The authors cited several studies indicating that lower levels of suicidal thoughts and behaviors are present when an adolescent maintains good communication with, and feels understood by, his or her family.

Possible Questions

You need to strike a balance when asking questions about possible resources. If you don't probe, you may never find out about an ability or a person that, if accessed, could contribute significantly to the client's safety. But if you probe too much, particularly about possible resources that don't, in fact, exist, then your questioning could inadvertently heighten the client's hopelessness. For example, given Leslie's apparent isolation, it doesn't seem likely that anyone in her social world is particularly empathic. It's possible that there is someone you don't know about, so it would be worth pursuing, but not with a question that imposes implicit assumptions about the presence of resourceful people in her life:

- "Of all your friends and family, who do you find to be the most accepting of you for being you, of not needing you to be any different?"

Given the circumstances, a more circumspect inquiry would be more appropriate:

- "Know anyone who accepts you as is?"

Other viable possibilities:

- "Jeremy understood you intellectually and perhaps even aesthetically, at least to some degree. Anyone you know who gets you emotionally?"
- "Has anyone in your family struggled with depression? So do they kind of have a feel for what you've been going through?"

iv) Supporting the Client's Medical/Mental Health Treatment

Sometimes our clients show up in our offices feeling torn. They recognize that they need professional assistance, but they are contending with significant others who discount the relevance or integrity of their coming to see us—family members who are adamantly opposed to medications or psychotherapy; peers in an Narcotics Anonymous (NA) or Alcoholics Anonymous (AA) group who are advising them that all substances, including psychiatric medications, are to be avoided at all costs; or some other authority figure who frowns on all mental health treatment as dangerous or a waste of time. We continually maintain sensitivity to the social context of our clients, and, when necessary, we offer to make phone calls or invite significant others into our offices as a means of facilitating interpersonal support for our clients' efforts to change. We and our clients are most often successful when significant others endorse the therapeutic process.

Possible Questions

Leslie's parents were originally opposed to her taking the antidepressant and mood stabilizer prescribed by the psychiatrist back home. However, they are now promoting rehab, so clearly they aren't opposed to all mental health treatment, and if they knew more about the intensity of their daughter's suicidality, they might become supportive of her doing whatever would help her, for the time being, more safely negotiate the dangerous situation she is currently facing. Were they to endorse the possibility of Leslie's continuing in therapy and taking medications, she might be encouraged to venture beyond her most recent self-medicating attempts to deal with her despair.

- "Is there anyone who matters to you who considers your seeking help to be a sign of strength? If you were to decide to do even more for your well-being than you are already—maybe, say, giving some meds a chance to help—would they support you in that decision?"
- "If your parents come down to help you deal with all that's going on, do you think they could be convinced to come with you to see me? And if they don't come for a while, do you think they'd participate by telephone?"

TROUBLING BEHAVIORS

	Client	Client's Significant Others
Risks	L) Withdrawing from activities/relationships M) Substance abuse/Disordered eating N) Impulsive/Compulsive behaviors O) Harming self/others	f) Participating in the client's troubling behaviors g) Unhelpful attempts to regulate the client's troubling behaviors
Resources	6) Engaging in activities/relationships 7) Participating in therapy/rehab 8) Finding alternative behaviors	v) Reaching out to the client vi) Facilitating recovery/safety

CLIENT RISKS

L) Withdrawing from Activities/Relationships

Comparing depressed adolescents who have not made a suicide attempt with those who have, Kienhorst, De Wilde, Diekstra, and Wolters (1992) concluded that those who made attempts were significantly more withdrawn from people and activities. This finding is in keeping with Trout's (1980) contention that "social isolation has a primary and direct role in suicide" (p. 19). It also prefigures Stravynski and Boyer's (2001) finding that the subjective feeling of loneliness among their subjects was correlated with a 12-fold increase in suicide attempts over individuals with no such feelings. As the authors put it, "The possibility of attempted suicide as well as suicide itself seems to increase with the deepening of the sense of loneliness—especially when combined with the facts of living alone and having no friends" (p. 39).

Possible Questions

By moving into her own apartment, Leslie was spared the daily pain and humiliation of living in close quarters with the person who had rejected her. Nevertheless, though her dog Mahler may ameliorate her loneliness somewhat, she no doubt feels acutely Jeremy's absence and the isolation of being on her own.

- "What's it like being in your apartment by yourself? Does Mahler provide companionship?"
- "How lonely do you feel?"
- "Are you staying connected with people other than Jeremy via e-mail or Facebook?"

M) Substance Abuse/Disordered Eating

For over a year, we worked with a suicidal client in our center who was self-medicating with opiates prescribed by his pain specialist. He started taking them for fibromyalgia, but when he discovered that they reduced his emotional pain as well, he found a pain doctor who supplied him with additional pills. This worried us for several reasons, not the least of which was that he now had a reserve that gave him ready access to a lethal means of taking his life.

Analyzing data from the National Comorbidity Survey, researchers determined that substance abuse confers a significantly elevated lifetime risk of suicide attempts and suicidal ideation (Borges, Angst, Nock, Ruscio, & Kessler, 2008). A similar conclusion was reached by Oyefeso, Ghodse, Clancy, and Corkery (1999), who found that the risk of suicide among addicts in Britain was 4 times higher for male addicts and 11 times higher for female addicts than for individuals in the general population. Younger addicts (ages 15–34) were 6–8 times more likely to die by suicide than persons of the same age in the general population.

In a chart review of patients seen in a psychiatric emergency room of a large metropolitan hospital, Adams and Overholser (1992) identified patients who had suicidal ideation or suicide attempts and compared them to nonsuicidal control patients. Those who had attempted suicide were significantly more likely than nonsuicidal patients to have a history of drug abuse, and those with suicidal ideation were significantly more likely to have a family history of alcohol abuse.

Cornelius et al. (1995) determined that people suffering from both alcoholism and depression were at significantly higher risk of suicidal ideation, death wishes, or suicidal behavior than those who were struggling with either alcoholism or depression alone. It appears that alcohol heightens risk even among those not struggling with addiction. Drawing on a literature review and clinical cases, Frances et al. (1986) concluded that "alcohol use has been found to be associated with 50% of suicides and to increase the risk of suicidal behavior both for alcoholic and nonalcoholic populations" (p. 316). Having conducted a more recent literature review, Sher (2006) estimated that the risk of suicide for people with alcohol dependence is 60–120 times greater than it is for the general population.

Suicide by overdose is not only a problem for individuals struggling with addiction, however. A report from the National Violent Death Reporting System (National Center for Injury Prevention and Control, n.d.) noted that less than half of those who died by suicide with an alcohol and/or drug overdose between 2005 and 2007 were known to have an alcohol or substance abuse problem (p. 3). The report went on to say that 79% of suicides involving substance overdose during the same period were due to prescription drugs only. Among those individuals who died by ingesting a single medication, the majority took an opioid, benzodiazepine, or antidepressant. Over-the-counter drugs such as acetaminophen were the second leading substance type used in suicides, representing 10% of suicides due to single substance overdose; street or recreational drugs accounted for just 2% of single-drug overdoses. Alcohol and prescription drugs were ingested in 31% of the suicides involving multiple-substance overdose.

Individuals diagnosed with anorexia nervosa have significantly higher rates of completed suicide than the general population, and those diagnosed with bulimia nervosa have a significantly elevated rate of suicide attempts (Franko & Keel, 2006). Based on a meta-analysis of suicide in individuals with anorexia nervosa, Pompili, Mancinelli, Girardi, Ruberto, and Tatarelli (2004) calculated that the suicide rate among patients with anorexia is almost 8 times higher than that of the general population. According to the authors, "suicide is the major cause of death among individuals with anorexia nervosa, refuting the belief that starvation is the primary cause of death" (p. 102). Papadopoulos, Ekbom, Brandt, and Ekselius (2009) reached the same conclusion, confirming that suicide was the most frequent main cause of death in their study of individuals with anorexia nervosa.

Possible Questions
We know that Leslie has been abusing the opiate prescribed to her for back pain. Normalizing this overuse with an empathic statement could help her feel less defensive about the plight she's in.

- "I imagine that when you're feeling desperate and strung out, it's pretty easy to take an extra pill or two or three to try to slow down your thoughts and ease your edginess."

Given that she's been buying part of her supply on the black market, we don't know the number of pills she has available to her, should she decide to make a suicide attempt.

- "How many pills do you have at the moment? When your prescription runs out before the refill date, how long does it take you to make up the difference on the black market?"

We also don't know whether she is ingesting her opiate together with alcohol or other substances.

- "Do you ever try to take the edge off in more than one way at a time? Pills *and* alcohol? Pills *and* pot? Or some other cocktail?"

As always, even as we are attempting to get a feel for her level of risk, we are also curious about any variations in her abuse patterns and to what extent these variations can be linked to her resourcefulness.

- "Sometimes you take too much pain medication and sometimes you avoid it altogether. What determines which direction you head?"

The pain specialist needs to be alerted to Leslie's suicidality so that he can provide her with a safer medication or limit the number of pills she is able to obtain at any one time. Of course, you could only contact this person if Leslie were to give you written permission to share information, and even if the two of you were in contact and the doctor changed her prescription, Leslie could always choose to buy what she wants from her own sources. Nevertheless, we'd still do our best to obtain permission to talk.

- "I'd like to coordinate what you and I are doing with the treatment being provided by your pain doc. Would you be comfortable signing a release so we can keep each other apprised and not work at cross purposes?"

Leslie is eating less than usual. It isn't yet clear if her grieving and anxiety are manifesting in a loss of appetite or interest in food, or whether her restricted consumption is the result of over consumption of pain meds or indicative a pattern of disordered eating.

- "What are you eating these days? How much and how often?"
- "When you do eat, are you doing so because of hunger pangs or just the knowledge that it's time you had some sustenance?"
- "Have you ever struggled with your weight?"
- "Ever been involved in treatment to help you with how you were relating to food?"

N) Impulsive/Compulsive Behaviors

The potential for impulsive action is important to keep in mind, as not all suicides are the result of careful or sustained planning. In a study of 82 patients who had attempted suicide, Deisenhammer et al. (2009) discovered that for almost half of them, the elapsed time between the most recent thought of suicide and the attempt was 10 minutes or less. Simon et al. (2001), defining impulsivity as an elapsed time of less than 5 minutes between the decision to attempt suicide and the actual attempt, found that 24% of their 153 subjects attempted impulsively. Characterizing impulsivity as a "tendency toward rapid, unplanned responses" (p. 1680), Swann et al. (2005) similarly determined that those people in their study who had a history of the most severe suicide attempts scored highest in measures of impulsivity.

Further support for the importance of impulsivity can be found in a study conducted by Dumais et al. (2005). The researchers assessed the impulsivity of 104 males who had completed suicide and 74 living depressed male comparison subjects. For each of the living subjects, they obtained data directly from the man himself and from an informant; for each of the deceased subjects, they gathered information from two informants. They concluded that a measure of high impulsivity was significantly greater for the men who had completed suicide.

We've seen several clients who became suicidal after being rejected by long-term partners and who were struggling to contain compulsive urges. One man kept driving by his former girlfriend's apartment, looking to see if an unfamiliar car (of a possible new boyfriend) was parked outside. Another client, a young woman, would go out to bars where she both hoped and dreaded to see the ex-boyfriend who had left her for another woman. In both cases, the urge to keep some form of contact simultaneously satisfied a deep longing and intensified their desperation.

Possible Questions

The pattern of Leslie's monitoring and texting of Jeremy appears to have both impulsive and compulsive characteristics. She feels compelled to text him several times per day, seemingly without editing the contents, and she hasn't been able to keep herself from continually monitoring his status updates on his Facebook page. Does she have any experiences that contrast with this, experiences of checking her impulses instead of checking on Jeremy? If so, does she prefer what happens when she, say, extends the time between thought and action? Would she be interested and willing to experiment in implementing such slowing as a strategy for coping with her pain and anger?

- "These texts you've been sending to Jeremy—you dash them off before you think twice? I wonder if the texts would turn out any different if you were to decide to intentionally insert a pause for a breath or two, or time for a second look, in the space between the writing and the sending?"
- "Are there other areas of your life where you're more likely to pause and evaluate an impulse before acting on it?"
- "I would imagine that heading to Jeremy's Facebook page is both anxiety relieving and anxiety provoking. What do you think might happen if you were to take your desire to know what's up with him and channel that focused curiosity somewhere else?"

O) Harming Self/Others

As a means of broaching possible suicidality, some clinicians ask their clients whether they have been thinking about hurting themselves. We tend not to do this, because some people don't think of death by suicide as a form of self-harm but, rather, as relief from suffering. Nevertheless we *do* ask about harming thoughts and behaviors, as there are significant correlations between these and suicidality (Hawton, Zahl, & Weatherall, 2003).

In a study of adolescents admitted to an in-patient ward, researchers found that 70% of those who had inflicted damage and/or pain on themselves in the previous year also, at some point in their life, had made a suicide attempt (Nock, Joiner, Gordon, Lloyd-Richardson, & Prinstein, 2006). Those who reported lower levels of pain while engaging in the self-harming had a life-time history of more suicide attempts, as did those who had been engaging in the self-harm for longer and/or had used different methods of inflicting the harm.

Whitlock and Knox (2007) noted a positive correlation between frequency of self-harm and suicidality. With more than 40% of the study's adolescent subjects who had engaged in self-injurious behavior also reporting a history of suicidality, the authors concluded that self harming is "strongly predictive of suicidality" (p. 636) and recommended that, upon discovering such behavior, the clinician should initiate a suicide assessment (p. 634).

Clinicians need to be concerned about suicide risk not only when they encounter clients who are harming themselves, but also when they are harming others. For example, Flannery, Singer, and Wester (2001) noted an almost threefold increase in the risk of suicidality among adolescent females who had behaved violently in the previous 12 months.

Possible Questions
Leslie has given no indication that she is engaging in self-harming behaviors or fantasizing about hurting others. We'd thus want to broach such topics tentatively. We wouldn't want her feeling accused or interrogated; however, since she is so intensely angry with Jeremy, it would be important to inquire into the possibility of homicidal thinking. If you were to become sufficiently concerned about Jeremy's immediate safety, you'd need to strongly consider hospitalizing Leslie at this point and contacting both Jeremy and the police.

- "You've been hurt by others, both physically—with the car accident—and emotionally, with the breakup. Do you ever find yourself hurting yourself?"
- "More often that you'd like, you find that you can't stop thinking about how badly Jeremy has hurt you. When that happens, or at other times, do you sometimes think about hurting him in return, wanting to ensure that he suffers as much as you?"
- "Any thoughts about hurting anyone else?"

CLIENT RESOURCES

6) *Engaging in Activities/Relationships*

In an epidemiological study of adolescents, researchers found that engagement in physical activity and sports correlated with decreased suicide risk (Taliaferro, Rienzo, Miller, Pigg, & Dodd, 2008). The results demonstrated that "sports participation was significantly associated with reduced odds of hopelessness and suicidal behavior among both genders" (p. 549). Vigorous physical activity alone provided an ameliorative effect for boys, but involvement in organized sports contributed an additional protection for both genders.

According to Joiner (2005), feeling connected to others and feeling effective in life are both protective against suicidality. This idea is backed up by Lapierre, Dubé, Bouffard, and Alain (2007), who showed, in a study of recent retirees, that developing goals and engaging in goal-oriented activities not only significantly improved overall psychological well-being, but also decreased suicidal ideation.

One way of measuring engagement in relationships is to look at family mealtimes. Fulkerson et al. (2006) studied the high-risk behaviors of high school seniors, tracking how they varied in relation to the frequency of family dinners. The researchers found that the more often families ate together, the less their teenagers engaged in high-risk behaviors, including suicide attempts.

Possible Questions

If Jeremy didn't belong to the orchestra, Leslie might find rehearsals and performances more of a respite from her distress. Nevertheless, it would be worth exploring whether during the time she's actually playing, she gets any benefit from the activity of playing or from the musical relationships with her colleagues.

- "Even though the orchestra has been a disappointment for you, you continue to rehearse with the other members—you continue to play music together. Do you notice any relief from your suffering when you're in the midst of playing?"

If there aren't any relationships with people that are assisting Leslie, perhaps her relationship with her dog, and the exercise possibilities that come with pet ownership, are making a difference.

- "Do you take Mahler for walks? Does he sometimes decide that *you* need to go out? How successful is he in convincing you to get outside?"

7) *Participating in Therapy/Rehab*

Several studies have linked therapeutic involvement with a lowering of suicidality. Patsiokas and Clum (1985) demonstrated that two different therapeutic approaches—one, cognitive restructuring; the other, problem solving—
both led to a reduction of suicidal intention and hopelessness among patients
hospitalized for a suicide attempt. Diamond et al. (2012) found a significant
reduction in suicidal ideation in lesbian, gay, and bisexual adolescents treated
with attachment-based family therapy. And in another study, substance-
abusing suicidal adolescents showed significantly reduced numbers of suicide
attempts, psychiatric hospitalizations, emergency room visits, and arrests after
engaging in an integrated outpatient cognitive–behavioral program (Esposito-
Smythers, Spirito, Kahler, Hunt, & Monti, 2011).

The benefits of treatment appear to hold true not only for psychotherapy,
but also for rehabilitation. In a study involving more than 8,000 patients at
nearly 150 treatment sites in the Department of Veterans Affairs health-care
system, researchers found that the more patients actively participated in
treatment for their substance abuse, the lower their risk of making a suicide
attempt after 1 year. Indeed, among the most-at-risk group, those who participated most were half as likely to make a suicide attempt as those who
participated least (Ilgen, Harris, Moos, & Tiet, 2007).

Possible Questions
Leslie's involvement in therapy hasn't, to date, demonstrated a commitment
to change, but she faithfully comes to her appointments—a fact that can be
used as a stepping-stone to explore other possible resources.

- "Despite feeling so overwhelmed, you've been continuing to see me
  regularly. What seed of hope keeps you coming?"

She might be able to commit more to therapy if she knew she was respected
as a discerning consumer of services who can help direct treatment.

- "With this recent deal with Jeremy, you're using more pain meds and
  you feel like things are spiraling down. What do you think would help
  make our sessions more helpful? Anything I could be doing differently? Anyone else we should get involved?"

By legitimizing Leslie's pain, we can legitimize her struggle, which might
open the way to her considering rehab.

- "You said that rehab is for junkies, so you're not interested in going. If
  you recognized that rehab is for people who, through no fault of their

own, have legitimately become physically dependent on medications that have been necessary for pain management, would you remain so adamantly opposed to getting that kind of help?"

If she were to remain adamant about eschewing traditional treatment modalities, you could explore legitimate alternatives, at least for some aspects of her suffering or troubling behaviors.

- "Have you explored treatments other than medication for your pain? Hypnosis? Acupuncture? Physical therapy?"

8) Finding Alternative Behaviors

Troubling behaviors are those that complicate the potential for safety. When clients are coping with stressors and suffering in ways that put them at further risk, we explore with them the possibility of finding alternative behaviors. Even though their inclination is to retreat from the world, avoiding activities and withdrawing from friends and family, we ask if they would be willing to head *out*, rather than *in*. Even though alcohol provides temporary relief, would they be willing to head to the gym, rather than the bar? Even though cutting is a short-term solution to the numbness they've been feeling, would they be willing to explore slower-acting but longer-lasting antidotes? If they are at least open to seeking alternatives, this may provide a means of enhancing safety.

One of our clients, a survivor of her husband's suicide the previous year, was herself suicidal. Her primary way of coping with her still-raw grief was to marinate herself with mixed drinks while scrutinizing photographs (dating from his childhood through to the most recent times they had shared) and documents (including the will and his detailed suicide note). She accepted and followed a suggestion to find an alternative grieving ritual, one that didn't require excessive amounts of alcohol to inure her to explicit reminders of painful memories. Her desperate sense of loss began to soften, her head began to clear, and the possibility of committing to life beyond her husband's death made its way into her repertoire of choices.

Possible Questions
We start with the assumption that our clients aren't committed to their troubling behaviors, but rather to the temporary relief they experience when engaging in them. Our curiosity about alternatives is thus structured by a dual respect, implicit in everything we ask. We communicate our appreciation for the necessity of relief *and* we underscore our commitment to safety.

- "Other than or in addition to the medications, what helps you sleep?"
- "Before you got so overwhelmed, what did you do to help you feel balanced or calm?"
- "Have you ever felt like making someone pay for hurting you—that first boyfriend of yours, maybe, or Jeremy, or someone else—and then found yourself letting go of that thought, of that desire? How did it happen?"
- "How would you manage your emotional pain if you no longer needed to rely on the pain meds?"

SIGNIFICANT-OTHER RISKS

f) Participating in the Client's Troubling Behaviors

Earlier in the chapter we mentioned an incident involving a suicidal young woman being seen in our center who went home for the holidays, hoping to benefit from the warm ministrations of her parents. Instead, she was confronted by a mother who proposed that they jointly kill themselves. In this particular case, our client recoiled from the idea, becoming more determined than ever to find alternatives to her hopelessness. However, we've seen many other clients whose troubling behaviors were exacerbated by their parents' involvement in them. For example, one young man who died from a drug overdose had been smoking marijuana with his father for years prior to his death. Other family members believed that the father's inability to get his son into rehab for his cocaine and opioid addiction was a direct result of their habit of getting high together.

Possible Questions
Given the parents' dismissive attitude toward medications and Leslie's pain and dependence on the pain medications, it is possible that they have a history of substance abuse in their families or in their own experience.

- "Sounds like your parents have a lot of concerns about medications and about the potential for addiction. How did they come to hold such strong views?"
- "Who is most worried about your use of pain medications?"

Notice in the question below that when inquiring about possible parental anxiety regarding Leslie's limited eating, we don't ask if they are concerned about weight *loss*. We wouldn't want to fail to find out if one or both of them struggle with their own weight and so are actually *relieved* that she is losing weight.

- "Are your parents concerned about your weight? How do they let you know? Has it always been like that?"

g) Unhelpful Attempts to Regulate the Client's Troubling Behaviors

Afraid for the well-being of their child, spouse, parent, or friend, significant others will, at times, attempt to limit or stop the client's troubling behaviors in ways that intensify, rather than lessen, his or her danger. Just as threats or criticisms are seldom helpful, so are anxious entreaties to "just try" to change. Most of us push back against those who impel us to do something different, and, in this, suicidal individuals are no different. Even if clients are ready to take action to change (see Prochaska, DiClemente, & Norcross, 1992, regarding "stages of change"), they may refuse to do so in order to protect their integrity from the demands of significant others.

When we have the opportunity to meet with concerned significant others, we invariably ask about what they've been trying to do to help. Is it working to actively assist a depressed daughter to complete her homework and get to class? Does it help to angrily demand that your son get up and attend university when you are continuing to pay for the high-speed Internet connection that he uses up to 20 hours per day to advance his standing in an online game? If you are a son with a depressed mother needing to get back up and running after a suicide attempt, does it help to give her good advice about what she should do? And if you're the daughter, does it help to call her multiple times per day and to turn down a promotion that would take you out of state? Sometimes, when significant others come to recognize that their efforts to regulate the behaviors of the client are making matters worse, they find it possible to do something demonstrably different.

Possible Questions

Leslie's parents didn't want her to take the medications originally prescribed for her mood disorder, and they are now advocating that she go to rehab to get off her pain meds. We would want to scope out the degree to which their efforts to influence Leslie's choices have been contributing to her well-being, and to what extent they have exacerbated her struggles.

- "Your parents were against your taking the antidepressant and mood stabilizer that the doctor back home originally prescribed. Did you agree with them at the time? And now?"

Some brilliant comedian (we forget which one) defined maturity as "doing the right thing even though your mother thinks it is a good idea." It would be helpful to know if Leslie is making choices about rehab in opposition to, or in agreement with, her parents' position.

- "Your parents have been pushing hard to get you to go into rehab. How does their worry affect your decision about whether or not to go?"

And to what extent are the parents' views on Jeremy complicating or helping Leslie's emotional responses to the split?

- "What advice have your parents been giving you about Jeremy? Do you agree with them?"

SIGNIFICANT-OTHER RESOURCES

v) Reaching out to the Client

A college senior came to our Student Counseling Center, devastated by the recent suicide of a friend she'd known since they'd roomed together as first-year students. Our client, along with many others, had known that her friend was struggling and had been providing ongoing support for several months. But then the challenges of school and problems with her boyfriend had swallowed up our client's time, and she'd become less diligent in checking in and asking her friend to get together. The more the friend had withdrawn, the easier it had been to not quite get around to reaching out. After the death, dozens of people attended the funeral, and our client was left with an agonizing question: What would have happened if she and all the others who were able to make it to memorialize a lost life had been as active in showing up when her friend needed them? Would the friend still be alive?

Possible Questions

Leslie's social network is limited, in part because she is relatively new to the city and in part because she doesn't respect her fellow musicians. But there may be people available to her that aren't immediately apparent, people who might make a point of contacting her *because* they haven't heard from her.

- "Who has helped you the most through this breakup with Jeremy? What have they done that has made a difference?"
- "To what lengths would your friends or family go to in order to help you make it through this horrible time?"
- "When you've had crises in the past—the car accident, your abusive

first boyfriend—did you reach out to your family for help? How about to friends? Did they reach out to you?"

vi) Facilitating Recovery/Safety

We've worked with clients struggling with serious alcohol or drug dependence who needed more than what we had to offer. Despite our recommendations that they seek more intensive treatment, they didn't follow through until concerned friends and family banded together to convince them to move forward. We've also witnessed parents step in and proactively place their college-attending children in treatment facilities when their troubling behaviors reached a dangerous threshold. One time, the parents of two substance-abusing roommates who were both suicidal took action simultaneously, finding respective in-patient dual-diagnosis programs, figuring out the insurance, and arranging with the school for medical withdrawals. In another situation, we obtained permission to call the parents of a client whose disordered eating had put her life in danger. They provided the necessary financial assistance for her to participate in a specialized treatment program at another facility.

Sometimes the only significant others available are professionals. We were seeing a suicidal client once who was abusing his narcotic pain medication. For several months, we urged him to augment his therapy with us by working with an addictions specialist to reduce his dependence on the opiate. He would half-heartedly agree that it was a good idea, but he never quite got around to making the call. We were particularly concerned because his current suicidal ideation and an attempt a few years earlier involved overdosing on this same medication. We met with the entire clinical staff to discuss treatment options, and we decided that we would offer the client the option of meeting with all of us, all seven clinicians, as a group. Intrigued, he agreed. During the course of the session, we addressed his suicidality and his use of the drug as an emotional anesthetic. He was able to hear from a variety of positions that we recognized the extent of his pain *and* saw his drug dependence as a dangerous roadblock to moving forward in his life. Within a week, he had contacted the specialist his therapist had earlier recommended, and over the next 6 months, he eliminated his abuse and lessened his dependence on a medication that had been keeping him within arm's reach of death.

Possible Questions
Not unlike other clients we've seen, Leslie resents her parents' concern about her abusing the pain medication. She sees them as meddling, but their vocal

insistence could make the difference between her getting the help she needs and spiraling further down.

- "Your parents have been insistent about wanting you to get help to become less reliant on your pain meds. This irritates you, obviously, but I'm wondering the degree to which you recognize their concern as a commitment to your safety. How else have they let you know that they care?"
- "If things get too difficult here, would your parents or any friends be okay with your staying with them for a while?"

DESPERATION

	Client	Client's Significant Others
Risks	P) Hopelessness Q) Intense desire for relief R) Intention/Plan to act on suicidal thoughts S) Communicating about suicidality T) Having/Gaining access to means U) Preparing for/Attempting suicide	h) Suicidality i) Ignorance/Denial of the client's suicidality j) Dismissive response to the client's suicidality
Resources	9) Hope/Reasons for living 10) Variability in suicidality 11) Willingness not to conceal suicidality 12) Active participation in developing and implementing a safety plan	vii) Compassionate response to the client's suicidality viii) Active participation in a safety plan

CLIENT RISKS

P) Hopelessness

Thanks to the groundbreaking work of Aaron Beck and his colleagues, hopelessness has long been recognized as a critical factor in suicidality. Beck et al. (1974) developed a 15-item scale to measure hopelessness, which they defined as a negative view of the self in relation to the future. Aish and Wasserman (2001) subsequently conducted a factor analysis of this scale, arguing that a single item—"The future looks dark to me"—measures the essential aspects of hopelessness.

Various studies have determined that suicidal intent is more closely related to hopelessness than to depression (Beck et al., 1979; Minkoff et al., 1973) and that hopelessness among suicidal inpatients is significantly correlated with suicide completions (Beck, Steer, Kovacs, & Garrison, 1985).

Marsha Linehan and colleagues have cautioned clinicians to recognize that when clients complete self-report inventories of hopelessness and depression, their desire to be viewed in a positive light (what they term "social desirability") results in their underreporting the level of their distress (Linehan & Nielsen, 1981, 1983; Strosahl, Linehan, & Chiles, 1984). Such misrepresentation is not the result, the authors say, of intentional dissembling; rather, clients, sensitive to the social implications of being seen negatively, feel the need to present themselves in the most favorable light possible. As a result, clinicians may dangerously underestimate the degree of risk. Subsequent research by others has painted a more complex picture of the relationship between social desirability and reports of suicidality (e.g., Ivanoff & Jang, 1991); however, the concern for clinicians remains: It is essential to help clients feel comfortable enough during the assessment to be open about their experience. Our contention throughout this book is that an empathic connection with the client is the best insurance in this regard; however, the research to establish whether this is, in fact, true has yet to be conducted.

One way we temper the possible confounding effects of social desirability is by normalizing clients' potentially shameful thoughts or behaviors:

- "Sometimes when people feel desperate, they just want to give up."

Clients' shame and psychological isolation can diminish a little when they learn that other people have had similar experiences and when it sinks in that you aren't shocked by or discounting of what they've told you. Take care, though, that in acknowledging the commonality of suicidality, you don't make it out to be an expectable phenomenon that doesn't warrant serious attention and intervention:

X "Sometimes I wonder if *any* undergrad gets through college without going through some kind of suicide phase."

You also don't want to inadvertently *sanction* or *endorse* it, as the following statements might do:

X "It makes sense that you're feeling suicidal. Many people in your situation would be, as well."

✗ "It would be understandable if you were to make an attempt on your life."

Possible Questions

Leslie sounds quite hopeless. She worries that she may have missed the window of opportunity for finding a position with another symphony, she is reeling from and not looking beyond her breakup with Jeremy, and she has seen no improvement in her physical pain. Empathizing with her about her overwhelming experience is a good place to start.

- "You're devastated and edgy and physically and emotionally exhausted. As I've learned from other clients, it's incredibly difficult to see beyond your pain at times like this."

When you're depressed about being depressed, the spiraling can be intense. You can always ask directly about hopelessness.

- "A lot of people facing what you are would be feeling pretty hopeless at this point. What about you?"

However, we're more likely to inquire about whether a client has any semblance of hope or can imagine a future that has a chance to be positive.

- "How hopeful are you that things might improve?"
- "How long do you think it will take before your heart opens to the possibility of finding a new lover, one who is a better fit than Jeremy?"

If Leslie has no hope and can't imagine getting beyond her pain, she'd probably just respond negatively to these questions and you'd get a sense of her hopelessness; however, by inclining our inquiries toward hope, we invite her curiosity about the presence, rather than absence, of possibilities.

Q) *Intense Desire for Relief*

Hendin, Maltsberger, and Szanto (2007) compared information on 36 patients who died by suicide with information from 26 patients who were depressed but not suicidal. They determined that whereas 30 of the 36 patients who took their life had, in the 3 months prior to their death, evidenced an "urgent need for relief from pain or distress that has become intolerable" (p. 365), none of the nonsuicidal depressed patients had expressed this intense desire. This result accords with what we've noticed about the vast majority of our suicidal clients. Unable to see outside their despair, they desperately seek relief from—a way out of—what they view as intolerable circumstances, unremitting suffering, spiraling failure. With their imagination shut down and their choices impossibly constrained, they fixate on suicide as the only available solution.

One of our clients, a middle-aged woman, agonized by jealousy and fury when her husband cheated on her, started "walking the aisles" at the local pharmacy, stocking up on what she hoped would be lethal medications. Another client, a young woman, drank bleach when she could no longer tolerate her nonstop paranoid thoughts and hallucinations. And a third client, a former CEO who was unable to pay gambling debts and unable to still attract the young woman who had been enchanted by his willingness to live beyond his means, sealed the doors of his garage and started his car. All three told us how desperately they had needed fast *relief*. They were not necessarily committed to ending their life; they had just wanted to end their suffering.

Possible Questions
Leslie's pain—both physical and emotional—is excruciating, making her desperate for relief. You could broach this issue tentatively (the first question, below) or more directly (the second question).

- "The pain pills you've been taking provide some help for your pain, but not enough for you to feel comfortable. What other ways have you considered as means of finding relief?"
- "Sometimes when people are dying for relief from their pain, they literally think about dying. Does that ever happen to you? Does it scare you? Comfort you?"

The more direct approach of the second question is tempered by normalizing the experience of a person having such thoughts: "Some people" think this way when they are in agony. As we said in an earlier section (*Harming Self/ Others*), suicidality is sometimes not experienced as a desire for self-harm but the very opposite—the desire for an absence of pain.

R) Intention/Plan to Act on Suicidal Thoughts

Shahar, Bareket, Rudd, and Joiner (2006) made note of the close interrelatedness of hopelessness, depressive symptoms, and suicidal ideation, highlighting the importance of all three in the evaluation and treatment of suicidal individuals. Nevertheless, suicidal ideation has been identified as a risk factor for chronic, not acute, suicidality (Busch & Fawcett, 2004). As Lieberman pointed out (1993), the high prevalence of suicidal thoughts in the normal population undermines the potential for suicidal ideation to serve as a predictor of suicidal behavior. Indeed, he argued that "the phenomenon [of suicidal ideation] may have as much or more to do with affirmation of life and immunity to actual suicide. It may be a part of normal, healthy adult development" (Lieberman, p. 173).

Lieberman's view is echoed in the results of a 10-year study that tracked people who, at baseline, had a history of suicidal ideation (Borges et al., 2008). More than a third of the subjects continued having such thoughts over the course of the research, and for those who at baseline hadn't evidenced a previous plan or attempt, their subsequent thoughts were *negatively* correlated with subsequent plans or attempts. That is, the more likely they were to have suicidal *thoughts*, the less likely they were to make *plans* or *attempts*. The authors concluded that their results provide "empirical support for the clinical view that persistent suicide ideation in the absence of making suicide plans or attempts does not increase the risk of suicide plans and attempts, and may actually decrease such risk" (p. 31).

Existing evidence doesn't support the position that suicidal thoughts alone predict a future suicide attempt or completion; however, the research *does* support the raising of concern when there is the intent or a plan to *act* on such thoughts. Researchers conducted a longitudinal study of 224 patients who had attempted suicide during a 7-month period in 1990 (Suominen, Isometsä, Ostamo, & Lönnqvist, 2004). Initially establishing the patients' level of suicidal intent with Beck's Suicide Intent Scale (SIS), the researchers followed them for 12 years. They found that the 17 (8%) who subsequently died by suicide had higher SIS scores and that these values were the most powerful predictor of eventual suicide.

Harriss, Hawton, and Zahl (2005) similarly found that high SIS scores among individuals presenting to a hospital after self-poisoning or self-injury were associated with a higher risk of subsequent suicide, particularly for women and, for both genders, within the first year following the attempt. Brown, Henriques, Sosdjan, and Beck (2004) determined that the patients in their study "were more likely to make a lethal suicide attempt when they had both an accurate expectation of the lethality of the attempt and a higher level of intent to commit suicide" (p. 1172).

Possible Questions
Leslie has indicated in several ways that she's been having suicidal thoughts. She said she'd rather die than go to rehab; she fantasizes about Jeremy finding out "too late" that he made a mistake in breaking up with her; she mentioned giving him "a parting gift"; and she suggested that her parents and Jeremy would be relieved if she "were no longer here." Your task at this point would

be to find out whether she has the intent to act on these thoughts and whether she has concretized any plans for how she would do so.

- "You sometimes fantasize about Jeremy realizing too late that he made a mistake ending your relationship. What happens in the fantasy? How does he discover that it's too late?"
- "You mentioned the idea of giving Jeremy the musical manuscript as a 'parting gift.' How were you envisioning that 'parting' coming about? By taking a job somewhere else? Or by taking your life?"
- "When you think about 'no longer being here,' do you mean no longer here in this city and in this orchestra, or no longer on the planet? How do you imagine that coming about?"

Some clients focus on only one possible method for suicide, whereas others are considering any number of means. We are first interested in pursuing the details of the specific methods they divulge, but we also want to ask more broadly about other possibilities they have considered. It is impossible to construct a safe safety plan if you don't have a clear conception of what you and the client are protecting the client from. For example if, in response to the last question, above, Leslie told you that she'd been thinking about overdosing on her pain pills, you'd want to extend your curiosity:

- "It makes sense that when you're thinking about ending your suffering that you'd consider using the pills. Have you also thought about other ways?"

Shea (2002) advocates the importance of exploring alternative means with clients, making note of possibilities, one by one, and having them either affirm or deny each method as it is listed. We're more likely to mention, in a casual way, some other possible means and carefully note the clients' responses. If they indicate, if only nonverbally, that they have other methods in mind, then we are prompted to get more specific and thorough.

- "Some people who are thinking about ending their life only ever consider one way to act on those thoughts, but others consider different ways—jumping, hanging, using a gun. . . . What about you?"

S) Communicating about Suicidality

In 2003, David Rudd, Thomas Joiner, and several of their colleagues participated in an expert working group, convened by the American Association of Suicidology, to create a list of warning signs for imminent suicidality, which they considered distinct from less acute, but still important, risk factors (Rudd, 2006).[6] The group considered communicating about suicidality—including "Someone talking or writing about death, dying, or suicide" and "Someone threatening to hurt or kill themselves" (p. 259)—to be among the most serious indicators of an imminent attempt. This assertion was borne out by Hendin et al. (2007), who reported that 17 of the 36 people (47%) who died by suicide in their postmortem study had expressed suicidal preoccupation in the 3 months before their death.

Possible Questions

As far as we know, Leslie hasn't directly communicated an intent or plan to die to anyone. We know that she has been dropping hints, which are worrisome enough to be considered communications, but we'd want to know if she has been more explicit with anyone.

- "You've been texting Jeremy a lot. Have you sent him any texts that you think may have worried him? Have you ever mentioned to him a desire or plan to take your life?"
- "What do your parents know about how desperate you've been feeling?"
- "If you got to where you were seriously considering taking your life, who would you tell? How would you tell them?"
- "Have you written anything to Jeremy—in a text, maybe, or in a note or letter—about why you're planning to give him the manuscript? If you did, do you think he would construe it as a suicide note?"

T) Having/Gaining Access to Means

Some clients have ready access to means by virtue of their circumstances and the method they are considering using to take their life—a driver who fantasizes about steering into oncoming traffic; an anesthesiologist who has thoughts about injecting himself with a lethal dose of potassium chloride; a mountain climber who has nightmares of jumping to her death. Other clients take specific action to obtain access to means—a man who buys a gun; a teenager who steals rope from his father's boat; a woman who buys a ticket for an ocean cruise.

Firearms are the most common method of completed suicide for all demographic groups in the United States (Brent, 2001), and availability of guns translates into increased risk of death. In a study of the relationship between suicide and gun ownership, Kellerman et al. (1992) examined 803 suicides occurring over a 32-month period in Tennessee and Washington. The presence of one or more guns in the home was associated with an approximately fivefold increase in the risk of suicide. Similarly, Brent et al. (1991), examining the presence and accessibility of firearms in the homes of adolescents who died by suicide, concluded that the risk of dying in an attempt was double in homes where guns were kept.

Epidemiological studies have demonstrated that reducing access to means results in fewer deaths by suicide. When legislation in the United Kingdom limited the number of analgesic tablets that consumers could buy at one time, it significantly reduced the number of deaths due to acetaminophen and salicylate self-poisoning (Hawton, 2002). This effect mirrors a similar reduction in the United Kingdom when, between 1960 and 1971, coal gas, with a high (10–20%) carbon monoxide (CO) content, was replaced with natural gas, which has virtually no CO (Kreitman, 1976). Not only did the suicide rate for CO poisoning drop to almost zero, the overall rate of suicides in the country also declined. Young people of both genders looked for and found other means to take their lives, but such efforts were less dramatic among the older population.

Possible Questions

We know that Leslie has access to enough pain pills to put her in significant danger of making a lethal attempt. This is probably the case, even if she hasn't made any special effort to stockpile. Of course, if she is actively procuring pills, we would be even more concerned.

- "How many tablets of the pain medication do you have right now? Do you have any extra pills saved up?"
- "What other medications do you have?"

Influenced by the research literature, we ask about access to guns even when our clients haven't mentioned firearms as a method they've been considering.

- "Do you have a gun in your apartment? Any thoughts of getting one?"

U) Preparing for/Attempting Suicide

Some people orient themselves to the possibility of suicide by mentally preparing for it or even rehearsing it. Many clinicians judge the giving away of prized possessions and putting one's affairs in order to be important warning signs for suicide; however, to date the empirical evidence to support such judgments is lacking (Mandrusiak et al., 2006).

There are other ways to prepare for a suicide attempt. In Joiner's (2005) view, "people who have hurt themselves before (especially intentionally but also accidentally), who know how to work a gun, who have investigated the toxic and lethal properties of an overdose drug, [and] who have practiced tying nooses . . . are . . . at substantial risk for suicide" (pp. 50–51). Such "provocative experiences" can allow them to become "fearless, pain-tolerant, and knowledgeable about dangerous behaviors" (p. 47).

Analyzing data from a U.S. community sample, Kuo and Gallo (2005) calculated that "compared to people without a history of attempts, former attempters had much higher odds of completing suicide" (p. 633). Indeed, according to Harris and Barraclough (1997), a nonfatal suicide attempt is the strongest clinical predictor of eventual suicide. Nevertheless, "previous suicide attempts . . . tend to predict suicide during a span of years, not acutely, with 6% to 12% of patients committing suicide during the 5 to 10 years following their first attempts" (Busch & Fawcett, 2004, p. 357). Suominen et al. (2004), having conducted a 37-year follow-up study of 98 individuals in Finland who had attempted suicide, similarly concluded that a suicide attempt history "appears to be an indicator of high risk for completed suicide throughout the entire adult lifetime" (p. 563). There is evidence that among those people with an attempt history who eventually die by suicide, most employ the same method in their last, fatal attempt as they did in their first (Runeson, Tidemalm, Dahlin, Lichtenstein, & Långström, 2010).

Possible Questions
It isn't clear if Leslie has made any preparations for taking her life, and we don't know if she's ever made an attempt. Given that researchers believe many suicide attempts and completed suicides are misclassified as accidents (Florida Statewide Office of Suicide Prevention, 2008), it would make sense to inquire whether her car accident 3 years ago was actually an attempt to take her life. You could broach this possibility either indirectly—

- "You must have been disoriented when you woke up in the hospital after the car accident. Were you surprised that you survived the crash?"

—or more directly:

- "How did the car accident happen? Were you having any thoughts at the time about wanting to end your life? Did anyone interpret the crash as a suicide attempt?"

Regardless of whether the car accident is understood as a suicide attempt, you would still want to ask about (other) previous attempts.

- "Have you ever attempted to take your life? What did you do? What happened?"

CLIENT RESOURCES

9) Hope/Reasons for Living

Marsha Linehan and her colleagues pioneered the idea that just as you can access suicide risk by inquiring about hopelessness, you can get a sense of resiliency by asking clients about their sense of hope and other reasons for living. Their notion, grounded in the cognitive–behavioral recognition that people's actions are profoundly influenced by their beliefs, resulted in the creation of the Reasons for Living Inventory (Linehan et al., 1983). Rather than examining risk factors that predisposed individuals to suicide, this work focused on resources that help suicidal people to live, such as survival and coping beliefs, responsibility to family, child-related concerns, fear of suicide, fear of social disapproval, and moral objections. Such an approach to understanding suicidality has received empirical support. Studying 84 inpatients with a diagnosis of major depressive disorder, Malone et al. (2000) administered the Reasons for Living Inventory and found that those who identified more reasons for living were less likely to act on their suicidal thoughts at vulnerable times.

Possible Questions

Despite Leslie's desperate circumstances and thoughts, she *has* been coping.

- "You've been feeling really down, really desperate. How have you managed to survive? What's kept you going?"

Does Leslie hold any beliefs or fears that could protect her from making an attempt?

- "If you were to be on the verge of taking your life, what would stop you?"
- "I knew a client once who was profoundly suicidal, but her religious beliefs kept her from taking that final step."

We'd want to find out not only about intrapersonal reasons for keeping going, but also interpersonal (and interspecies!) reasons.

- "What would happen to Mahler if you were no longer here?"
- "Who would suffer most if you were to die?"

10) Variability in Suicidality

Suicidality is best thought of not as a constant state but, rather, as a pattern of interaction, encompassing the person's response to circumstances, suffering, and relationships with people. Because so many of these elements can be in flux, the suicidality itself can vary in both duration and intensity. As Simon (2006) recognized, "persons who attempt or complete suicide are usually am-bivalent about dying, some to the very last moment. . . . Suicide intent often remains an uncertainty to the last moment" (p. 299). The commitment to dying can wax and wane, not only as a result of ambivalence, but also in re-sponse to shifts in external realities and internal perceptions. We thus go in search of variations, and we attempt to discern what is going on both inter- and intrapersonally when the client is feeling less suicidal.

Possible Questions

- "When your most despairing thoughts come, how long do they typi-cally last? What makes them last longer? What helps them pass?"
- "What causes the despair to intensify? What helps it diminish a little? If it does diminish, how much of a break do you get from it before it comes back? Anything that helps it forget to come back?"
- "What are your thoughts like when you're playing a piece of music you love?"
- "Have you ever had a thought or an urge to do something desperate and then found a way not to act on it? How did you do it?"

11) Willingness Not to Conceal Suicidality

A client's ability and willingness to share with significant others his or her suicidal ideation, or details of his or her suicidal behavior or planning, can be crucial for ensuring safety. A young man attending our university's coun-seling clinic for students was trying to keep his parents from worrying about his despondency. Limiting face-to-face contact and putting on a brave front during brief telephone conversations with them had succeeded in keeping them in the dark. However, as his despair deepened, it seemed to us that his struggle was too overwhelming for him to handle on his own. We proposed, and he agreed, that he should call his parents and fill them in on what he was experiencing. They had previously discounted the seriousness of his depression, but in response to our call, they realigned their approach and took appropriate and timely action to help. The client, surprised and some-what relieved, was able to consider them as resources as we collaboratively created a safety plan.

Possible Questions

Wanting to protect themselves from shame and interpersonal pressures, clients who have been keeping their suicidality to themselves are never thrilled when we suggest alerting key significant others. We usually introduce the possibility by empathizing with their reluctance and then underscoring the importance of safety.

- "I know your parents have said some things that have put you on edge, so I imagine talking to them about what you're going through would be pretty tough. But I'm thinking that if they knew, it could help you stay safe. Would you be willing for us to give them a call?"

Jeremy is a vitally important significant other, but given that Leslie's relationship with him is over, we wouldn't suggest that she inform him of anything.

12) *Active Participation in Developing and Implementing a Safety Plan*

Researchers have demonstrated that safety plans effectively reduce suicidality (e.g., Henriques, Beck, & Brown, 2003; Huey et al., 2004). Henriques et al. incorporated early safety plan development in their cognitive therapy approach to working with adolescents and young adults who had attempted suicide. They described the safety plan, which was tailored for each individual patient, as "a hierarchically arranged written list of coping strategies, developed collaboratively by the patient and therapist, which the patient can do if a crisis situation arises" (p. 1261). Preliminary results showed a statistically significant reduction in subsequent suicide attempts of 50%.

Huey et al. (2004) developed an alternative to hospitalization for suicidal youths with psychiatric emergencies. Their program, an approach they named *multisystemic therapy*, implemented core strategies to minimize the risk of self-harm, including the development of a safety plan with the family so that potentially lethal suicide methods could be secured or eliminated. The researchers found that their program was significantly more effective than psychiatric hospitalization at reducing attempted suicides over the course of 16 months.

Our approach to safety planning, which is described in depth in the next chapter, similarly includes the co-creation, with the client, of a list of practical strategies. Whenever possible, we actively encourage the participation of significant others.

Possible Questions

The first step in developing a safety plan is determining whether the client is willing and able to collaborate with us.

- "What steps have you already taken to help ensure your safety?"
- "I'm thinking it might be helpful to brainstorm together some ways of feeling and being safe, even when you're feeling really bad. Would you be up for working together on some ideas?"

SIGNIFICANT-OTHER RISKS

h) Suicidality

After reviewing adoption, twin, and family studies, Brent and colleagues (Brent & Mann, 2005; Brent & Melhem, 2008) concluded that "suicide and suicidal behavior are familial, and appear to be heritable, through at least two components—liability to psychiatric disorder, and liability to impulsive aggression" (Brent & Mann, p. 22). They also elaborated on possible environmental factors contributing to what they termed the *familial transmission* of suicide behavior, including abuse, adverse family environments, and imitation.

Regardless of how the propensity for suicidality is passed on or shared, we make sense of our clients' current experience within the context of their interactions with family and friends, both in the past and in the present. We've worked with many clients who were making choices for themselves, informed not only by the previous attempts or completions and current desperation of family members, but also of non-family significant others.

Possible Questions

There is often so much shame attached to suicide that clients are reluctant to talk about any history of suicidality among their significant others. We thus make empathic statements and ask a variety of questions designed to open the door to addressing it.

- "We work a lot with clients who are survivors of suicide—living with the effects of someone close having taken their life. They have so many unanswered questions and so much grief to process."
- "Are you or is anyone you know a survivor?"
- "Anyone in your family ever attempt suicide? Die by suicide?"
- "How about friends? Anyone else you've known who took their life?"

i) Ignorance/Denial of the Client's Suicidality

Significant others who are kept in the dark or turn a blind eye to the client's suicidality can't act as resources, and their lack of information can actually make matters worse. Len once consulted on a case of a hospitalized suicidal teenager who hadn't revealed his sexual identity to his mother. The two of them lived alone in a small apartment and hadn't been in contact with the father for many years. The boy had become suicidal at the prospect of his mother figuring out that he was gay, and thus he was doubly committed to secrecy. As a result of the hospitalization, she became aware of his dilemma, whereupon she was able to become supportive.

Another hospitalized young teenager had unsuccessfully tried to handle her intensifying suicidality on her own. Experiencing flashbacks and other PTSD symptoms related to a rape she'd been subjected to when she was 6 years old, she kept her symptoms to herself in an effort not to burden her mother. In the process, she put herself at heightened risk. As in the case just discussed, the hospitalization was instrumental in the mother's discovering what had been going on. The girl was relieved of the burden of bearing her pain alone, and once she could talk with her mother, her suicidality resolved and did not recur.

Possible Questions

Jeremy may be ignorant of Leslie's suicidality, or he may just not want to know. Although painful to Leslie, his not showing concern is at least keeping the complications of the breakup from getting even more severe. She has been texting him a lot, so he no doubt appreciates that she's profoundly upset, but we wouldn't want to encourage her to be contemplating him anymore than she already is. We'd thus keep our questions focused mostly on her parents or we'd pose them in a general way.

- "Do you think your parents' demanding that you go into rehab is a result of their suspecting that you're suicidal, or does it reflect that they don't have a clue?"
- "Who is most worried about your safety?"

j) Dismissive Response to the Client's Suicidality

Family members or friends who have been contending with a chronically suicidal loved one can find themselves pulling back and/or lashing out. Exhausted by constant anxiety and uncertainty, angry with the client for not "snapping out of it," they, like the client, may be thinking that his or her death would bring some much needed relief. Such an attitude can dramatically increase the client's risk.

Len conducted a suicide assessment of a preteen boy who was having frequent thoughts of shooting himself. After the child revealed that he had access to guns in his home, Len called the father, who took offense at the suggestion that he remove the weapons. Criticizing his son for "making up" his suicidality, he said that he would rather get rid of the boy than his guns. Given the father's dismissive attitude, Len deemed the child's risk of acting on his thoughts to be dangerously elevated. He notified the police of the danger in the home, and the boy was hospitalized.

Possible Questions

So much depends on the tone significant others use when responding to the suicidal person. Not having talked to Leslie's parents yet, we don't know if they are as exasperated as she suggests or have been well meaning but clumsy in their efforts to help.

- "It sounds like you think your family has kind of thrown up their hands. Would they agree with that assessment?"
- "You figured your folks were pretty angry and demanding when they told you to get your butt to rehab. Do you think they would have used that tone if they knew how dark your thoughts have been?"

SIGNIFICANT-OTHER RESOURCES

vii) Compassionate Response to the Client's Suicidality

The word *compassion* comes from the Latin stem *compati*, meaning to suffer with or suffer together. Compassion takes significant others inside the suffering of the suicidal person, providing them with an empathic grasp of his or her pain. It is thus more emotionally involving than pity, which affords significant others some emotional distance. When they feel pity, they feel bad *about* the client, rather than *with* him or her. Compassion is thus a more positive involvement, but sometimes family and friends find that pity is all they can muster.

Therapists, too, recognize that compassion takes *effort*, an effort that, although at times overwhelming, can make a profound difference in the lives of those at risk. Richman (1979) told a story about a suicidal client who called him to cancel an appointment she had earlier scheduled for the next day:

> I acceded and upon hanging up the phone experienced a sense of relief thinking that I would just as well not be burdened by her troubles. Realizing the rejection implied by my acquiescence, I called back to say I thought she should keep her appointment. "Oh good," she replied, "I was just about to jump out the window with my little son." (p. 135)

When we've been fortunate enough to be able to bring friends or family members into a suicide assessment, we have sometimes witnessed the genuine communication of compassion. Such absence of resentment and the expression of caring bode well for the involvement of these significant others in a workable safety plan; however, sometimes other demands prevent them from actively participating in the day-to-day burden of ensuring safety. Nevertheless, knowing that the emotional support is there may contribute to the client's stability.

We once saw a first-time client who was overwhelmed by her boyfriend's decision to move out of their apartment and to quit the job where they both worked. Her fever-pitched talk and her divergent speaking pattern had us worried. During the appointment, she took a phone call from her mother, during which she delved into the details of the situation and worked out some of the logistics of what she was going to do next. The mother had a not-dissimilar manner of speech, yet she was treating our client's concerns with an almost bored matter-of-factness, which suggested to us that she was quite accustomed to hearing her daughter in this state of mind and was thus not put on alert by it. Of course, having a parent not taking her seriously could have exacerbated the client's distress, but this didn't happen. After talking with her mother for a few minutes, our client became somewhat calmer.

Listening to the mother–daughter conversation helped us put our observations in a broader interpersonal context, which somewhat lowered our concerns. And it helped us realize that a response that isn't ostensibly heartfelt can still be, in its non-reactivity, uniquely compassionate.

Possible Questions
Leslie has described her parents in a negative light, characterizing them as shrill and angry. Such a response is, however, open to being therapeutically reframed as evidence of caring.

- "Have your parents always felt your pain so deeply? They seem to care a lot."
- "It sounds like your parents are worried even without knowing all the details of what you're going through."
- "Of your friends and family, who would be the first to jump on a plane if they knew how desperate you are?"

viii) Active Participation in a Safety Plan

When significant others have the availability, commitment, and wherewithal to actively participate in keeping the client safe, their involvement can mean the difference between hospitalization and going home. Two cases we saw in our center highlight the difference such significant others can make, even when they aren't family members.

Panicked by thoughts of shooting himself, Steve (to whom we return in Chapter 5) came to therapy in our center, wondering if he needed to be hospitalized. He didn't want to die, but he was an avid gun enthusiast with several weapons in his apartment, so the opportunity to impulsively act on his thoughts was dangerously available. The night before his appointment, he was so disturbed by his suicidal ideation that he'd gone to stay with his good friend, Aaron. As the therapist and Steve began to develop a safety plan, they explored the possibility of Aaron's being a resource. Steve endorsed the idea; however, he revealed that Aaron also owned guns. Steve and the therapist called Aaron, who readily agreed to remove the guns from both his own and Steve's apartment. Together, they worked out that Steve would, for the time being, continue staying with Aaron.

Another client, Michelle, had persistent thoughts of jumping off the balcony of her 11th-floor apartment. Her parents lived in another country and she'd recently become alienated from many of her friends, so the availability of helpful significant others was limited. However, she still had one friend, Vanessa, who had stood by her, and Michelle felt comfortable contacting her as part of a safety plan. Vanessa lived in the same building on the ground floor, and she readily agreed to have Michelle stay with her. Michelle refused to impose to that degree; however, she proposed taking the elevator down to Vanessa's place whenever thoughts of jumping reached a threshold of intensity or persistence that scared her. This part of the safety plan felt safe enough to both women and the therapist, so they proceeded with implementing it.

Possible Questions
You could venture the therapeutic possibility that Leslie's parents' pushiness is the result of deep caring, but before you moved forward to enlist their help in a safety plan, you'd need to see if Leslie and they themselves would accept this perspective. If not, attempting to involve them in a safety plan could put Leslie more at risk. If you were to get her permission to contact them, you'd then want to spend time filling them in and gauging their reaction. Do they express shock? Deep concern? Anger? Frustration? Do they ask about how they can help? Do they seem capable of taking tangible action? The questions below offer first steps toward gathering this essential information.

- "Whom can you count on to really be here for you and help you through this time?"
- "If you had to get out of here for awhile—to get a much-needed break from all this—would your folks be willing to put you up for a few weeks?"
- "Given what you're facing at the moment, I think we need to enlist the help of your family. Would you be willing for us to give them a call now and fill them in?"
- "This seems to me too big for you to do alone. Which of your parents would be more likely to come and stay with you for a while?"

In the next chapter we focus exclusively on the issue of safety. We offer an engaged, empathy-informed means of coming to a decision about whether the client presently has the requisite intra- and interpersonal resources to stay safe outside of the hospital. We present an eight-step guide for brainstorming and writing down the details of a comprehensive and collaborative safety plan. And we explore how you can use the process of developing a safety plan as an opportunity to gather further information for making the safety decision.

NOTES

1 The research literature is overwhelmingly skewed toward the exploration of individual risk factors. Thus, our identification of individual resources and of the risks and resources of significant others has, of necessity, relied most heavily on our clinical experience.

2 Although grounded in an actual RSA we did in our center, the case we present has been substantially modified, not only to protect the confidentiality of the client, but also to provide the necessary range and depth of relevant information to warrant the posing of empathic queries under each of the 51 topics of inquiry.

3 See Chapter 2.

4 They will usually tell you when you're on target by responding to your statement with comments such as "Right!" or "Exactly."

5 See Chapter 2.

6 We'll return to this distinction in the next chapter.

4

SAFETY

YOU INITIATE A suicide assessment when you're concerned that a client could be in imminent danger of making an attempt; you conclude it when you're satisfied that you needn't be on heightened alert or, having recognized that concern is indeed warranted, you've taken relevant steps to help protect the client's safety. In the time between, you gather the necessary information about intra- and interpersonal risks and resources to make what we call a *safety decision*, an empathy-informed resolution about how best to proceed, and then you implement this decision, putting it into action. The implementation might entail collaborating with the client on the creation of a *safety plan*, an idiosyncratic resource-based to-do list that, as we explain below, differs in important respects from a no-harm contract. Or, in situations where you aren't convinced that the client has the necessary resources available to safely negotiate the challenges he or she will be facing in the coming days, it may involve your making a collaborative, or, if necessary, unilateral, decision for the client to go into the hospital.

The entire assessment and decision-making process, from beginning to end, can take anywhere from a few minutes to well over an hour, depending on several factors:

- *How the client is feeling.* A client once showed up at our center, shaking, thirsty, and hungry. She hadn't eaten (or slept much at all) in the last couple of days, so before we started even thinking about asking her questions, we got her some water and a couple of items out of the vending machine. Once she was feeling more comfortable, we were able to begin a conversation.

If clients are upset, agitated, or disoriented, we don't want to contribute to their distress any more than necessary, and, if possible, we want to help them feel calm enough to thoughtfully engage with us. An assessment that goes on too long can prove taxing to folks struggling emotionally, so you'll want to temper your curiosity with an ongoing awareness of how they're holding up.

• *How experienced you are.* The more thoroughly you know the topics of inquiry within the RSA categories of experience (*Disruptions and Demands, Suffering, Troubling Behaviors,* and *Desperation*) and the more experience you have in conducting assessments with these in mind, the more efficient you can be in gathering and digesting information, making a safety decision, and, when relevant, developing a safety plan.

• *How much time you have or can make available.* Depending on your profession and practice setting, time constraints may be more or less pressing. A multitasking ER doctor generally won't be able to devote the same amount of time to an assessment as a psychotherapist in private practice. Regardless, in both settings, clinicians need to protect the necessary time to make an adequate assessment, and to do that, they will find it necessary to triage, prioritizing immediate life-threatening danger over less seriously ill patients or clients.

• *Whether this is a first-time, stand-alone assessment.* When we haven't previously met clients and particularly when they are sitting in our office at someone else's urging, we make sure to start off slowly. We ease into the conversation, introducing ourselves, orienting them to our setting, and empathizing with their plight. This obviously takes time, but not rushing at the beginning can facilitate a more efficient conversation later on, once they have relaxed a little into the process. Although the reason for the conversation requires us to attend primarily to the current crisis, we intentionally widen the focus of our curiosity, especially at the beginning of the interview, as we want as much as possible to encounter our clients as richly complex *people.* Devoting time to asking them about aspects of their lives that seemingly have nothing to do with their suicidality sometimes yields important information relevant to securing safety, but it also allows them to recognize that we are interested in who they *are*, not just with how they're dealing with what they're facing.

• *How forthcoming the client is in answering your questions.* Our first thought when encountering reticent clients is not that they're being uncooperative but, rather, that we're attempting to move too fast. If they are distrustful of you and/or the process, then your responding with patience, empathic understanding, and cautious curiosity may help assuage their concerns and allow them to participate more fully.

• *The complexity of the client's circumstances and suicidality.* In some cases, we're able to quickly determine that a client is not in danger; in others, that a client needs to be in the hospital. A comprehensive assessment is only necessary when you can't be quick because you're not yet sure. When the client's story and motivations are complex, we desire a detailed understanding of the person, as such particulars help us grasp both their desperation and possibilities for safety.

• *The complexity of the safety plan.* Occasionally, the safety plan that you and your client come up with will be easy to lay out and straightforward to implement. But sometimes everything hinges on a significant other you're having trouble reaching or on figuring out complex steps, say, of securing weapons and preventing access to other lethal means. Certain steps can't be rushed.

For ease of explanation, we have divided the discussion of the assessment process into three parts. In the previous chapter, we explored the intricacies of gathering information related to both risks and resources; in this one, we tease apart the complexities of making a safety decision and then of developing a safety plan. However, such divisions are somewhat misleading, as no part of an assessment is a discrete stage in a linear progression; each overlaps and is recursively linked to the others. The making of a safety decision isn't an encapsulated event at the end of the assessment but an ongoing process of comparing, considering, and digesting that is dependent on, but also interwoven with, the gathering of information on risks and resources. Curiosity about danger *and* safety gives rise to questions that delve into suicidality *and* implicitly frame therapeutic possibilities. This danger–safety double focus is essential when you're working out the details of a safety plan with the client. And, in turn, the process of co-constructing such a plan allows you to obtain further information—about the client's resolve and resilience—that can turn out to be critically important when making the safety decision.

COMING TO A SAFETY DECISION

It is possible to accurately predict long-term trends and the behavior of groups, but, as we discussed in Chapter 1, it is impossible to predict the short-term behavior of an individual. How, then, do you figure out whether the person you're assessing is in imminent danger of making an attempt? According to Simon (2006), you can't: "Suicide risk likely varies from minute to minute, hour to hour, day to day. This makes any prediction about imminent suicide illusory" (p. 299). Holding this understanding in mind is a good antidote to any hubris you might be harboring, but it doesn't alter the fact that when you're assessing a suicidal individual, you have the clinical responsibility to indeed attempt the impossible.

Conventional wisdom has it that when faced with this kind of high-stakes decision-making, you should rely on rational thinking, as it is ideally suited for parsing complexity and forming objective, logical conclusions. If this were true, then, as discussed in Chapter 1, you'd ideally use a paper-and-pencil instrument to gather empirical data on clients' suicidality and then analyze it with a formula that assigned differential weights to various answers, making it possible to derive a reliable and valid "danger score" on which to base your conclusions and interventions.

Unless this is the first page you've read of our book, you already know that we don't embrace such an approach. Rather than attempting to be exclusively rational, we are committed to being *relational*—tuned into relationships between clients and therapists; between clients and significant others; between risks and resources; between dangers and possibilities for safety; and between desperation and tangible, achievable steps for protection and future prevention. And rather than impartially objective, we strive to be emotionally intersubjective—empathic—in our efforts to learn about our clients' experience.

Support for our orientation can be found in the work of the neurologist Antonio Damasio, who says that it's impossible to be devoid of feeling while making decisions: "Emotions are a crucial part of the decision-making process. . . . A brain that can't feel can't make up its mind" (as cited in Lehrer, 2009, p. 15). A similar point is made by neuroscientist Joseph LeDoux, who notes that emotions are actually organizing much of what we think and are themselves a form of thought: "Every feeling is really a summary of data, a visceral response to . . . [nonconscious] information that can't be accessed directly" (as cited in Lehrer, p. 23). Recognizing that "our emotions are deeply empirical" (as cited in Lehrer, p. 41), we treat our emotional responses during an assessment as valuable sources of information. We thus listen to them closely as we attempt to make sense of the complex stories our clients offer.

Another way of addressing the importance of emotional thinking is to examine the phenomenon of expert intuition. Drawing on the groundbreaking work on decision-making by Herbert Simon, Daniel Kahneman (2011) construes intuitive decision-making to be a form of pattern recognition. If you develop expertise in an area, then you can rely on the ability to recognize patterns to intuitively inform your choices: "When confronted with a problem . . . the machinery of intuitive thought does the best it can. If the individual has relevant expertise, she will recognize the situation, and the intuitive solution that comes to her mind is likely to be correct" (Kahneman, p. 12). Indeed, according to Ap Dijksterhuis, conscious decision-making is only preferable when making simple decisions. When faced with complex situations, the prefrontal cortex gets overwhelmed with too much information. In such circumstances, it is actually *preferable* to rely on emotional thought processes, allowing yourself to digest the information unconsciously. As long as you have adequate experience, then "whatever your intuition then tells you is almost certainly going to be the best choice" (as cited in Lehrer, 2009, p. 237).

Until you've acquired sufficient experience in suicide assessment, you'll be limited in how much you can be guided by an intuitive sense of your clients' orientation to dying. You have to be able to distinguish, for example, between the anxiety you're empathically picking up from your client and the anxiety you're feeling as a function of being in the midst of such a high-stakes interview. And you need enough assessments under your belt to know that something about this particular client feels different in a way that either unsettles or reassures you.

An experienced colleague of ours (and Douglas's wife), Dr. Shelley Green, a family therapist, was providing live supervision from behind a one-way mirror of the first session of a therapy case. The client was a middle-aged man who had recently lost his daughter—his only child—in a traffic accident. A few months before that, cancer had taken his wife. Devastated and terribly lonely, unable to breathe, he had let his consulting business slide, so his financial stability was crumbling. He talked to the therapist about having lost the will to live. Shelley went into the therapy room at this point to conduct a suicide assessment, and as she conversed with the man, he spoke eloquently about the emptiness that overwhelmed him. A less experienced clinician, recognizing his hopelessness and fearful of the darkness of his thoughts, might have taken steps to have him admitted to the hospital, but Shelley didn't do that. She spoke to him at length, listening carefully and empathizing with his pain, and she scheduled a follow-up therapy appointment. She didn't perceive the need for a safety plan.

When he returned a week later, the client mentioned the profound grief he still felt, but he went on to explain how he had begun organizing his house and how he had taken steps to restart his business. Within a month his finances were in good-enough shape that he was confident he wouldn't lose his house to foreclosure, and he had donated most of his wife's and daughter's clothes to charity. He was alive and he was living.

We asked Shelley how she knew that she didn't need to implement a safety plan or facilitate the client's hospitalization. She said that it came down to how she felt while he, maintaining soft but intense eye contact, was telling his story. He was clearly experiencing deep pain, she said, but his eyes communicated something like relief at being able to speak about it, at hearing the essentials empathically reflected back to him, at making a human connection. Shelley saw a spark, and her gut registered its importance.

You can't learn this kind of body-informed discernment directly from a book. It comes with experience, lots of it, and that experience can be hard to come by. Although suicidal thinking is common enough that most clinicians encounter it fairly often in a busy practice, suicide attempts are more rare, and completed suicides rarer still. To learn most from the cases you see and the assessments you perform, you'll want to get whatever follow-up information you can on what transpired after you conducted your assessment. On occasion you'll be able to determine that a client you sent to the hospital or who worked with you on a safety plan is, several weeks, months, or years later, still alive and well. Of course, you can never be certain that your involvement was the deciding factor in his or her survival, but you'll have some degree of confirmation that you were accurate in your reading of the situation. And if you learn on follow-up that a client who you didn't think was profoundly suicidal ended up making an attempt soon after seeing you, you'll want to devote time to analyzing what you missed and how you missed it.

It will take time and practice for you to develop the ability to trust your pattern-recognizing intuition, but you *can* begin building the knowledge base for that expertise by thoroughly acquainting yourself with the topics of inquiry in the RRIG (see Chapter 3), informed as they are by the research literature and clinical experience. You can also learn from your clinical work with a variety of highly distressed, *nonsuicidal* individuals, as they can serve as an informative background when someone comes along who grabs your attention as somehow different. We'll return to this issue below.

Trusting your gut, trusting your intuition, begins with and always depends on knowing what information to listen for, ask about, delve into, and return to. A working group of experts (Rudd, Berman, et al., 2006), convened by the American Association of Suicidology (AAS), came to consensus on warning signs for suicide, distinguishing these from risk factors by virtue of their indicating near-term risk (p. 257), the presence of an active suicidal crisis, and the demand for specific and immediate intervention (p. 258). They developed a hierarchically structured list, including, at the top, the following indicators (Rudd, Berman, et al., p. 259):

- Someone threatening to hurt or kill themselves
- Someone looking for ways to kill themselves: seeking access to pills, weapons, or other means
- Someone talking or writing about death, dying, or suicide

Further down they listed these (Rudd, Berman, et al., p. 259):

- Hopelessness
- Rage, anger, seeking revenge

- Acting reckless or engaging in risky activities, seemingly without thinking
- Feeling trapped—like there's no way out
- Increasing alcohol or drug use
- Withdrawing from friends, family, or society
- Anxiety, agitation, unable to sleep, or sleeping all the time
- Dramatic changes in mood
- No reason for living; no sense of purpose in life

We endorse the development and publicizing of such lists; the more familiar clinicians and the general public are with key signs of suicidality, the better. Working within the *categories of experience* and *topics of inquiry* of the RRIG, you will similarly put yourself on heightened alert when you have a client who is—

(a) Showing signs of *desperation*:
   - Feeling hopeless
   - Possessing an intense desire for relief
   - Intending and/or planning to act on suicidal thoughts
   - Communicating suicidality to others
   - Having or gaining access to a means of suicide
   - Making preparations for or attempting suicide

and/or is—

(b) Engaging in *troubling behavior(s)* that complicate the situation:
   - Withdrawing from activities or relationships
   - Abusing substances (e.g., alcohol) or engaging in disordered eating
   - Acting impulsively or compulsively
   - Self-harming

and/or is—

(c) *Suffering* with one or more physical or mental health conditions that undermine the ability to cope:
   - Depression
   - Anxiety
   - Conflicted identity, shame, burdensomeness
   - Psychotic experiences
   - Insomnia, pain, or illness

and/or is—

(d) Experiencing *disruptions and demands* that could precipitate a suicide attempt:
- Loss of an important relationship
- Overwhelming expectations or obligations
- Precipitous loss of social or financial status
- Trouble with authorities
- Trauma stemming from abuse, bullying, or some kind of peril (e.g., car accident, combat)

However, as we discussed in depth in Chapter 3, we don't think that assessing for suicide can be adequately accomplished if you're not also assessing for possibilities of *safety*, and you can't do that without attending to the interpersonal context of the individual—to the importance and involvement of family, friends, and other professionals—or without listening for and asking about *resources*.

This is a foundational assumption of relational assessment: Everything you do—the questions you ask, the understanding you develop, and, most relevant to this chapter, the safety decision you come to—needs to be grounded in the *juxtaposition of idiosyncratic details*. You explore and make sense of this particular risk of this particular person at this particular point in time *in relation* to other particular intra- and interpersonal risks and resources. The point of your interview is to help you derive a contextually sensitized grasp of what the person is facing, contemplating, and capable of doing, and to help you decide what, if anything, you need to do to bolster safety.

Just as our semistructured interview approach is indebted to the qualitative data-gathering practices developed by ethnographic researchers (e.g., Spradley, 1979), so too our approach to deriving a safety decision owes something to the data-analysis procedures initiated by ethnographers (Spradley) and grounded theorists (Glasser & Strauss, 1967) and then nuanced, adapted, and evolved by naturalistic inquirers (Lincoln & Guba, 1985), postpositivist-grounded theorists (e.g., Charmaz, 2006), and other qualitative researchers (Coffey & Atkinson, 1996; Dey, 1990; Miles & Huberman, 1994; Tesch, 1990). We must hasten to add that the motivations, settings, and responsibilities of researchers are profoundly different from those of clinicians. Analyzing data from one or more qualitative research interviews is a methodical process that can take days, weeks, even months; it may be aided by specialized computer programs; and it usually culminates in the composition of a monograph. Analyzing information in a suicide assessment is an extemporaneous process, with the time frame measured by a clock, not a calendar; it relies on brain-and-body wetware, rather than computer software and hardware; and it facilitates the making of a decision, not the writing of a text. However, in both activities, something significant *emerges* from the *juxtaposition of information*. In qualitative research, the constant comparison (Glasser & Strauss; Lincoln & Guba) of decontextualized bits of data (Dey, 1993; Tesch) allows for new, recontextualized (Dey; Tesch) connections to be made and categories to emerge (Glasser & Strauss). In a suicide assessment, the clinician's constant, empathic comparison of idiosyncratic risks and resources allows for a decision to emerge. In both cases, it is continual juxtaposition that makes possible the realization of something new, whether it be a category or a decision.

We talk about *coming to* a decision or about a decision *emerging* or *being realized*. Such descriptions are intended to underscore the synergistic effect of continual juxtaposition of relevant information over the course of the interview. Research suggests that even when you think you are in conscious control of your decisions, you are experiencing something of a mirage (Bode et al., 2011); nonconscious parts of your thinking and feeling are much more involved in the process than you recognize. Up to 10 seconds prior to what you think of as consciously deciding something, areas of your brain responsible for relational reasoning have already made and registered the decision (Soon, Brass, Heinze, & Haynes, 2008). Your conscious awareness might take credit for actively making up your mind, but it is more the passive recipient of a decision already formed through the ongoing juxtaposition of information from both the rational and emotional parts of your brain (Lehrer, 2009).

Gregory Bateson (1979) was interested in the benefits that accrue from juxtaposition, or what he called *double description*—"the bonus or increment of knowing [that] follows from *combining* information from two or more sources" (p. 67). He pointed out that with binocular vision, data collected from one eye is compared with data from the other, and the difference between these two sources creates the perception of depth, the phenomenon of three-dimensional seeing. Extrapolating from this particular means of knowing to knowing in general, he concluded that "in principle, extra 'depth' in some metaphoric sense is to be expected whenever . . . information [from two separate] . . . descriptions is differently collected or differently coded" (p. 70).

Juxtaposition, constant comparison, and double description all make use of *relationship* as the basis for understanding, deciding, and acting. As such, they are integral to any relational suicide assessment, including the tasks involved in making and implementing a reliable and valid safety decision: juxtaposing what you've learned as a professional with what you learn from the client, juxtaposing your emotional thinking with your knowledge of the facts, and thinking twice about whatever safety decision you come to before acting on it.

JUXTAPOSING PROFESSIONAL KNOWLEDGE
WITH CLIENT INFORMATION

You begin a suicide assessment in possession of professional information—including both your clinical experience and your acquired understanding of risks and resources. In the course of the interview, you come to possess information from and about the client, empathically listening not only for the details being communicated, but also to *how* they're being communicated. Your depth of understanding, to the degree that you are able to acquire it, depends on your juxtaposing these two different sources of knowledge—what you bring into the process as a professional and what you gather empathically from the client.

This bringing together of professional and client experience doesn't automatically facilitate depth of understanding. This will happen only if you equally value both sources. If you use your knowledge about risks and resources to quiz clients on their state of mind, fitting their responses into categories you have readied in advance of the conversation, then the information you collect will have limited utility. As a character in John Irving's (2012) novel, *In One Person*, says, "Please don't put a *label* on me—don't make me a *category* before you get to know me!" (p. 198). To come to a decision that most accurately reflects your professional competence *and* your client's unique circumstances, experiences, and possibilities, your expertise needs to inspire your curiosity in an interactive conversation, not narrow your focus so much that you ask questions to confirm what you believe you already know.

JUXTAPOSING YOUR EMOTIONAL RESPONSE
WITH YOUR KNOWLEDGE OF THE "FACTS"

Emotions can be understood as the body's way of thinking and communicating about context and relationship. You, like most people, tend to relax in safe, predictable circumstances and around trustworthy others; get angry when social status or well-being is questioned or expectations are thwarted; and become anxious when safety is threatened and wariness is warranted or when desired prediction and control of the future is not possible. By paying attention to your emotional responses to your client, you're giving your body a chance to contribute to your decision-making, to serve as an important listening device and interpreter.

Of course, for you to trust your emotions as a reliable source of information, you have to be sure that they are differentially reflective of relational elements of your client's communication, rather than uniformly registering the contextual urgency of the situation. If, for example, your anxiety varies throughout the interview, increasing and decreasing in sensitive response to what you're learning about the client's circumstances and mindset, then you can probably rely on it as a valuable source of information. If, however, your anxiety begins before the interview starts and remains steady throughout, it may be telling you more about how scary it is to conduct such assessments than about any particular dangers you're sensing from the client.

We put the word *facts* in quotes to highlight the idea that all the details you learn in an assessment are subject to contextual interpretation. This notion then provides another way to bring juxtaposition into your decision-making process. One way to juxtapose feeling and thinking information is to consider each within the context of the other. How does the sensation in your gut inform your understanding of the "facts"? And how can the "facts" help you make sense of what your gut is telling you? Searching for and finding answers to such questions is essential for body-informed decision-making, as "bodily experience is the primal basis for everything we can mean, think, know, and communicate" (Lakoff & Johnson, 1999, p. xi).

THINKING TWICE ABOUT YOUR SAFETY DECISION

According to Lehrer (2009), the brain's "decisions often feel unanimous . . . but the conclusions are actually reached only after a series of sharp internal disagreements. While the cortex struggles to make a decision, rival bits of tissue are contradicting one another. . . . The mind is an extended argument. And it is arguing with itself" (pp. 198–199). Given that "even the most mundane choices emerge from a vigorous . . . debate" (Lehrer, p. 199), it makes sense to us to formally invite second-guessing or counterarguments as a means of ensuring that you are making a reliable and valid decision.

We thus suggest that once you've settled on a safety decision but before you implement it, you find a way to take a second look. You might do this by bringing a supervisor or colleague into the process, sharing with him or her what you've gleaned and how you're planning to proceed, and then taking his or her response into account. You might invite this person into the session, filling him or her in on what you've understood so far, and asking the client to correct or elaborate on your characterization. Alternatively, you may prefer to provide the supervisor or colleague with a synopsis in a room separate from the client (if it's safe to leave him or her alone or talking to someone else for a few minutes) and use whatever feedback you receive to either support your direction or broaden your perspective and take other possibilities into account.

If you don't have the benefit of having other professionals available for immediate consultation, you might engage in something of a counterargument thought experiment. Ask yourself, "For me to make a different decision than the one I've come to, what new information would I need or how would I need to view the existing information differently?" If it's feasible to do so, make the necessary inquiries to see if you can obtain such information and then use it to reevaluate your decision. Or see if you can find an alternate frame to make sense of the information that has been inclining you in a particular direction. If, in posing such possibilities to yourself, you can confidently assert that nothing could, at this point, shift the direction you're heading, then your thought experiment has successfully allowed you to think twice about what you're doing, and you can proceed with a depth of confidence provided by the juxtaposition of the two possibilities. If, however, your second-guessing opens up another way of viewing the situation, a way that leads you to a different decision, then allow the juxtaposition to continue, to inspire new questions, and to bring you, possibly, to a different decision.

RSAs provide the means for you to explore broad ranges of human experience, but they are designed to lead, inevitably, to one of three decisions. (1) If your head and your gut are in agreement that the client is in imminent danger of making a suicide attempt, and, despite your best efforts, you've been unable to identify the necessary intra- and interpersonal resources for the client to stay safe, then immediate hospitalization will come to the foreground as the best course of action. (2) If your head and gut concur that the client is in danger of making a suicide attempt, but you have been able to identify intra- and interpersonal resources that will make it possible for him or her, at least for the short term, to safely negotiate the danger, then you'll work with the client to construct a detailed safety plan. And (3) if neither your head nor gut register significant concern about immediate safety, you might recommend that the client seek therapy or pursue some other form of treatment, but you won't consider a safety plan relevant or necessary. We'll address each of these three decisions, but in reverse order.

WHEN NO SAFETY PLAN IS NEEDED

Several years ago, at the beginning of sixth grade at a new school, with a social studies teacher who didn't yet know him well, Douglas's 11-year-old son Eric turned in a class assignment. At the bottom of the page, for reasons that made sense to him but completely eluded his teacher, he had written, "I think I'll kill myself," next to which he had drawn a smiley face. His logic may have gone over the teacher's head, but his scribbling made it onto her radar. Before long he was called down to the guidance office. While a guidance counselor met with him, the office called his mother, Shelley, and asked her to come in immediately for a meeting.

By the time Shelley arrived at the school, Eric, subjected to a good 40 minutes of intense questioning, was exhausted and distraught. His repeated claims that he wasn't suicidal could now be corroborated by his mother, who reassured the counselor that he was a well-adjusted, happy kid with a sometimes twisted sense of humor. The counselor, no doubt unprepared for and unnerved by the assessment responsibilities she shouldered, scolded Eric for thoughtlessly and needlessly creating such a kerfuffle, and she admonished Shelley to feel grateful for the perspicacity of Eric's teacher and the responsiveness of the school.

The school was indeed wise to take the scribbled note seriously; after all, it could have been a conflicted cry for help. However, the assessment needlessly became an inquisition-like, shame-inducing experience, rather than an opportunity to connect with a new student, explore risks and resources in a nonthreatening way, and touch base with his parents to get a feel for his interpersonal context. When it became clear that Eric wasn't at risk, the counselor could have increased the likelihood that he would access professional help in the future, should he feel the need, by letting him know that she cared about his safety and would welcome seeing him again anytime he felt stressed out. Instead, he left feeling rebuked, determined to never return. At least she didn't suggest that they create a safety plan for him, as both he and his mother would have been offended by the idea that he needed one.

You will occasionally find yourself in similar circumstances, asked to assess someone who, it turns out, isn't at risk. However, you will more commonly encounter clients who tell you they are fine but whose reassurances are belied by the distress evident in their voice and body. Because you'll be attending not only to what clients say but also to how they say it, you'll be prepared to use such reassurances as a reason to continue, rather than stop, the conversation.

If you do decide that a safety plan is not necessary, document in your note how you came to this decision as a result of your assessment. You don't want your records to give the appearance that you neglected to follow up on an indication of danger.

WHEN A SAFETY PLAN IS NECESSARY AND POSSIBLE

We start thinking that a safety plan is necessary whenever we have concerns about our client's ability to otherwise negotiate the challenges he or she faces. Arriving at this thought then prompts two considerations: Does the person possess the requisite intra- and interpersonal resources to make the development of a viable plan possible? And, if so, is he or she interested in co-developing and implementing a plan? Often, clear answers to these questions come only during the process of developing and writing down the steps of the plan.

• *Do available resources make a viable plan possible?* In Chapter 5 we present a transcript of an RSA that is based on one we conducted with a depressed and distraught young man at our Student Counseling Center. This client owned several guns, and he was contending with ongoing thoughts and urges to shoot himself. Nevertheless, as a former competitive downhill ski racer, he was an expert at handling dangerous situations, and he had a close friend who was willing to take responsibility for removing all the weapons from the apartment. These and other intra- and interpersonal resources became the foundation for a safety plan that got him through a rough time without having to go to the hospital. Had he not had this sense of his own competence or had his friend not been available or willing to help, then, given the level of danger he was facing, a safety plan would probably never have made it onto the table as an option.

• *Is the client interested in co-developing and implementing the plan?* Fisch, Weakland, and Segal (1982) and de Shazer (1985) underscore the importance in therapy of not getting ahead of your clients when offering to help them change. They distinguish between, on the one hand, "window shoppers" (Fisch et al.) or "visitors" (de Shazer)—clients who come in for a session but have no investment, yet, in doing anything different to alter their situation—and, on the other hand, "customers"—clients who are committed to doing what it takes to change their situation. Prochaska and his colleagues (e.g., Prochaska et al., 1992) similarly suggest that we tailor our interventions to clients' stages of change: Are they prepared to take action, or have they even started wondering about the possibility of doing so? Informed by the work of these therapists and researchers, we never *urge* clients to work on or implement a safety plan. We float the idea of developing one and see how they respond. An example of this can be seen in the following dialogue with a young person in danger of taking an overdose.

Therapist: The most important thing is for you to be safe.

Client: I hate it. Hate it.

Therapist: Yeah. And at the moment you don't feel safe.

Client: Not at all.

Therapist: So if you had a plan—if we were to toss around some ideas and create a plan—for some things you could do to help you be safer, do you think that would help?

Client: I don't know. Yeah, maybe. Like what?

Therapist: Well, for starters, figuring out who can help you do something about that stockpile of pills you've got stashed in your apartment.

Client: How do you mean?

Therapist: As long as those pills are within arm's reach, you're in danger. If your mom or your dad or your brother were to help you clear those bottles out of there and then, for the next little while, help you manage your pain meds so you didn't have enough in your apartment to make an attempt, then your urge to take them might change in some way.

Client: You think it would? The urge, I mean?

Therapist: I don't know. There's a way to find out. It would mean you and I contacting one of those people and seeing if they would be willing to help. Making them part of a plan to keep you safe.

Client: My brother would do it.

Therapist: So if you were up for calling him, we could see if he'd get on board, and if he would, then we'd include that as the first step of a safety plan.

Client: And the other steps?

Therapist: Well, those will depend on what your brother says, but if we can get ahold of him, explain what's going on, and he would be willing to come here, then we could work some of those other steps out while we wait for him to show up.

Even when we're sure about the necessity of a plan, we tentatively introduce it as a possibility, never as a forthright request or encouragement. A safety plan can't be safe if the client feels herded or coaxed into working on it.

You won't always create a safety plan when conducting an RSA. In cases where immediate hospitalization is obviously necessary, attempting to develop a plan could waste valuable time or exacerbate the client's distress. Alternatively, if you have a client who you believe would benefit from constructing a plan with you but who dismisses the idea as pointless or trivial, then you wouldn't be able to pursue it very far without undermining your working relationship.

Carlos was struggling intermittently with repetitive, intrusive suicidal thoughts, and he often daydreamed about methods for taking his life. His therapist, a clinician in our Student Counseling Center, inquired on a few different occasions about the possibility of his collaborating with her on a plan for what to do if the thoughts became more insistent or he felt closer to putting the images into action. But Carlos consistently refused. He said that if he were to get to where he was going to kill himself, he absolutely wouldn't reach out for help. He wouldn't call us, wouldn't call his family, wouldn't call a hotline or 9-1-1, wouldn't consider getting to someplace safe—he'd just go ahead and act. Any talk of a safety plan, he said, would therefore be a waste of the therapist's valuable time. Such stipulations complicated the assessment process, but it didn't prevent the therapist from deciding that Carlos didn't, at least for the time being, need to be in the hospital.

WHEN A SAFETY PLAN IS NOT ENOUGH

Sometimes you will know early on in the assessment that a safety plan won't be enough to keep your client from making an attempt, and so you won't even broach the possibility of creating one—for example, if the client is having command hallucinations to commit self-harm, believes you're part of a conspiracy and thus doesn't trust you, or has just made a serious attempt and is disappointed to still be alive. But at other times, you won't know that a plan isn't enough until you get some way through developing one and realize that it will end up being impossible to implement, perhaps because it is too much for the client to handle, or perhaps because it places too many demands on his or her personal or professional significant others. The plan can't require the client to attend follow-up appointments that are too frequent or expensive or far away from home, and it can't make demands on family members or professionals to sustain a frequency of contact or level of responsibility that's beyond their capacity to provide.

Sometimes a safety plan will work well for a period of time but then, at some point, for any number of reasons, becomes inadequate. Perhaps during a follow-up visit you'll recognize that the person's ability to cope has decreased as his or her desperation has increased. If the client has stopped following the plan, if critically important significant others aren't participating as originally agreed, or if the parameters of the plan have otherwise become inadequate, you may look at modifying it in some way, but you will more likely conclude that it is no longer sufficient for keeping the person alive.

When you decide that a safety plan is not enough to effectively reduce the risk of the client's making an attempt, you arrive, by default, at the conclusion that hospitalization is necessary. No one considers the hospital a long-term solution for suicidality, but that doesn't undermine its importance as an effective short-term method for preventing attempts.

It isn't unusual for clients to emerge from a stay in the hospital believing it to have been an alienating, depressing, disruptive waste of time and money.

But at least, except in rare incidents, they emerge *alive*. Given the variable nature of suicidality, the hospital can serve, if nothing else, as a safe haven, a place where an intense desire to die can be safely experienced. At best, a hospital operates as a vestibule, a transitional space to initiate a shift from a commitment to dying to a commitment to living.

When telling our clients about our having decided that hospitalization is, for the time being, necessary, we always start with an assertion of our concern for their well-being and our willingness to do whatever is necessary to keep them alive. Below is a smattering of ways you can communicate the decision so as to improve the chances of preserving your relationship with the client. The first example, like others that follow, begins with an empathic statement, demonstrating to the client that you grasp something of his or her experience. It asserts a commitment to safety and connects safety to the hospital.

- "You crave relief, and it seems like you've come to believe that suicide is your only way of getting it. I too want you to get relief, but without your having to go to the trouble of dying, first. The best, the *safest*, way for that to happen is going to be for you to spend a little while in the hospital."

We prefer to give clients the rationale for our decision, and we often introduce the idea of the hospital as a place to safely begin or regulate medications. Our office then becomes a place to which clients can subsequently return:

- "You're in an impossible situation, and you're feeling so desperate— unable to sleep, crying so much, looking for ways to take your life. You've let some of your medications slide and have been doubling up, or more, on some others. We need to be sure that you're safe while your medications get reevaluated and adjusted, so I'm going to arrange for this to get started in the hospital. Once you're feeling a little better, we'll see you back here and continue our work together."

By making reference to what you and other professionals know about suicidality, you can normalize the client's danger and hopelessness, and invite expectancy for how the hospital can serve as a means for providing safe passage to a better time:

- "We know that when people feel the way you're feeling now, they sometimes do, in fact, make an attempt to end their lives. But we also know that if we can get you through this very difficult time, there will be opportunities for turning things around, opportunities that you can't see, believe, or even imagine at this point. The tragedy would be if we didn't make it possible for you to get to where you could grab hold of those opportunities. To get you there, we have to make sure you stay alive, and at this point, that means spending some time in the hospital."

Sometimes a dramatic, simple statement can galvanize clients to think about their plight and their options in a different way:

- "I want to see you next week in my office, not in a casket at your funeral."

Suicidal clients often feel abandoned by, or a burden to, significant others. You can't simply convince them otherwise, but you *can* make clear that your decision is based on their mattering to *you*:

- "I know you feel like you want to die and that nobody cares about you, but *I* don't want you to die, so we're going to work very hard to keep you alive and help you get through this. And if it takes your going to the hospital right now to do that, then that's what we'll do. Later you won't need to be in a hospital, but right now you do."

When a client responds well to such statements, agreeing that going to the hospital is the best option, you may be able, in some circumstances, to arrange for voluntary hospitalization. If we could, we would always choose voluntary over involuntary hospitalization: It maintains the client's autonomy and legal rights of self-determination; it is consistent with our ethical commitment to always choose the least restrictive environment for keeping the client safe; it fits with our resource-based approach; it avoids our taking on a social-control function; and it better preserves our relationship with the client. However, it is only safe to offer voluntary hospitalization as a possibility if the client and a reliable significant other have the necessary resources to ensure admission.

When a client can muster only reluctant agreement that going into the hospital is a good idea, we are much less likely to seriously consider voluntary admission a viable option. Given the determination and patience it can take to get admitted, we aren't willing to risk subjecting tentative clients to the gauntlet they may need to endure. We once collaboratively decided with a client that she needed to be in the hospital, and we agreed that she had the necessary resources to go voluntarily. She was committed to using her stay there to get some much needed sleep and to make it through the anniversary of a tragic past event, the anticipation of which had filled her with an overwhelming desire to die. However, her resolve to be protected in the hospital steadily diminished—and her anger swelled—as she sat for the next 6 or 7 hours in the waiting room of the admitting department, largely ignored by the clinical staff, despite her making several trips to the reception desk. Unwilling to tolerate such treatment any longer, she took it upon herself to leave.

When you are considering voluntary hospitalization, think through how your client will fare when he or she runs into barriers that need to be overcome or is detoured by a change of heart. Our client's response to the situation made perfect sense—*and* her choice wasn't safe.

If the client's resolve wavers after leaving your office, an assertive significant other who endorses the necessity of hospitalization can be the deciding factor in ensuring that the original plan is carried out. Although we have each in the past supported voluntary hospital admissions for clients who, at the time, had no significant others available to help out, we've come to the conclusion that the journey from office to hospital is too rife with danger to negotiate alone.

To better ensure that the client arrives safely at the hospital, we prefer that he or she head there directly from our office, rather than first going home, getting something to eat, or rendezvousing somewhere with a significant other. We thus ask his or her significant other to come in and meet with us and the client before embarking. This gives us a chance to check out the means of transport—Will they be going by car? Does the vehicle have sufficient gas and reliability to make the trip? If not, do they have cab fare?—and to strategize responses to some worst-case scenarios: What if the client develops second thoughts about going? What if there is an inordinate wait? What if the client's anxiety escalates?

The process may be further streamlined, and thus less traumatic for the client, if you have already established a good working relationship with the hospital. That way, when you call and alert them that the client is on the way, they take you seriously. Better yet is to know a colleague who has admitting privileges. Usually the intake worker won't turn the person away if he or she either has insurance or the ability to self-pay, and if a doctor has agreed to oversee his or her stay. Voluntary hospitalization of indigent patients is significantly more difficult.

Be sure that the case note you write details the reasons you thought it necessary for the client to be in the hospital, why you ruled out involuntary hospitalization, the steps you took to facilitate a safe admission, and what you discussed with the client regarding postdischarge follow-up.

Voluntary hospitalization isn't always possible or even advisable, and when it isn't, we are willing to facilitate involuntary hospitalization as a way of keeping our client alive. As we said in Chapter 1, if we need to restrict our client's ability to choose in the present so he or she is still alive to exercise that choice in the future, then we feel ethically bound to do so. However, we should clarify that the term *involuntary hospitalization* is something of a misnomer. Licensed clinicians have the ability to arrange for a client to be involuntarily transported to a receiving facility for evaluation, but the person doing the assessment there at the hospital may end up not admitting the client. It would thus be more appropriate to refer to the process as *involuntary evaluation.*

We initiate involuntary evaluation when, based on our thorough assessment, we consider the client to be in imminent danger of making an attempt, unable to be safely treated as an outpatient, and unwilling or unable to agree to voluntary hospitalization. When Len worked at a community mental health clinic, he provided medication management for a man with bipolar disorder. Sven, a strong, 6-foot 4-inch, 240-pound man, enjoyed the physicality of his job as a manual laborer. Friendly and cooperative when his mood was stable, he could become agitated and irritable when in the throes of a manic episode. For periods of time he would regularly attend scheduled appointments, but then he might miss a session and not return for several months.

During one such return, Sven reported feeling like he was going crazy. He hadn't been taking his medication and had been drinking heavily for the better part of a week in an unsuccessful attempt to get some sleep. He did his best to answer Len's questions, but he was having trouble holding his thoughts together, and he couldn't sit down. Pacing back and forth in the small office, he spoke rapidly and loudly, expressing his anger, describing his loneliness, and proclaiming his certainty that his plight would never improve. He hadn't formulated a plan to take his life, but he had been thinking a lot about the benefits of being dead.

Given that Sven appeared to be experiencing a mixed manic–depressive episode (a particularly high-risk state for suicide), Len introduced the subject of hospitalization into the discussion. Sven immediately embraced the idea, acknowledging that he desperately needed to rest. They discussed advantages in addition to the opportunity for sleep: Sven would have no access to alcohol, so he could get a start on his goal of staying sober; he'd be in a safe environment where he couldn't harm himself; and the doctor there could get him back on his mood-stabilizing medications. Somewhat relieved but still agitated and pacing, Sven despaired at the logistics of getting to the hospital. Having walked several miles to his appointment at the clinic, he would rather not have to hoof it all the way there, he said, but he wasn't sure whether any of his family members were home and available to drive him.

Len was concerned about Sven's ability to arrive safely at the hospital.

Walking was out of the question, but even if it turned out that a family member was available and could offer to take him, no one would be a match for his size, strength, and resolve should he change his mind on the way there. And then there were the legalities of the situation. Given Sven's current state, he wasn't legally capable of giving his informed consent for voluntary admission. Len thus initiated involuntary hospitalization, making a call to the police for them to transport him.

When told of this decision, Sven loudly endorsed it, and when the police arrived, he treated them respectfully, standing at attention in the manner of a soldier following orders from his commanding officer. Restless as he was, he couldn't remain in this position for long, but he cooperated fully as the police escorted him to their car.

Upon release, Sven returned for a follow-up appointment, feeling rested and with his mood stabilized. He said he found his hospital stay helpful. He'd gotten several nights of good sleep, had enjoyed the food(!), and had taken advantage of the time there to do some thinking. He was relieved to be back on his medication, he said, and wasn't sure why, some months back, he'd stopped taking it.

Sven's full cooperation with the process of involuntary evaluation was unique, an exception. More commonly, clients will accept your decision only grudgingly, if at all. Many become anxious; some, angry or confrontational. Such responses can be ameliorated by your underscoring your commitment to their safety and continued existence, but clients will still often consider your decision to be unnecessary or even a betrayal.

Elisa, a woman in her early 20s, arrived one day at our Student Counseling Center for a follow-up appointment. She had been coming to the center for a few months, addressing concerns that she was overweight and unattractive (a judgment her therapist disagreed with), that her friends were shunning her, and that she couldn't keep up with her professors' unreasonable demands. Prescribed an antidepressant a month earlier, she had been taking it faithfully, she said, but she hadn't noticed any improvement in her mood, and now she was experiencing great trouble falling and staying asleep.

During the session, Elisa revealed that she'd been having relentless suicidal thoughts for over a week. On her way to see us, she'd been gripped by the idea of driving her car into oncoming traffic, and she speculated that she might actually do it on her way home, as she was still in thrall to the thought. She was vague and ambivalent in response to questions about her wish to die, but also to questions that attempted to establish resources. Withdrawn from friends, unwilling to let her parents know what was going on, and convinced that no one could help her, she felt hopeless, with little reason to live. We broached the possibility of her going to the hospital for a short stay as a means of getting some much needed rest and to ensure that her thoughts didn't put her in harm's way. She scoffed. She'd rather be dead, she said.

Taking everything into account, we decided that involuntary evaluation at the hospital was necessary to prevent the too-high possibility of an intentional car accident. When we informed Elisa of this, she strongly disagreed with us, telling us that we were mistaken and criticizing us for being more concerned about our liability than her well-being. We reiterated our deep concern for her life and, despite her protests, arranged for her to be transported to the hospital. Once there, she was admitted and stayed a little over a week, during which time she slept, participated in psychotherapy, and had her medication adjusted. Upon her return for a follow-up appointment, she said the hospital had not been helpful; however, she acknowledged a slight improvement in her mood, and she was no longer having suicidal thoughts. Still angry at the safety decision we'd made, she told us she wouldn't be coming back for subsequent appointments. We made recommendations for other providers in the community, which she accepted.

When committing someone to an involuntary evaluation, you always risk losing him or her as a client; however, we must say that we've been heartened many times by clients who return from their stay in the hospital and thank us for following through with the safety decision we had made in the face of their strong objections. We've come to believe that at least in a few cases, our clients' angry disputations and accusations are a form of face-saving, allowing them to benefit from the protection the hospital provides while vigorously asserting that they aren't in need of it. In contrast to a *death-by-cop* scenario, where a desperate individual tempts fate by provoking police to open fire, we think of what sometimes happens in our offices as a *life-by-shrink* scenario, where a desperate individual tempts fate by trying to convince a clinician not to hospitalize him or her.

Esme, a nursing student, had just found out that she was once again pregnant a week after she'd discovered that her long-time boyfriend, whom she disparagingly referred to as "the sperm donor," had been cheating on her for the better part of a year. He had paid for two previous abortions, but now she'd kicked him out and had vowed never to talk to him again, so she didn't know how she could afford another procedure without help from her disapproving parents. In the past few days, dwelling on the idea of terminating the pregnancy by ending her life and finding it almost impossible to concentrate on studying for her first-year finals, she had procured a sizable number of over-the-counter sleeping pills. And then, that morning, she had walked into our center, brought by her concerned roommate. The office manager facilitated an immediate appointment, and the assigned therapist conducted a suicide assessment.

At some point during the conversation, the therapist broached the possibility of Esme's taking a leave of absence from school and spending some time in the hospital. Esme dismissed both ideas outright. She didn't want to reveal to her program administrators that she was struggling—What if they stopped her from graduating?—and she couldn't imagine going as a psych patient to a hospital where she might later have to do a clinical rotation. At this point, the therapist got Douglas involved, who quickly came to the conclusion that, Esme's potential professional humiliation notwithstanding, involuntary evaluation at the hospital was the only safe alternative.

Esme told him that he was making a ridiculous mistake, a mistake that would make her life immeasurably worse. If he would only reconsider, she said, she promised to flush the pills and redouble her efforts to study. She'd figure out what to do about the fetus after finals were over. But if he followed through with his threat to ruin her professionally, Esme said, she would simply kill herself when she was released from the hospital. Expressing concern for her safety and empathizing with the impossibility of her situation, Douglas proceeded with having her involuntarily transported to the hospital.

Esme returned to our center several weeks later and met with Len for medication management, as well as with the therapist who'd seen her for the emergency appointment. She'd been granted a semester's medical leave of absence from the nursing school, had terminated her pregnancy (with money from her ex), and had started taking an antidepressant. She spoke about how hopeless, mortified, and angry she had felt when Douglas sent her to the hospital, but she also said that if her roommate hadn't brought her to see us or if she'd been given the chance to go home, she would have downed the pills with a bottle of vodka she had purchased for the purpose.

When you come to the decision to have a client involuntarily evaluated at a hospital, you'll want to be sure in your case note to explicate the reasons for choosing that course. Once the client has left our office, we call the receiving facility and ask to speak to the charge nurse, letting him or her know that we have sent a client for evaluation and providing, in more detail than the paperwork accompanying the client allows, our impressions and concerns.

Let's return now to the second of the three possible decisions you can arrive at when conducting a suicide assessment: constructing a safety plan. After introducing you to the process, we'll walk you, step by step, through a guide we've developed for developing such a plan with your clients.

CONSTRUCTING A SAFETY PLAN

You begin constructing a safety plan when you're concerned about the client's risk of making an attempt and you have the sense that, if necessary resources could be accessed and sufficient measures taken, the client could safely negotiate the dangers of the coming days and weeks. In this sense, the development of a plan is something of an ongoing experiment, part virtual and part real world. But we're getting ahead of ourselves. Before saying more about what a safety plan is and how to construct and make use of it, we need to clarify what it is *not*.

From the mid 1970s until recently, clinicians concerned about the suicidality of a client would commonly, as a matter of course, have him or her sign a no-harm or no-suicide contract (Lewis, 2007; Rudd, Mandrusiak, & Joiner, 2006). Therapists generally assumed that the use of such contracts would help reduce their clients' risk of making an attempt and their own risk of malpractice lawsuits; however, research to date has failed to support either assumption (Garvey, Penn, Campbell, Esposito-Smythers, & Spirito, 2009; Lewis; Rudd et al.; Simon, 2007). Indeed, if a no-harm or no-suicide contract were used in the absence of, or as a replacement for, a comprehensive assessment, it could actually prove harmful (Garvey et al.; Kelly & Knudson, 2000), as it would offer a false sense of security.

Even if you were to conduct a thorough assessment first and only then introduce a contract for the client to sign, we would still be concerned about possible detrimental effects. As you know from Chapter 3, suicidal individuals are typically overwhelmed by multiple and often conflicting demands. Once you fully grasp the complexity and impossibility of these personal and contextual obligations, you will avoid imposing yet another obligation—a requirement to sign a pledge not to act on suicidal thoughts—in an attempt to secure safety.

In contrast to a no-harm or no-suicide contract, a safety plan, as we define and use it, delineates explicit steps the client helps invent and agrees to undertake so as to heighten protection and prevent an attempt. The client's engagement in this process of ensuring safety is not demonstrated by way of his or her signature at the end of a quasi-legal form but, rather, is given expression throughout the collaborative creation of a personally meaningful plan of action. Our approach to the development of a safety plan bears some similarity to Rudd, Mandrusiak, et al.'s (2006) use of what they call a *crisis response plan* (CRP), which provides specific instructions for the patient on what to do during periods of crisis (p. 248). Both types of plan focus on action-oriented steps; however, Rudd and his colleagues use their CRP in conjunction with having the client sign a handwritten and individualized commit-ment-to-treatment statement, which we, for the reasons articulated above, do not. Whenever we can, in keeping with Huey et al.'s (2004) multi-systemic family therapy approach, we involve the family (and, in our case, additional significant others) in helping to carry out certain elements of the safety plan, and as with Henriques et al. (2003), we include in the safety plan a "written list of coping strategies, developed collaboratively, . . . which the patient can do if a crisis situation arises" (p. 1261).

In Chapter 3 we offered the semistructured Risk and Resource Interview Guide (RRIG) to assist in the organization of the assessment process; in this chapter, we lay out the format for its companion—the Safety Plan Construc-tion Guide (SPCG). The SPCG lists eight action steps designed to assist you in developing, when clinically appropriate, a comprehensive means of keep-ing the client out of the hospital and out of harm's way. We recommend that you consult the SPCG portion of the Backpocket RSA (see Appendix) as you and the client begin figuring out a plan; this will help ensure that what you create is as encompassing and detail-oriented as is necessary and possible. The goal is to create a clearly delineated, uniquely relevant to-do list for the client, one that he or she can access and refer to during difficult times in the coming days and weeks. Although the plan is co-created with the client, we ourselves, drawing on the SPCG, take responsibility for what needs to be in-cluded, and we also do the actual writing down of the steps. If you have easy access to a laptop or tablet, you might type out and print what you and the client come up with; if not, then you'll want to write clearly enough for the client to be able to read your handwriting.

We mentioned earlier that the construction of a safety plan is itself an op-portunity for further assessment, as it allows you to get a sense of the client's willingness and ability to find and implement meaningful safeguards. Some-times the safety decision you make will hinge on whether you're able to co-create a safety plan with your client that lives up to its name—that actually feels safe. Can everyone involved implement the steps you're developing to-gether? Can you and the client count on designated significant others to come through? You don't want to create a plan that looks good on paper but fails to hold up when put to the test. One way to get a sense of the plan's vi-ability is to exercise your empathic imagination and engage in a virtual ex-periment. If you were the client, and you were—tonight, say—to find yourself facing and experiencing the sorts of challenges that have proven to be so overwhelming to him or her, would you be able to draw on the plan and do something different?

You can keep this virtual experiment running in the back of your mind as you make note of how the client is responding to what the two of you are developing together. Is he or she calming down—or becoming more distracted, agitated, or frightened? Showing enough resolve to put the plan into action—or not really motivated or interested? By asking yourself such questions (and listening to the answers you arrive at), that is, by taking a second look at the developing safety plan and the client's response to it, you provide yourself with the means of assessing the viability of the plan and the reliability of your safety decision.

If you decide it is safe enough to proceed, then before ending the assessment, make some copies of the plan. Put one in the client's file and give the others, along with the original, to the client. One or more significant others may need a copy, and the client may benefit from having at least one backup copy in case the original gets misplaced. Make reference to the plan in your case note for the session; its presence in the file helps to establish that you've taken seriously the client's suicidality and are taking demonstrable steps to address it.

The real-world testing of the safety plan comes into play when the client takes it home and puts it into action. At the next appointment (or sooner, if you maintain between-session telephone contact with the person), get follow-up information. Did the client carry out the actions described in the plan? Did they help? How? Was there anything that didn't help? Why? Were the client's significant others as available and involved as they said they would and could be? Based on what you learn, assess whether the client is able to safely continue managing his or her suicidality without hospitalization. If so, update and adapt the plan as necessary and schedule the next appointment. Treat the plan as a living document—one that you will continue modifying as needed. If the plan is not enough at the moment for the client to safely manage his or her suicidality, then a modified version may prove helpful later, after the client is released from the hospital.

SAFETY PLAN CONSTRUCTION GUIDE

The following eight guidelines offer a structure for brainstorming and co-constructing safety plans with your clients. Detailing issues to address and how to address them, the guidelines range from the general to the specific, covering critical dangers to consider; personal, interpersonal, and professional resources to access; stress-reducing options to explore; and emergency contact information to include. As with the RRIG, we encourage you to exercise flexibility as you develop safety plans with your clients. You must be sure to address all relevant safety issues, but you needn't address them in the order they appear below. Attending to the flow of the unfolding conversation, bring to the foreground next whatever issue can be dealt with most expediently and meaningfully.[1]

> **Guideline I.** *Identify resourceful significant others who could assist in implementing relevant details of the safety plan. If they are in the waiting room, bring them into the session. If not, phone them. Determine their willingness and ability to help, and engage them accordingly.*

Given that suicidality is often occasioned by a sense of alienation, it isn't surprising that some clients won't be able to identify any significant others who could or would be helpful in protecting their safety. However, we always ask whom they might contact, as there may be someone who hasn't been mentioned earlier in the interview who nevertheless could be a resource if called upon to contribute. If it is reasonable and possible to speak directly to resourceful significant others, we do so. A life is at stake, so as much as possible, we want direct confirmation of availability and commitment. And if we can be in conversation with them, we can get a sense of whether they have the wherewithal to participate in a critically important way.

In the last chapter we mentioned several cases where significant others were contributing to the client's risk, rather than serving as resources. Keep this disconcerting possibility in mind; you want to be confident that the person(s) suggested by the client can actually be relied upon. We have made a point of *not* contacting a significant other whom we believed would possibly complicate or compromise the client's safety.

When significant others *can* be relied upon to function as an important part of the safety plan, they may be the deciding factor in keeping the client out of the hospital. However, take care not to burden them with more responsibility than they can realistically be expected to manage. Simon (2007) makes the point well: "The patient's family or partner should not be burdened with the impossible task of providing constant one-to-one supervision of the patient. Exceptions to constant supervision are invariably made by family members" (p. 525).

> **Guideline II.** *Work out how the client and resourceful significant others can prevent and/or restrict access to means for making a suicide attempt. Put measures in place to safeguard against any method the client has been considering (e.g., shooting, hanging, jumping, overdosing, suffocation, carbon monoxide or pesticide poisoning, cutting, drowning, crashing a car or stepping in front of a vehicle, electrocution).*

The last barrier to suicide is the most critical to maintain. Even if a client's commitment to living is still tenuous, even if suicidal thoughts are still pronounced, and even if an impulsive urge to make an attempt rises up, safety is still possible, as long as the person doesn't have access to a means of taking his or her life. If you are working on a safety plan, rather than choosing hospitalization, then you've decided that it is logistically possible to collaborate with the client and resourceful significant others on their taking proactive steps to create a protective barrier between the client and whatever method(s) of suicide he or she has been considering.

Be thorough in your planning. If you arrange with significant others to secure a weapon, for example, make sure that they call to confirm that the task has been successfully completed. As Simon (2007) puts it, "the essence of gun safety management is verification" (p. 525). More broadly, the essence of restricting or preventing access to means is collaborative anticipation and planning, consistent follow-through, and verification. With our clients' endorsement, we've worked with significant others, for example, to take responsibility for holding and issuing scheduled medications, thereby limiting access to dangerous quantities of pills; to remove guns and other weapons from a client's home (see Chapter 5 for an example); to take over driving responsibilities and lock up car keys; and to provide ground-floor accommodation for a client with an urge to jump (see Guideline 4, below).

> **Guideline III.** *Identify troubling behaviors the client has been using to cope with distress (e.g., withdrawing from activities/relationships, substance abuse, disordered eating, impulsive/compulsive actions, harming self/others), and, if appropriate, explore temporary alternatives (e.g., walking, exercise, music, meditation, prayer, reading, writing, reaching out).*

As therapists, we are loath to dole out the kind of good advice that family members or friends might be expected to offer someone who is depressed and lonely:

- X "How about instead of drinking tonight, you watch something funny on TV and then make an early night of it? You'll sleep better, anyway."
- X "Exercise is one of the best things you can do for depression—why don't you go for a nice long walk and clear your head a little?"
- X "You've been so isolated lately—you should call one of your friends and get out of your apartment for a change."
- X "When was the last time you picked up your guitar? Playing a few

tunes would do you a world of good—it'll get your mind off your trou-
bles."

X "I don't remember the last time you meditated. You know you feel better when you do that regularly. Why don't you try sitting on your
meditation cushion instead of lighting up a joint?"

We recognize that although suggestions such as these seem like sage advice to the significant others proffering them, the recipients of such well-
intended efforts to help typically end up feeling misunderstood and even
more alienated. If it were that simple for them to institute a change, they
would have taken these sorts of actions long ago.

So why, then, are we suggesting that you explore with the client the possibility of engaging in safer alternatives to troubling behaviors? Will these
explorations not also fail to help and, in the process, leave the person more at
risk? Possibly, particularly if the client feels imposed upon and hemmed in.
But effective safety plan development is built on a foundation of collaboration, and the alternatives you come up with together will be more acceptable
and viable if they are understood as temporary experiments, rather than permanent commitments. Frame clients' troubling behaviors as well-intended efforts to cope with impossible circumstances and suffering, and invite their
involvement in figuring out safer alternatives. Here's an example:

Therapist: If you drink enough, it blocks out the thoughts enough for you to
fall asleep.

Client: Yes.

Therapist: But then the alcohol messes with the quality of your sleep, so you
wake up feeling hung over and strung out.

Client: I don't sleep much, anyway.

Therapist: The alcohol helps you de-stress.

Client: Yeah.

Therapist: But it is also problematic in another way. People who have been
drinking are more likely to act impulsively. So if your thoughts about taking
your life hit you hard when you've had a few beers too many, you could make
a choice that you wouldn't make if you were sober.

Client: I've done some pretty stupid shit when I'm drunk.

Therapist: Who hasn't? So what ideas do you have for what you could do—
for now, while you're having these thoughts—when you're stressed out? Do
you always reach for a drink?

Client: Most of the time.

Therapist: Not always?

Client: Probably not.

Therapist: When you don't, what do you do, instead?

If the client isn't coming up with many ideas, you may need to introduce some, but we suggest that you offer them tentatively, getting the client's endorsement before including them as part of the safety plan.

Client: I don't know. I just don't.

Therapist: If you don't drink, the thoughts get you feeling pretty agitated.

Client: Prickly, yeah.

Therapist: Can't sit still?

Client: I gotta move. It's like I'm coming out of my skin.

Therapist: Pacing around?

Client: Oh, yeah.

Therapist: In your room, or what?

Client: Yeah, mostly, I guess.

Therapist: Do you ever walk?

Client: Of course. I don't have a car. I walk to the bus.

Therapist: I mean, do you ever walk just to walk?

Client: I have, I guess.

Therapist: Sort of like pacing, but you don't have to change directions so often.

Client: *(laughs)* Pacing, but in a straight line.

Therapist: Exactly.

If you were to have a conversation such as this, you'd need to make sure that if the client were to do some walking, it wouldn't introduce new dangers. Is the neighborhood safe? Would walking put him or her at increased risk of stepping in front of a vehicle or jumping from a bridge?

Client: No way I'm walking at midnight.

Therapist: Of course not, no. I'm wondering whether you might find it a bit easier to sleep at night, without needing so much alcohol, if you walked some of that agitation out of you earlier in the day.

Client: Maybe.

Therapist: Is that something you'd be interested in putting on the safety plan? Maybe engaging in some straight-line pacing during the day?

Client: Yeah, sure. Maybe.

Therapist: If you were having thoughts about wanting to die and you were out walking, how safe would you be?

Client: What?

Therapist: You told me that the image that plagues you is of you hanging yourself.

Client: Yeah.

Therapist: So if you were out walking . . .

Client: . . . would I go looking for a rope? Nah, I don't think so.

Therapist: Okay, but would other methods loom up?

Client: What, get myself run over? No way. No way.

Therapist: Or finding a bridge?

Client: Are you kidding me? I'm terrified of heights (*laughs*)—no way!

Therapist: Okay. So I'll write it down. "Walking during the day." That's something you could experiment with doing, for now?

Client: Put "straight-line pacing." I like that.

Therapist: But then we need to come up with some ideas for what to do at midnight if the walking you did earlier in the day isn't enough.

Client: It won't be enough.

Therapist: So what might help then? Got any friends who would still be awake?

> **Guideline IV.** *Identify safe havens the client could, if necessary, access for a limited time (include contact information, if relevant):*
> * *In the client's, a family member's, or a friend's home*
> * *In the hospital*

In Chapter 3 we briefly described developing a safety plan with one of our clients, Michelle, who needed a safe place to go when tormented by thoughts of jumping off her 11th-floor balcony. With her permission, we contacted her close friend Vanessa and asked her to join us in the session. Vanessa, who lived on the ground floor of Michelle's building, readily agreed. When she arrived, we explained the situation and explored the possibility of Michelle's going to her apartment if the thoughts became too intense. Vanessa was completely fine with the idea, so we wrote her and her apartment into Michelle's safety plan, but not before Douglas made sure that Michelle would take advantage of the availability of the safe haven:

Douglas: (*to Vanessa*) So, according to Michelle, these thoughts could happen pretty much any time—in the middle of the afternoon or the middle of the night. How comfortable would you be with her showing up, unannounced?

Vanessa: Completely. It wouldn't be a problem.

Douglas: If it were during the day, you might not be there, so you'd be fine with Michelle having a key?

Vanessa: Of course.

Douglas: And if it were the middle of the night, you wouldn't get scared if you heard the door being unlocked and someone coming in?

Vanessa: I'm a deep sleeper, so *(to Michelle)* you could come in and I probably wouldn't even hear you. And if I did, I would know it was you.

Douglas: *(to Vanessa)* Do you already have a spare key, or will you need to get one made?

Vanessa: I have one in the apartment. *(to Michelle)* I'll give it to you as soon as we get home.

Michelle: I can put it on my key ring.

Douglas: Okay, that's great. Now, let's talk about one more thing to make sure this is going to work. *(to Vanessa)* Michelle tells me you have a boy-friend.

Vanessa: Yeah, Tyler—but she knows him well.

Douglas: *(to Michelle)* That probably helps.

Michelle: *(nods)*

Douglas: *(to Vanessa)* And does Tyler sometimes sleep over?

Vanessa: Sometimes. Not often.

Douglas: *(to Michelle)* Okay, well, so how comfortable would you be with Tyler knowing what's going on? Because I'm thinking that if you're feeling the need to take the elevator down to Vanessa's at 11:00 at night but you think Tyler might be there, and you think he'll think it's weird if you were to just show up unannounced, then, I don't know, you might be reluctant to go.

Michelle: I'm okay with him knowing.

Douglas: *(to Vanessa)* Are you?

Vanessa: Sure. He'll be totally fine with it.

Douglas: *(to Vanessa)* Excellent. So can you tell him today? *(to Michelle)* Or would you rather be the one to tell him?

Michelle: No, I don't care. I don't ever just call him. I don't want to be the one to explain it.

Vanessa: I'll do it. It's fine.

Douglas: Great. And maybe you can let Michelle know once you've talked to him so she isn't wondering.

Vanessa: Of course.

Douglas: Great, so one last thought I have, one more thing I want to check out. (*to Vanessa*) Michelle is a sensitive person.

Vanessa: Yes, very. Too much, maybe.

Douglas: Very sensitive. Yes. So I'm thinking, if I'm Michelle, and I'm feeling the need for some first-floor safety, so I'm heading to the elevator, but I'm worried that if I just arrive unannounced, I might barge in on you and Tyler making out on the living room couch or something, and if I'm worried about that, I just might not push that first-floor button in the elevator.

Vanessa: That won't be a problem. I promise you.

Douglas: (*to Vanessa*) Great. So you can talk to Tyler and say, "For the time being, sex happens in the bedroom with the door closed," and he'll be cool with that?

Vanessa: Absolutely.

Douglas: (*to Michelle*) So if Tyler knows that for a while Vanessa's place is your place whenever you need it, and if you know that you don't have to worry about interrupting a romantic interlude by heading down the elevator and turning the key, does it feel safe to you to set up Vanessa's place as a safe haven, a place you can go to whenever you feel the need, no second thoughts necessary?

Michelle: Yes. I would go down there, for sure. I *will* go down if I need to.

Douglas: And it would be nice to know that you didn't have to wait until the thoughts were really intense before you made the trip to the elevator. That you could feel comfortable heading down if the thoughts were just annoy-ing—before they started really scaring you.

Michelle: I might spend the night down there sometimes.

Douglas: Right, good point, so (*to Vanessa*), would it be possible to put a sheet and a blanket and a pillow on the couch, so if Michelle felt moved to come down and stay the night, that she wouldn't have to mess with getting settled, that everything would be right there?

Vanessa: Sure, of course. I'll just leave them at the end of the couch.

Douglas: (*to Michelle*) Sound good to you?

Michelle: (*looking relieved*) Yes. Very good.

As we continued to work out details, Michelle ended up deciding to desig-nate Vanessa's apartment as her "second-choice safe haven," the place to go when her first choice, what she described as her "first line of defense," wasn't working "to keep the thoughts at bay." Her first choice was her walk-in closet—the place to which she'd long retreated to meditate and "chill out" when life felt like it was just too much to deal with. With those two havens established, we then designated a third—a hospital not too far from her apartment. We always include at least one hospital on our safety plans, noting down the phone number and address so that the person can go there for a voluntary admission if necessary. Here's how this part of Michelle's safety plan read:

Safe Havens

1. If thoughts too much: walk-in closet and meditate.

2. If need more safety: elevator to Vanessa's. No need to call—key in purse.

3. If need more safety: Memorial Hospital: 350 Smith Street: 222-333-2000

When Michelle returned for a follow-up appointment a few days later, she told her therapist that she had taped her safety plan to the wall in her walk-in closet. She said that having it there and reading through it, knowing she had options, was itself effective in helping her feel safer.

> **Guideline V.** *Consider enlisting the client's work supervisors and/or school administrators to at least temporarily alter the client's schedule, reducing his or her workload, and/or granting a leave of absence.*

Many of the suicidal students we saw in our Student Counseling Center were in crisis, in part, because they were overwhelmed with the demands of their programs of study. And, over the years, we've also assessed suicidal clients who weren't in school but who felt pushed to the edge by their ridiculously stressful jobs. When we have broached the possibility to such clients that they alter their schedule in some way, perhaps cutting back on their course load, reducing their work hours, or taking a leave of absence from school and/or work, their initial reaction is invariably negative. Afraid of the consequences of being perceived as weak or flawed, unable to conceive of slowing down or, worse, delaying the pace of their involvement and progress, they assert that they have no choice but to continue on as they have been. But, of course, the conviction that there are no options for even slightly relieving the demands they face is precisely what contributes to their viewing suicide as "the only way out." We thus persist beyond the initial dismissal of our suggestion, and we offer that if the client were to give us a signed release, we would be quite prepared to make a phone call or write a letter, explaining to their program administrator and/or boss that a lighter schedule, a medical leave, or personal leave (depending on what the client is willing to consider and would be most comfortable with our saying) is, at the moment, essential.

When clients are willing to take us up on our offer, we take it as a good sign that they are recognizing that surviving their suicidality will take a significant shift in orientation.

> **Guideline VI.** *Determine, if warranted and appropriate, if the client would consider initiating, resuming, or continuing relevant treatment:*
> - *Therapy*
> - *Medication(s)*
> - *Detox/rehab*
> - *Inpatient or outpatient program(s)*

Many of the suicidal clients we see are avoiding, or at least delaying, getting help for mental health and/or substance abuse problems. In such cases, when appropriate, we propose including in the safety plan the possibility of checking out treatment options. Johanna was one such client in our Student Counseling Center. Following a painful, messy divorce a year earlier, she'd become chronically depressed, with recurrent suicidal ideation, and she'd started abusing opiates, supplied by one of South Florida's notorious pill mills. By the time she came to see us, her suicidality had intensified, she was taking up to six oxycodone pills a day, and she was drinking, in the evenings, at least a few times a week.

Len assessed for suicide and came to the decision that hospitalization wasn't immediately necessary, in part because she was open to seeing a therapist in our center for weekly sessions and to starting on an antidepressant. She wasn't, however, willing at the moment to consider detox and rehab, as she was in the last year of an intense program of study and thus couldn't afford the interruption it would mean to her schedule. She wouldn't be able to graduate on time, and her yearlong "dream internship," which was lined up and waiting for her, would slip through her grasp.

Len put the names and phone numbers of two different addiction treatment facilities on Johanna's safety plan so that she could call in the event of a change of heart, and over the coming weeks, he and Johanna's therapist kept close tabs on the effects of her substance abuse on her depression and desperation. As the end-of-year demands of school increased, so did Johanna's oxycodone use and, with it, her suicidality. Nevertheless, she continued to adamantly refuse inpatient treatment options for her addiction.

With Johanna's situation becoming more and more dangerous, Len consulted with an addictions specialist in the community, a psychiatrist who was the medical director of a rehab center. The psychiatrist and Johanna agreed to meet for a consultation, during which they decided that she would work with him as an outpatient to gradually reduce her dosage of the oxycodone, and they would keep an inpatient stay on the table as perhaps a necessary option. Committing to this arrangement had a beneficial effect on Johanna's suicidality, and she continued working with the specialist through and beyond graduation.

> **Guideline VII.** *Generate a list of personal resources the client could call if necessary (include contact information for each):*
> - *Family members and/or friends*
> - *Members of the client's religious or spiritual community*
> - *Peers and/or mentors*

When we're generating a list of personal resources with clients, we suggest that they brainstorm for trustworthy, reliable people even beyond their usual inner circle, and we obtain and write down the phone numbers for each contact, even when the clients already have them in their phone or address book. Anticipating that they might most need to reach out when they're feeling inordinately distraught or disorientingly inebriated, we want the list to be as many layers deep (i.e., including backup people, in case the first-choice resources aren't available) and as fail-proof as possible.

> **Guideline VIII.** *Identify emergency resources the client could access if necessary (include contact information for each):*
> - *Doctor(s)*
> - *Therapist(s)*
> - *Crisis line(s) and 9-1-1*
> - *Nearby emergency room and/or hospital*

When we had our Student Counseling Center, we offered the students a 24/7 crisis line, which gave them immediate access to the staff counselor who was on call for the week. That counselor, in turn, had access to both of us for backup consultation. We made up for the sleep we lost during and after emergency phone calls by sleeping easier over all, knowing that our suicidal clients had our crisis-line phone number on their safety plans and were willing to reach out when desperate. Not every clinician has this luxury, of course. However, 9-1-1 is always available, as is 1-800-SUICIDE (1-800-784-2433), the number for the National Suicide Prevention Lifeline and Veteran's Crisis Line. We continue to put both on all safety plans, and we include the names and daytime phone numbers of relevant professionals, along with the number and address of nearby emergency rooms and psychiatric receiving facilities, in case clients decide prior to their next appointment that they need to voluntarily hospitalize themselves.

Over the course of the chapter, we've raised issues and identified procedures to help you ensure your clients' safety. Now, before concluding, we'd like to briefly discuss how you can best ensure *your* safety if, despite your best efforts, a client with whom you've been working dies by suicide and the family takes legal action against the mental health clinicians involved in his or her case. Successfully defending your professional competence in court will depend, in large measure, on the degree to which you have thoroughly documented in your case note the details of your suicide assessment, including the steps you took to establish and bolster the client's safety. Depending on your profession and place of employment, the format and content requirements for this documentation will vary somewhat, but a case note describing a relational suicide assessment should minimally include the following:

- A detailed description of the client's intra- *and* interpersonal risks *and* resources.
- The safety decision you arrived at—whether 1) to hold off on developing a safety plan; 2) to involve the client in constructing and implementing a safety plan; or 3) to arrange for the client's immediate admission to a hospital.
- A rationale for your safety decision that makes clear how the information you gathered—regarding risks, resources, and safety—influenced the decision you made.
- The steps you took to implement the safety decision, such as contacting other clinicians and/or clinical facilities; scheduling dates for follow-up appointments; enlisting the help of significant others in implementing a safety plan; providing emergency contact numbers to the client; facilitating hospitalization; and so on.
- A copy of the safety plan (if you and the client constructed one).

In the next chapter we offer an annotated transcript of a suicide assessment that illustrates the process of delving into risks and resources, exploring possibilities for safety, and making a safety decision. Interspersed throughout is a commentary that describes what the therapist was thinking and doing as the conversation unfolded. At the end we provide a case note for the session, which includes a co-created safety plan.

NOTE

1 In the Foreword (pp. xi–xiii), Donald Meichenbaum offers a set of abbreviations as a mnemonic for keeping in mind the eight components of safety plan construction.

5

RSA IN ACTION

UP TO THIS point in the book, we've provided the foundational ideas and therapeutic principles informing our approach to suicide assessment (Chapters 1 and 2, respectively), as well as a structure for conducting interviews that attend to risks, resources, and possibilities for safety (Chapters 3 and 4). Now it's time to show you how an assessment is *done*—how it all plays out in action. Below you'll find an annotated transcript, based on an assessment we conducted in our Student Counseling Center, with a client we are calling "Steve."[1]

Our annotations are designed to help you connect the process of the conversation to the structure of the Risk and Resource Interview Guide (RRIG) and the guidelines of the Safety Plan Construction Guide (SPCG). To facilitate such connections, we've included both guides, first introduced in Chapters 3 and 4, respectively, prior the beginning of the transcript. You'll notice that each topic of inquiry under each of the four categories of suicidal experience in the RRIG (*Disruptions and Demands, Suffering, Troubling Behaviors*, and *Desperation*) has a unique identifier (e.g., 1.A; 2.3; 3.f; 4.vii), as does each of the numbered guidelines from the SPCG (e.g., SP.II; SP.VII). Throughout the transcript, we've placed these identifiers in square brackets in order to allow you, if you're interested, to track the topics being addressed over the course of the conversation.

Not every area of concern and topic of inquiry in the RRIG is covered in the transcript, because not all were relevant to the person we interviewed. However the transcript and commentary do show the therapeutic sensibility informing the overall approach; the interweaving of topics; the use of empathic statements; the techniques involved in broaching, delving into, and coming back to critical issues; the gradual emerging of a clinical decision; and the development of a safety plan.

RISK AND RESOURCE INTERVIEW GUIDE

1. DISRUPTIONS AND DEMANDS

		Client	Client's Significant Others
Risks	A) B) C) D) E)	Loss/Failure of relationship Overwhelming expecta- tions/obligations Loss of social position/fi- nancial status Legal/Disciplinary troubles Abuse/Bullying/Peril	a) Distressing expectations/demands of the client b) Abandoning the client c) Abuse/Bullying of the client
Resources	1) 2)	Effective problem solving Positive personal/spiritual connections	i) Reasonable expectations/encour- agement of the client ii) Helping the client meet obligations

2. SUFFERING

		Client	Client's Significant Others
Risks	F) G) H) I) J) K)	Depressed/Manic mood Anxiety/Anger/Obsessive thinking Conflicted identity/Shame/ Burdensomeness Hallucinations/Delusions Insomnia/Nightmares Pain/Illness/Injury	d) Viewing the client as flawed/a burden e) Limited awareness of/Unhelpful re- sponse to the client's suffering
Resources	3) 4) 5)	Engagement in medical/ mental health treatment Variability in psychologi- cal/physical symptoms Effective response to suffer- ing	iii) Empathic response to the client's suffering iv) Supporting the client's medical/ mental health treatment

3. TROUBLING BEHAVIORS

	Client	Client's Significant Others
Risks	L) Withdrawing from activities/relationships M) Substance abuse/Disordered eating N) Impulsive/Compulsive behaviors O) Harming self/others	f) Participating in the client's troubling behaviors g) Unhelpful attempts to regulate the client's troubling behaviors
Resources	6) Engaging in activities/relationships 7) Participating in therapy/rehab 8) Finding alternative behaviors	v) Reaching out to the client vi) Facilitating recovery/safety

4. DESPERATION

	Client	Client's Significant Others
Risks	P) Hopelessness Q) Intense desire for relief R) Intention/Plan to act on suicidal thoughts S) Communicating about suicidality T) Having/Gaining access to means U) Preparing for/Attempting suicide	h) Suicidality i) Ignorance/Denial of the client's suicidality j) Dismissive response to the client's suicidality
Resources	9) Hope/Reasons for living 10) Variability in suicidality 11) Willingness not to conceal suicidality 12) Active participation in developing and implementing a safety plan	vii) Compassionate response to the client's suicidality viii) Active participation in a safety plan

SAFETY PLAN CONSTRUCTION GUIDE

I. Identify resourceful significant others who could assist in implementing relevant details of the safety plan. If they are in the waiting room, bring them into the session. If not, phone them. Determine their willingness and ability to help, and engage them accordingly.

II. Work out how the client and resourceful significant others can prevent and/or restrict access to means for making a suicide attempt. Put measures in place to safeguard against any method the client has been considering (e.g., shooting, hanging, jumping, overdosing, suffocation, carbon monoxide or pesticide poisoning, cutting, drowning, crashing a car or stepping in front of a vehicle, electrocution).

III. Identify troubling behaviors the client has been using to cope with distress (e.g., withdrawing from activities/relationships; substance abuse; disordered eating; impulsive/compulsive actions; harming self/others), and, if appropriate, explore temporary alternatives (e.g., walking, exercise, music, meditation, prayer, reading, writing, reaching out).

IV. Identify safe havens the client could, if necessary, access for a limited time (include contact information, if relevant):
   • In the client's, a family member's, or a friend's home
   • In the hospital

V. Consider enlisting the client's work supervisors and/or school administrators to at least temporarily alter the client's schedule, reducing his or her workload, and/or granting a leave of absence.

VI. Determine, if warranted and appropriate, if the client would consider initiating, resuming, or continuing relevant treatment:
   • Therapy
   • Medication(s)
   • Detox/rehab
   • Inpatient or outpatient program(s)

VII. Generate a list of personal resources the client could call if necessary (include contact information for each):
   • Family members and/or friends
   • Members of the client's religious or spiritual community
   • Peers and/or mentors

VIII. Identify emergency resources the client could access if necessary (include contact information for each):
   • Doctor(s)
   • Therapist(s)

- Crisis line(s) and 9-1-1
- Nearby emergency room and/or hospital

RELATIONAL SUICIDE ASSESSMENT WITH STEVE

Douglas: Hi, Steve. I'm Douglas Flemons. Jennifer told me that she's concerned about you and asked if I would step in and talk with you.

Steve, a law student, had been in a session with Jennifer, his regular counselor, when he mentioned that he was having suicidal thoughts. We had a policy in our center that in such circumstances, a supervisor would be contacted to conduct an assessment.

Steve: Okay.

Douglas: So what's going on? How did you decide to go ahead and come in this morning? [2.3]

Steve: I haven't been feeling too good the last few days.

Douglas: Having a rough time?

This was the first of many empathic inquiries offered throughout the assessment.

Steve: Yeah. I feel like crap.

Douglas: Too crappy to make it to class? You're in law school, right? Second semester?

Steve: I barely made it here.

Douglas: How did you?

Steve: What?

Douglas: Make it here. [2.3]

Steve: *(irritated)* I don't know. I just did.

Douglas's question implicitly credited Steve with agency (i.e., he managed to make it to the appointment), and it was a request for information about the nature of his resourcefulness. What quality did he possess that allowed him to take effective action in difficult circumstances? The impatient irritation in Steve's voice let Douglas know that he was getting ahead of his client, so he slowed down and empathized.

Douglas: It's hell to go to class when you feel crappy. [1.B]

Mirroring the client's language ("crappy") can help the therapist empathically appreciate the client's experience and help the client feel less isolated or separate from the therapist.

Steve: Yeah.

Douglas: The new semester started, what, yesterday, right?

Steve: Yeah, but the thing is, I didn't do too well on my exams last semester, so—

Douglas: —the pressure is on? [1.B]

This was an empathic hunch—it ventured an understanding a little beyond what Steve had so far offered.

Steve: Yeah, well. My GPA was high enough for me to enroll again, but I flunked a required class, so I have to take it over. But they don't offer it again till next fall, and it's a prerequisite for a class *this* semester, so it screws everything up. I bought the books for the classes I can take, but I haven't even opened them. They're still in the bag from the bookstore.

Douglas: I guess even thinking about opening them is anxiety provoking. [2.G]

This empathic hunch introduced the idea that thoughts can trigger anxiety.

Steve: I'm thinking I just need to withdraw.

Douglas: A leave of absence or withdraw completely? [1.1]

Douglas was gently probing whether Steve wanted to take a breather while he kept his options open (leave of absence) or wanted to walk away with no plans to return (withdrawal).

Steve: I don't know. Maybe a leave. I don't know.

He was indecisive but also not closed off to possibilities.

Douglas: Either way, it's a big step. [1.C]

Steve: Yeah, well.

Douglas: When you bought the books, you thought it [taking classes] was doable? But now the semester's started you're not so sure? [1.B]

Steve: The last couple of days have been the worst.

Douglas: Dr. Gralnik prescribed some medication a couple of months ago, right? Has it been helpful?

Steve: He changed the medication my primary doctor had prescribed.

Douglas: What were you taking before? [2.3]

Steve: Prozac and BuSpar. I don't think they were working.

Douglas: Did Dr. Gralnik agree that they weren't working?

Steve: He changed them. He raised the Prozac and stopped the BuSpar and put me on trazodone at night, which used to work for me, and it was working again when I started it this time.

Steve was more informed about his medications than many clients. His ability to remember and understand suggested a resourcefulness that could prove useful later.

Douglas: Have you been taking these, then? [2.3]

Steve: Not the past few days.

Douglas: So have you been getting any sleep? [2.J]

Steve's mention of a sleep medication gave Douglas the opportunity to ask about insomnia without disrupting the flow of the interview.

Steve: Not really. I go to sleep okay, but I'm up after an hour or two, and then forget it.

This would have been a good opportunity to ask about whether he was being awakened by nightmares, but Douglas failed to do so, thus missing an opportunity to find out about another important risk.

Douglas: Tied in knots, I'm sure. You must be wiped. [2.G; 2.J]

This was a decent empathic statement made with appropriately casual language. However, it would have been helpful to follow this up with a question about why Steve had stopped taking his medications. Was he discouraged that these, too, didn't seem to be working? Was he bothered by side effects? Was he embarrassed about taking them?

Steve: I'm fried.

Douglas: Yeah. Times like this, it helps to have someone who knows what's going on. Have you got anybody you've been able to talk to? [1.2; 2.iii]

This was the first of many questions Douglas asked about Steve's significant others, requesting information that could help make sense of Steve's struggles and possibilities for safety within his social context.

Steve: I stayed at my friend Aaron's place last night. I was really not feeling like being alone.

Douglas: You live by yourself?

Steve: I live by myself here near the school. My parents live in Miami, and I stay down there sometimes, but I really live up here. I have an apartment near the school.

Douglas: Does Aaron live alone too?

Steve: Yeah.

Douglas: How do you know him?

Was Steve reaching out to someone he didn't know that well (a classmate, a neighbor), or did he have a solid support system that he could rely on? Such distinctions are crucial when preparing to create a safety plan.

Steve: I've known him all my life.

Douglas: Is he in school, too?

Steve: He's working but he wants to go back to school. He's really probably smarter than me. He wants to go back and go to graduate school.

Aaron sounded solid, but Steve's compliment is also a self-criticism. Would Steve feel comfortable continuing to turn to Aaron for help if that became necessary, or would he be too intimidated?

Douglas: So he's finished his undergrad?

Steve: Yeah, he graduated a while ago and is working, but he wants to go back.

Douglas: Did it help to go over to his place? [1.1]

This is a common resource-finding question for us: "Did the action you take make a positive difference?"

Steve: It helped. It was good to not be alone. It helped. I still was not feeling good.

Douglas: It helps to be with someone when you feel lousy. What was going on?

Steve: I was having some bad thoughts.

The transcript can't capture the look on Steve's face when he mentioned having bad thoughts. Douglas's follow-up empathic inquiry, informed by this nonverbal communication, introduced a theme that ended up being elaborated throughout the rest of the interview.

Douglas: Bad thoughts that scared you? [2.G]

Steve: Yeah.

Douglas: Has that ever happened before?

Steve: Not like this. Maybe a little bit, but not like this.

Douglas: Have these thoughts been scaring you the last couple of days? [2.G]

Establishing the time frame of Steve's troubling experience will contribute to a contextual understanding of the situation.

Steve: For a few days, I guess, but really yesterday, and that's when I called Aaron.

Douglas: And he answered.

Steve: Yeah, he saw it was me.

Douglas: Uh-huh. And so when you called him and said, "I don't want to stay home tonight, I would like to stay at your place," he was cool? [2.iii]

Steve: Oh, yeah. I mean, yeah, that's like—we can do that. We're friends. If he needs something from me or I need something from him, yeah. He's very cool with that.

This further established Aaron as a resource for a possible safety plan.

Douglas: And he knows all of what has been going on with school—with the grades and so on? [2.iii]

Steve: He knows I've been having a rough time in school and not doing as well as I wanted to. He doesn't know that I'm looking at withdrawing.

We were still a long way from even considering the viability of a safety plan, but it is never too early to establish the resources of significant others. If the client is suicidal, these others can only be helpful if they are fully informed, so we want to find out both what the client has told them and what information he or she has not yet felt comfortable sharing.

Douglas: How long have you been seriously considering that [i.e., withdrawing] as an option? [1.C; 1.1]

Steve: A week or so.

Douglas: What led you to keep that from Aaron? [2.e]

Aaron's ability to be helpful will be limited if Steve feels too vulnerable to completely open up to him.

Steve: I think, I guess you can say I am ashamed of it, and I didn't think he could really help me with that. I mean, it's just something I have to—

Douglas: It felt better not to have to tell him? [2.H]

Steve: Right.

Douglas: How much does he understand then? If he doesn't know how bad it is at school, does he get how bad you're feeling? [2.e]

Steve: He gets that I'm really down, and he knows all about what happened with my girlfriend last August and what that did to me.

Douglas's asking about Aaron in a curious, nonthreatening way may have allowed Steve to feel comfortable enough to start talking about his girlfriend. Douglas followed Steve's lead and shifted from talking about shame to gathering information about a different risk—the loss of his relationship with his girlfriend.

Douglas: I saw that in the notes. Horrible timing—just as law school was about to start. And no warning? [1.A]

Steve: Maybe if I'd been paying better attention (*pause*). We were supposed to get married.

Douglas: And she decided to call it quits? [1.b]

Steve: Yeah.

Douglas: She have a reason? [1.b]

Steve: I guess. I don't know. She hooked up with somebody pretty soon after.

Douglas: You figure she had already met him before breaking up with you? [1.A; 1.b]

Steve: Yeah, but I didn't see it.

Douglas: Sideswiped. [1.A]

Steve: Pretty much.

Douglas: Have you had any contact with her since the breakup? [1.A]

Steve: I did at first and then it was sort of like we were trying to be friends, but then I just couldn't do it anymore.

Douglas: In the last, what, few months? [2.5]

Steve: Probably a month or two.

As we mentioned in Chapter 3, sometimes people in distress request help from people they can no longer trust, complicating the relationship and possibilities for safety. Despite the pain Steve was still experiencing from the loss of the relationship, he at least wasn't trying to rely on the person whose loss he was grieving.

Douglas: So Aaron knows about your ex and about your not wanting to be alone. But not really why? [2.e]

Steve: I didn't really tell him about the thoughts I've been having.

Given that Steve hadn't yet told his best friend about the bad thoughts, Douglas didn't want to risk shutting him down by asking too much about them too soon. The content needed to be known, but not yet. Nevertheless, Steve was being forthcoming in his responses, and he was maintaining eye contact. This engagement in the conversation augured well for the possibility of working on a safety plan together.

Douglas: Okay. And your folks, they don't know about what's being going on with school? [2.e]

Steve: No way.

The strength of his response suggested significant shame.

Douglas: And if Aaron knew about the school, how do you think he would react? [2.e]

Steve: I think he would be cool with it. I just haven't been able to tell him.

Douglas: It's a lot to face. It's a lot to hold on to by yourself, too. [1.B; 2.H; 2.e]

Steve: Yeah.

Douglas: Feels impossible to tell your family? [2.H; 2.e]

This empathic inquiry was informed by Steve's earlier strong assertion that his parents didn't know what was going on.

Steve: My dad is a high-powered lawyer.

Douglas: You're concerned he'll take the news hard? [1.a; 2.e]

Steve: Probably.

Douglas: What's his area?

Steve: He represents hospitals and doctors in lawsuits, and he does hospital mergers. That kind of thing.

Douglas: What did he think about your going to law school?

Steve: Oh, ecstatic. He was proud of me.

The greater the father's pride at Steve's getting in, the greater Steve's shame at the prospect of failing out.

Douglas: Kind of like following in the family business? [1.B]

Steve: Yeah. I used to work in his office and do clerk-type stuff. He never really . . . it was not something I planned as a kid to go to law school, so I think he was real happy.

Douglas: When did you decide you were going to go?

Steve: In college.

Douglas: He's successful?

Steve: Very.

Douglas: Making it all the more difficult to tell him that you're struggling? [2.H; 2.e]

A well-placed empathic hunch allows you to test your grasp of your client's predicament. If you're accurate, you effectively demonstrate that you've been listening, and if you're off base, your client has the opportunity to correct you.

Steve: I mean, well, I told him a little bit about, you know, my trouble studying and how I wasn't doing as well as I wanted and, you know, his advice was "Study harder," that kind of thing.

Douglas: If and when your parents find out about—I guess, they *are* going to find out at some point about the school if you withdraw—who do you think is going to have a harder time with it, your dad or your mother? [1.a; 2.e]

To develop a nuanced understanding of how the client perceives his or her social context, it helps to ask questions that differentiate significant others: Who would worry the most? Who would be least likely to support your decision? Who would be more intent on helping?

Steve: It's kind of weird when you think about that. I mean, it would seem like my dad would, but I don't know, sometimes my mom can go either way with those things, it's kind of hard. Sometimes she'll kind of be on my side and sometimes she'll also be kind of, you know, just kick me in the butt to get me doing things.

Douglas: Sounds like you're worried that they're going to think that you've done something wrong, or you didn't try hard enough. [1.a; 2.H; 2.e]

Steve: Yeah.

Douglas: When you worry about that, about them finding out about the school stuff, do the bad thoughts get worse? [1.a; 2.G; 2.H]

Steve: Yeah, I guess.

Douglas was already getting a clear empathic understanding of the client's hopeless situation: Steve was facing an impending precipitous loss of social status and an unbearable loss of face when his highly successfully father and sometimes critical mother found out about his failure.

Douglas: Can you talk to me about the thoughts? [2.G]

Notice the permissive way this question was posed.

Steve: Well, thoughts that maybe I shouldn't be here.

Douglas: Ahhh. Those are pretty scary. [2.G]

For the most part, we try to match our empathic comments and speculations with the probable intensity of the client's emotions. Douglas's "pretty scary" didn't do justice to Steve's level of fear. It might have been more effective to say something like this: "Ahhh. Those can scare the crap out of you."

Steve: Yeah.

Douglas: And you said that you've had thoughts in the past but nothing like this?

Steve: No, these are stronger. They don't go away. And they race. Too fast. Thoughts of maybe I should do something to not be here.

Steve's fear of the thoughts may have been contributing to the vague way he described them. It is less frightening to say that you're having thoughts about doing "something to not be here" than about doing "something to kill myself."

Douglas: Uh-huh, to take action? [4.R]

Steve: Right.

Douglas: In the past when you've had the thoughts about it maybe being better not to be here or something, they weren't as strong? Not as fast? No thoughts about making it happen? [4.R]

Douglas took care to use Steve's language to begin exploring his suicidality, asking about the thoughts of "not being here," rather than "thoughts about killing yourself" or "suicidal thoughts." Later, it would be necessary to inquire more directly about the nature of the thoughts, using descriptors that Steve hadn't introduced himself, but at this point, Douglas was still establishing trust, and he wanted to get a feel for how Steve was making sense of what was going on.

Steve: I used to have thoughts like, you know, if something happened to me it would be okay because things are not good in my life, but not thoughts of really doing anything.

Douglas: When you had the breakup just before school started, did you have those kinds of thoughts? [1.A; 4.R]

Steve: I had some. I got very depressed back then.

Douglas: But they weren't like this?

Steve: They didn't scare me like this.

Douglas: What is it about these thoughts now that's scaring you? The part about doing something? And that they don't go away? The racing? [2.F; 2.G; 4.R]

Detailed questions provide empathic entry into your clients' experience, offering, over the course of an interview, opportunities to gain a reliable sense of what your clients are thinking and feeling. But they are best asked one at a time! Because Steve was already feeling overwhelmed, he might have felt barraged by this rapidly delivered string of inquiries.

Steve: All of it. I mean, they go away after a while, but it takes a long time. When I called Aaron, I mean, it was taking a couple hours for them to go away. That scared me. They just wouldn't go away. I mean, I was thinking about it, and they just kept coming and coming.

Douglas: The thoughts themselves were scary and the speed of them was scary and that they just kept coming—that was scary, too. [2.F; 2.G; 4.R]

Steve: Exactly.

This response suggested that Douglas was accurate in his empathic understanding of Steve's experience.

Douglas: Was your heart racing as much as the thoughts? [2.G]

We want to ground our understanding not only in what our clients are thinking, but in what's going on in their bodies, as well.

Steve: I think I was having a panic attack.

Douglas: You've had those before? [2.G]

Steve: Oh, yeah.

You'll remember from Chapter 3 that panic attacks are associated with increased risk of suicidality.

Douglas: Did the panic set in and then the thoughts started coming, or did it seem to happen the other way—the scary thoughts spun you into this panicky place? [2.G; 4.R]

Douglas wanted to make sense of the panic as part of a more encompassing intrapersonal pattern of interaction.

Steve: The second one. The more I was thinking, it just freaked me out and then I couldn't get my breath and I was sweating and shaking.

Douglas: What was the nature of the thoughts themselves? What kind of scary action came to mind? [4.R]

Having confirmed that the thoughts were giving rise to symptoms of panic, Steve was able to then easily transition into clarifying what it was about the thoughts that prompted this level of anxiety. We want our clients to feel invited into exploring their experience, not interrogated about what they haven't yet revealed.

Steve: Shooting myself.

Douglas: The *idea* of using a gun? An image? [4.R]

If he was visualizing shooting himself, this could make it seem more real and thus more frightening.

Steve: Both. The thoughts are there and then I visualized it.

Douglas: Both. No wonder you were scared. Do you actually own any guns or have access to any? [2.G; 4.T]

Now that Steve had introduced a specific way of killing himself, it was necessary, but also easier, to directly address his access to means.

Steve: Yeah, I do. Target practice sometimes calms me down.

This was worrisome. His method of calming down involved taking in hand his imagined means of killing himself.

Douglas: Are the guns at your parents' place or in your apartment? [4.T]

Steve: Both.

Douglas: Your dad has guns of his own? [4.T]

Steve: My family—I've had guns, been around guns, all my life.

Douglas: Okay. You do target practice with your dad?

Steve: Yep. We used to a lot more, before I went away to college.

Douglas: Something you could share? [1.2]

Douglas was reassured that Steve and his father shared an interest outside the field of law, but given the circumstances, he couldn't imagine a worse scenario than the two of them going shooting together.

Steve: Yes.

Douglas: What about Aaron? [4.T]

Steve: Aaron has guns, too.

Douglas: Uh-huh. So, does he have guns in his place? [4.T]

Steve: Yeah. But he has them locked up, and I don't know where the key to the cabinet is.

Douglas: It [his place] felt, at least, safer than your place. [1.1]

Steve: A lot, yeah. I didn't know what I would do if I was alone.

Douglas: It makes sense, then, that you wanted to head over to his place. Did that provide you some relief, knowing that you didn't have a gun in arm's reach? [1.1; 4.10]

Aaron was obviously a source of safety—definitely an interpersonal resource—as was putting distance between himself and the means to kill himself. Douglas's empathic speculation helped establish that both were important.

Steve: Yeah, it did.

Douglas: Did he know that you were there as a way to protect yourself from the thoughts? [4.i]

Steve: No, I didn't mention that.

Steve was having explicit thoughts about shooting himself, he had access to the means to do so (at his own place, at Aaron's, and at his parents), and he hadn't told anyone except Douglas about his school failure or his suicidality. At this point in the conversation, hospitalization looked like it might be necessary for ensuring safety.

Douglas: How did you decide that it was time to go protect yourself? [1.1]

This resource-based question underscored Steve's decision to keep himself safe.

Steve: Well, when the thoughts wouldn't go away and when I could kind of picture myself doing it.

Douglas: Have you been experiencing the thoughts in any other ways? Sometimes people kind of hear scary thoughts like those, as if a voice is suggesting or even demanding that they kill themselves. [2.1]

Douglas normalized the possibility of hallucinations ("Sometimes people kind of hear . . .") so that if Steve were experiencing them, he would find it easier to acknowledge it.

Steve: No, nothing like that. Just the idea gets stuck in my head for a period of time.

This was reassuring—Douglas would have been much more concerned if Steve were suffering from command hallucinations to shoot himself.

Douglas: It sticks around, scaring the hell out of you, before it goes away? [2.G]

Steve: Yeah, exactly.

Douglas: When it does go away, how does that come about? [4.10]

Steve: No idea. I think I just get maybe so worn out that the way I think changes. It doesn't work to just decide to make it go away.

Douglas: And then when it does go away, how long do you get some relief before it comes back? [4.10]

Asking about variations in and exceptions to the symptom helps to further characterize it as a pattern and thus as something that can change. Such an understanding—an expectancy for change—could prove helpful the next time the thoughts showed up.

Steve: I don't know. It's different at different times.

Douglas: Okay.

Steve: Sometimes it'll come back in a few minutes, sometimes a couple of hours.

Douglas: So last night when you went to Aaron's, were you able to sleep any better than the previous few nights? [2.J; 2.4]

Steve: Not really, but I wasn't as scared.

Douglas: You found a way to feel safer. Man, that's so important. Have you found any other ways to feel safer? [1.1]

Steve: (*pause*) Coming here, I guess.

Douglas: Right. That makes sense. Anything else? [1.1]

Having identified key risks, it was also important, through persistent inquiry, to investigate resources, both for making a safety decision and, if appropriate, for developing a safety plan. Clearly, the danger was significant, but Steve had taken some important steps to keep himself from acting on the thoughts, and he was engaging with Douglas in the conversation. Both contributed to Douglas's sense that it might be possible to create a safe environment outside of the hospital.

Steve: Before, it would help if I could distract myself. Watching TV or something. Playing video games online with other people. But I haven't been able to do that so much.

Douglas: When you were with Aaron, you weren't alone with your thoughts, and you didn't have as easy access to a gun. But I guess if you really wanted to shoot yourself . . . [4.R; 4.T]

Steve: I guess I could figure it out. I mean, but Aaron knows all about—Aaron keeps his guns safe. He keeps them locked. He keeps them unloaded. I know that. He is a gun person. He knows how to secure guns, so I was not trying to find out where his guns were.

Douglas: All right. How about your own guns? Are they unloaded? Locked up? [4.T]

Steve: Yeah, unloaded and locked up, the whole deal. But the key's in my desk.

Douglas: So it wouldn't take long to have a loaded one in your hand. [4.T]

Steve: Exactly.

Douglas: Aaron doesn't know that you've been thinking about shooting yourself? [4.i]

Steve: I was kind of working up to telling him.

Douglas: I imagine he'd be pretty afraid if you told him. [4.vii]

Steve: His brother attempted suicide once, so he understands. But, yeah, he'd be afraid. But for me. You know, I don't think he would be afraid for himself or anything.

Douglas: He wouldn't be worried about you hurting him? [3.O; 4.vii]

Steve: No, I don't think so.

Douglas: Okay. Are you worried about that? [3.O]

Steve: No! Not at all.

Douglas: Are you worried about the safety of anyone else? Do your thoughts ever extend beyond taking your own life? [2.F; 3.O; 4.R]

Steve: You mean to killing someone else?

Douglas: Yeah.

Steve: No, never.

Douglas: Any images of that? [4.R]

Steve: Nope.

Sometimes thoughts of homicide can accompany, and exacerbate, thoughts of suicide, so it is relevant to ask about it. By bringing the issue up in the natural flow of the conversation, Douglas was attempting to keep Steve from feeling accused or put on the spot, while still making necessary inquiries.

Douglas: But sometimes images of shooting yourself. [4.R]

Steve: Yeah.

Douglas: Do those images or other images in your head or something ever get so scary or so involving that they feel real? [2.I]

Steve: I don't know what you mean.

Douglas: Sometimes when people haven't been sleeping and they're having scary thoughts, it's like they have dreams when they're awake. They [the dreams] feel real, but they're hallucinations. [2.I; 2.J]

Steve had already denied having hallucinations, but Douglas considered it important enough to ask about it again.

Steve: I had hallucinations once when I dropped acid in college, but it freaked me out so bad, I never did it again.

Douglas: It's frightening—eh?—when you can't tell whether something's real? [2.I]

Steve: Yeah, well, I hated it. I'll drink sometimes, but that's it.

Douglas: How about pot? [3.M]

Substance use combined with suicidal ideation increases the risk of taking impulsive, deadly action. It was necessary to find out more about the drinking; Douglas came back to it later.

Steve: Nah. It just made me depressed. I haven't smoked since I was a sopho-more.

Douglas: Depression is hell, eh? Before getting that medication from your primary doc and then getting it adjusted by Dr. Gralnik, did you ever get treated for depression? [2.F; 2.3]

Steve: No, never.

Douglas: So were you ever hospitalized for depression or something? [2.F; 2.3]

Steve: Nope.

Douglas: Thoughts of suicide have come and gone when you've been de-pressed before. [2.F; 4.R]

Steve: Yes.

Douglas: Ever make an attempt? [4.U]

Steve: No. I've had, like I said, some thoughts, but not this strong, and I never did anything.

Douglas: During those hard times when you were having thoughts about sui-cide, did anyone you care about—Aaron, your parents, anyone else—ever find out? [4.R; 4.i]

Steve: I never told anybody, no.

Douglas: Anybody in your family ever attempt or commit suicide? [1.A; 4.h]

Steve: I think maybe one of my aunts. I have a couple of aunts who've had depression and been treated for depression. I have one aunt that got real de-pressed after her son died, my cousin.

Douglas: Your cousin? [1.A]

Steve: Yeah.

Douglas: He died, but it wasn't suicide? [1.A]

Steve: No, that was an accident.

Douglas: Okay. She was really struggling with the tragedy, though?

Steve: Yeah, I'm not sure if she might have had a suicide attempt after that. I'm not sure. Somebody did, I don't know which aunt.

Without interrupting the fluidity of the conversation, Douglas was able, in a short amount of time, to inquire about substance abuse, psychiatric history, and Steve's personal and family history of previous suicide attempts. This was followed by the supportive statement, below, complimenting Steve's recent resourceful efforts, both intra- and interpersonal, to reduce his risk of self harm.

Douglas: Well, it's obvious you're taking some very important steps to stay safe. [1.1; 2.3; 4.10]

Steve: I'm trying. It doesn't—I don't know. I mean—

Douglas: Whether it's enough? [4.R]

Steve: I am trying. Right. I don't know.

Douglas: Have you thought at all about what else you might do to feel still safer? [1.1; 4.12]

Steve had done a lot to protect himself, but he'd need to be willing and able to take further steps if a useful safety plan were to be formulated and implemented.

Steve: I felt a little safer being at Aaron's house, but, you know, when I called him, I wasn't feeling safe.

Douglas: Yeah. But you were feeling safe enough not to tell him that you felt in danger of shooting yourself? [4.10]

This question positively framed Steve's reticence; however, continued concealment would jeopardize reliable safety. Steve would need to be willing to communicate his suicidality if they were to create a safety plan that was truly safe.

Steve: I really didn't see myself going out and doing a lot of big things to find a way to hurt myself.

Douglas: Okay. So at any point did you find yourself working up a plan or anything? [4.R]

Steve: I didn't think I was going to, you know, try to figure out where he keeps his guns locked up. I mean, I've never seen where he keeps his guns. I've been at his house, but I don't know. I didn't see myself going out and, you know, buying pills or anything like that, but I did have the thought and I kind of, like you said, an image of me shooting myself and, you know, my guns are there. That would be pretty easy.

Douglas: Sometimes when people feel too unsafe, they go into the hospital for a while. [2.3; 4.12]

By normalizing the hospital as a means of securing safety ("Sometimes when people feel too unsafe . . ."), Douglas was able to introduce it as a potential element of a safety plan.

Steve: Right.

Douglas: Is that something you've considered? [2.3; 4.12]

Steve: I've thought about that. I mean, I don't want to die. Okay. I really don't feel like I want to die. When I get these thoughts I get scared and I don't want to do that. So, if being in the hospital would keep me safe, I think that would be okay because I don't want to die.

When clients are open to the possibility of going into the hospital as a means of staying safe, it can help preclude its being necessary.

Douglas: That's interesting. You think about dying but you don't want to die? Has it ever happened that you get both? You get the thoughts and part of you does want to die? [4.R; 4.10]

Steve: No, I don't think so. I mean, part of me doesn't want to have to go through all this shit.

Douglas: Part of you doesn't want to die, and part of you is sick to death of all this shit. [4.Q; 4.10]

Steve: Yes.

Douglas: Ever wonder what it would be like for your parents if you ended up dying?

Steve: They're going to be disappointed in me either way.

Douglas: How do you mean? [2.d; 4.j]

Steve: I'm either the son who flunked out of law school or the son who offed himself. Either way, they don't get to brag about me to their friends.

Douglas: And then if you go to the hospital so you don't off yourself, you risk embarrassing your dad then, too. [2.e; 4.j]

Steve: Right, like, where would I go? You know, what if I ended up at a hospital where my dad knows people?

Douglas: I imagine that would be very difficult. [2.H; 2.e]

Steve: Humiliating.

Douglas: For you? Your dad? [2.H; 4.j]

Steve: Both, really. I think if they knew, I mean, you know, all the doctors there, they can look at the records.

Douglas: Man. When you have an option that could help you feel safer but the option itself feels emotionally risky—that could leave you feeling pretty stuck. [4.P]

Such scenarios worry us considerably. When the safest means of achieving safety (in this case, going to the hospital) ironically precludes and thus undermines safety (in this case, because of the potential for hospitalization to bring shame to Steve's father and himself), then suicide beckons as a way out.

Steve: Yeah, well. (pause) I kind of have this idea that things can get better. It's like a—I don't know how you would describe it, like an intellectual idea.

Douglas wasn't sure what to make of Steve's comment. He was expressing some degree of hope, but it was possible that he was offering reassurance rather than conviction. Nevertheless,

Douglas took his comment at face value and suggested that the idea of hope can turn into a feeling of hope.

Douglas: Like your body hasn't caught up with your head yet. [4.9]

Steve: I always believe it. I am trying to believe it, but there are times when I don't always believe things are going to get better. I kind of know from my experience that things should get better, but it gets hard sometimes to believe that.

Douglas: And when you work hard to try to make yourself believe it, has that ever worked? Have you ever been able to . . . [4.10]

Steve: It used to work. It's worked before. It hasn't been working so much recently.

Douglas: Were you believing that you were doing well in school? Was it a shock to find out your GPA and realize you'd failed that class? Or did you have some hints? [1.C]

Steve: I knew I was not doing as well as I should, so it was not a total shock. I mean, I kind of thought if I failed something that wasn't a prereq[uisite], then nobody would have to know, but now it will take extra time to graduate, even if I don't do a leave, so everybody is going to find out.

Douglas: Which is harder for you to think about, actually taking the course over or having to tell your folks? [1.B; 1.C; 1.a; 2.H; 2.e]

Steve: Telling my parents. My dad graduated third in his class.

Shame kept turning up as a determining factor in Steve's distress, which suggested that it would need to be addressed in some definitive way if safety was to be ensured.

Douglas: Hell to have to follow that act, eh? So do the thoughts get scarier when you think about talking to your parents? [1.a; 2.H; 2.e]

Steve: Yeah.

Douglas: Anything else that you've noticed gets the thoughts worked up? Anything in particular? [4.10]

Steve: When I think about my ex, that's part of it too.

Douglas: It feels like a double whammy then, like the breakup is still there and then the difficulty with school is piled on top of that. [1.A; 1.B; 1.C]

Steve: And then my ex finding out about me flunking out. Confirming her opinion [that I'm a loser].

Douglas: A triple whammy. Hard to catch your breath. [1.b; 2.H; 2.d]

Steve: I try not to think about it.

Douglas: Does that work? [1.1]

We always inquire whether the client's attempted solutions have ever been helpful. If they have been, we support their continuation; if they haven't, we know not to encourage them as part of a safety plan. Efforts to control, contain, or negate distressing symptoms (such as bad thoughts) typically exacerbate, rather than ameliorate, them (see Chapter 2).

Steve: Not really.

Douglas: Uh-huh. You want the relief that would come from being able to push the thoughts away, and then when that doesn't work, I imagine that makes the scary thoughts even scarier. [2.G; 4.R]

Steve: That's the scariest part.

Douglas: That you can't get them to stop. [2.G]

Steve: Or even slow down. You know, does that mean—I mean, I don't know, if you can't get them to stop, does that mean you are going to do it even if you don't want to? I don't know that.

Steve appeared to be afraid that the persistence of the suicidal thoughts would eventually wear down his defenses and he'd end up taking his life, even if he also wanted to live. The following question was designed to introduce the therapeutic idea that action doesn't necessarily have to follow thought.

Douglas: That's a great question. Have you ever had a thought that you were going to do something or a thought that you didn't like and you ended up not acting on it? Do you remember? [4.10]

Steve: Well, I guess I used to get thoughts like that when I was skiing, sometimes.

Douglas: Skiing? Waterskiing?

Steve: Snow.

Douglas: Oh, really. And do you still do that? I guess not too much in Florida.

We often look for opportunities, if contextually appropriate, to interject a humorous or amusing comment. This can reduce the tension of the interview and tell us whether the client is able to shift his or her outlook or mood, even if only briefly.

Steve: (*laughs*) No, no. I did it during college, mostly, in New York. I raced on the alpine ski team.

Douglas: Really. Which events?

Steve: Downhill and giant slalom.

Douglas: Which do you like better?

Steve: Giant slalom is more technically challenging, but I like the speed of downhill.

Douglas: How fast do you go?

Steve: In the giant slalom, 40, 45; downhill, 60 up to, like, 75 or 80.

Douglas: Miles per hour? Kilometers?

Steve: Miles.

Douglas: Whew. When you're traveling that fast, how do you keep yourself balanced? How do you deal with the speed and all the physical, technical demands? [1.1]

This might seem like a significant digression, but Douglas was in search of resources. If Steve had developed effective strategies for dealing with danger and anxiety while skiing, it was possible that these could be transported into the current danger and panic of encountering the bad thoughts. Confidence while purposefully going as fast as possible might be able to translate into confidence in responding to fast thoughts.

Steve: Well, people always say that, you know: How could you stay focused or whatever? How can you keep from panicking when you're going so fast and having to carve those turns? I mean, for me, it doesn't really feel dangerous.

Douglas: And you don't have to *try* to stay calm— [2.4; 1.1]

Steve: You get a rush from the cold and the competition and the speed— the rhythm of it or whatever. Waiting for the race to start is pretty nerve-wracking, but once you go, you don't really think about it.

Douglas: You said that skiing was an example of when you'd get a scary thought and then end up not acting on it. What did you mean? [4.10]

Steve: Sometimes before a race I'd get images of losing control or crashing hard. I'd worry about doing badly and then I'd think of something bad happening.

Douglas: Of letting that happen? [3.0]

Steve: I guess. But then once I'd push off, there was no time to think about that.

Douglas: Once the race started, you no longer were bothered about thoughts of getting hurt? [2.4]

Steve: Right.

Douglas: You said something very important a little bit ago. You said that you don't want to die. It seems like the thoughts about shooting yourself appear when the reality hits you that your parents are going to find out about school. Like if you were to die, you wouldn't have to see the disappointment on their faces or something. [2.H; 2.d; 4.R; 4.10]

This comment framed the suicidal ideation as a desperate solution for shame.

Steve: Yeah, I mean, I almost get that thought at the time that that would be better, I wouldn't have to deal with all of this.

Douglas: If you knew that your folks would handle it okay, maybe if they— [1.i; 2.iii]

Steve's risk for suicide was tied into his prediction of his parents' reactions to his school problems, so one way of assessing potential for safety was to explore the possibility of their changing their way of relating to Steve and his failure. Steve rejected the possibility of his parents taking the news well.

Steve: *(Shakes head no.)*

Douglas: —you don't think that's possible? [1.a; 2.d]

Steve: I don't think so.

Douglas: Would you be up for them coming to a session with Jennifer? She could maybe help you tell them about what's been happening. [1.1; 2.3; 2.e; 2.iv]

If Steve could entertain the possibility of a therapy session with his parents, Douglas could more easily imagine his not needing to go to the hospital, at least not immediately.

Steve: Maybe. I don't know. I don't think they could handle it.

Douglas: Could you? [2.H; 2.3]

Steve: I don't know how I would tell them.

Douglas: How are you thinking that they would have to find out, then? [2.e]

Steve: Well, if I drop out, I'm probably going to have to tell them about that. I don't think I can tell them about all this other stuff, at least not at first. I'll have to tell them about school some time.

He recognized that his parents would soon figure out that he wasn't going to class. He didn't want them to also find out about his suicidality.

Douglas: Their opinion of you matters a tremendous amount. [2.d]

Steve: Sure. I mean, definitely.

Douglas: Keeping secrets is really, really tough. [2.H]

Attempting to keep his parents in the dark had been adding considerably to his stress.

Steve: Yeah.

Douglas: If you end up discovering that law school isn't for you, do you have any ideas about what you would want to do instead? [4.9]

This was a question about hope. Perhaps the future could hold possibilities outside the world of law school.

Steve: I don't really want to think about that.

Douglas: I'm sure you don't, but could you, just for a minute? [2.5]

Wanting to be sensitive to, but not constrained by, our clients' anxiety, we at times ask clients to experiment with thinking about something that they have, up to that point, felt incapable of considering. Are they able to tolerate anxiety-provoking thoughts that provide an alternative to suicide? Note, though, that this was done to assess whether Steve could imagine hope on the other side of anxiety, not as an effort to impose hope. Douglas didn't encourage him to think positively.

Steve: *(pause)* I don't know. I don't know.

Douglas: You've had thoughts about shooting yourself as a way of getting relief from this nightmare. [4.Q]

Steve: Yes.

Douglas: Have you had any thoughts about achieving relief in a different way? [1.1; 4.10]

So far, the only solution Steve had come up with for dealing with his shame and despair was shooting himself. By framing his suicidal thoughts as a quest for relief, Douglas was able to open the possibility of finding other, safe, means of achieving the same end, such as pursuing a different life course.

Steve: I don't know what you mean.

Douglas: I don't know. Sometimes in the middle of a crisis, a new idea flashes. Finding a different path—different profession, different woman, different something. [1.1; 1.2; 4.9]

Steve: No.

This exploration of safe options for finding relief didn't lead anywhere, so Douglas shifted to inquiring whether Steve was at risk of dying by some other means.

Douglas: So far the idea of relief has been largely connected to thoughts about shooting yourself. [4.Q]

Steve: Yeah.

Douglas: Have you had thoughts of ending your life any other way? [4.R]

Steve: No. I mean, I guess if I did it I would use a gun.

Douglas: Uh-huh.

Steve: I don't want to do something that's, you know, not effective, I guess.

Douglas: Yeah. Uh-huh. All the more important to make sure that your way of staying safe is effective. When you were racing, did you take steps to be safe when you were doing that? [1.1]

Steve's commitment to lethality allowed Douglas to underscore the importance of safety.

Steve: Of course.

Douglas: So given this expertise, it doesn't surprise me that you've been taking steps to protect yourself the last few days. [4.12]

This exchange is a good example of how resources can be different from protective factors. No researcher has, of course, determined that experience as a competitive downhill skier affords a degree of protection for suicidality. But from a resource perspective, expertise in one area of experience may be applicable to another. By framing Steve as a person possessing expertise on safety, Douglas could characterize the taking of safety steps as a natural and expectable expression of this identity.

Steve: But I don't feel safe.

Douglas: Right, so it's going to be necessary to take some extra steps. Would you be up for that? [4.12]

Steve: Like what?

Douglas: You've been worried that if the thoughts about shooting yourself keep coming, you might end up doing it. [4.R; 4.U]

Steve: Right.

Douglas: You are going to start feeling safer when those thoughts aren't coming as often or aren't sticking around so long or aren't so graphic, or something. [4.10]

Notice the therapeutic expectancy present in this phrasing: "You are going to start feeling safer when."

Steve: That would help.

Douglas: But before that happens, it has to be safe to have the thoughts and know you don't have to worry about acting on them. Has there been any time when a thought about shooting yourself was accompanied by an urge to do it or a movement toward doing it? [4.R; 4.10]

Steve: I've kept my distance.

Douglas: From the guns?

Steve: Yeah. I've been too scared to get near them.

Douglas: Afraid you might pull the trigger if you had one in your hand? [4.R]

Steve: *(quietly)* Yes.

Douglas: So you didn't get to where you were headed to get a gun and had to hold yourself back? [4.R]

Steve: No. More that I was afraid I might.

Douglas: Must have been very scary.

Steve: Yes.

Douglas wanted to determine whether Steve was grappling with more than thoughts about taking his life. Had he intended to make an attempt but didn't follow through? Had he made any plans? The exchange above established that Steve wasn't having to hold back an urge to act, but Douglas could have done more to rule out the presence of an intent or plan to act on the thoughts. Still, Douglas's gut registered the significance of this absence of an urge to act. Yes, there were unrelenting, suicidal thoughts; yes, Steve had frighteningly easy access to lethal means; yes, he was still struggling from the loss of the relationship with his girlfriend and the impending loss of a career in law; yes, he had been drinking in response to the thoughts; yes, he was having panic attacks; yes, suicide loomed as an easy alternative to the shame of facing critical parents. And he was struggling against the thoughts; and he didn't have the urge to act; and he had taken steps to ensure his safety; and he had a solid friend; and it seemed possible he'd commit to therapy. The safety decision emerging from these juxtapositions suggested the possibility of developing a viable safety plan.

Douglas: One way to not have to feel so scared, to make sure that you feel safe, is to go into the hospital. When you're there, you can relax, knowing that regardless of your thoughts, you won't be able hurt yourself. [2.3; 4.12; SP.II; SP.IV]

This began the process of brainstorming the elements of a safety plan. By putting the possibility of hospitalization on the table early on and characterizing it in a positive way, Douglas made clear his commitment to safety, regardless of how it was to be achieved. In part he was assessing how Steve would respond to this prospect. Would he feel reassured or threatened by the idea of going to the hospital?

Steve: Okay.

Douglas: Another way is to create a safe environment outside the hospital, either so it is safe after you leave the hospital, or safe enough so you don't have to go in, in the first place. [4.12; SP.IV]

Steve: I'd rather not go.

Douglas: I'm sure not. Let's see if we can come up with a plan that feels safe.

Douglas wasn't yet sure that they could develop a safety plan that would be safe enough to prevent an attempt, given Steve's significant risks. However, if Steve were willing to communicate his suicidality to Aaron, then he, Aaron, could perhaps be brought on board as a significant contributor to Steve's safety. If nothing else, moving forward with constructing a safety plan would allow Douglas to gather more information for the making of a safety decision.

Douglas: If it seems like you don't need to go to the hospital, then great. If the plan doesn't feel safe enough, we'll hold on to the hospital as an option. [4.12; SP.IV]

Steve: Okay.

Steve didn't want to go to the hospital, but he was willing to not rule it out. This level of acceptance is uncommon. Many clients are afraid to go, whether because of prior experience, concerns about cost, worries about labeling and its effect on future academic and vocational pursuits, or fear of the unknown. Treating all such responses as legitimate, we talk with clients about what they can realistically expect, taking the position that sometimes the hospital is the only safe haven capable of providing reasonable protection. When helpful, a hospital stay provides an opportunity for rest, therapy, support, and relief. And even at its least helpful, it can provide clients with a bridge to a safer way of living and a commitment to change so they don't have to return.

Douglas: As we figure out a plan, a safety plan, I'm going to write it down. Then if it feels workable, you can take it with you. [4.12]

Giving the client the safety plan is itself a contribution to his or her safety. As we discussed in Chapter 4, we want the plan to be as specific and as full of resources as possible—a kind of road map for when the person feels lost inside his or her despair. We've had clients who carried it in their pocket or purse or posted it on a wall at home (such as the client we talked about in Chapter 4) so they could refer to it when they needed it most.

Steve: Okay.

Douglas: Okay. You stayed at Aaron's last night, and that felt safer than being at your place. [1.1; 4.10; 4.12]

Steve had shared a lot of information about Aaron, suggesting that he could be trusted. Without this background, Douglas may not have even broached the possibility of Steve's staying with him. If Steve endorsed the idea, the next step would be to talk directly with Aaron and confirm his availability, reliability, and willingness to help.

Steve: Yeah, a lot.

Douglas: Would that be a possibility? Can you camp out with him for a while? [1.1; 4.12; 4.viii; SP.IV]

Steve: If I wanted to stay with Aaron, you know, I am sure he would be cool with it as long as I needed to stay.

Douglas: Okay, so how about we call him? We could put him on speakerphone. Did he know you were coming here today? [4.12; 4.i; 4.viii; SP.VII]

Steve: No.

Douglas: So this call will be out of the blue for him. Are you okay with that? [4.11; 4.12; 4.i; SP.VII]

Steve: Yeah, it's okay.

Douglas had Steve sign a release, and then they called and reached Aaron, told him what was happening, and secured his support for participating in a safety plan. He welcomed the idea of Steve staying with him, and he agreed to immediately remove the guns from both his and Steve's apartments and to store them in what they termed "an undisclosed location." Then, before hanging up, they arranged for Aaron to come and pick Steve up from the clinic. While they waited for Aaron to arrive, Douglas and Steve developed the details of the safety plan.

Douglas: You're right—what a great friend. [2.iii; 4.vii; 4.viii]

Steve: I told you, right?

Douglas: Yeah. So with the guns taken care of for now, does that help? [4.10; 4.12; 4.viii]

Steve: Yeah, I think so. I mean, I just kept seeing myself going and getting one of my guns and loading it.

Douglas: So now you won't have to deal with that.

Steve: Right.

Douglas: Okay, so let's write that down. The first item on the safety plan (*reading what he is writing*): "I will stay at Aaron's until it feels safe to go back home." [4.12; 4.viii; SP.IV; SP.VII]

Steve: Okay.

Douglas: And then let's put in a second one that goes along with the first (*reading aloud*): "Aaron will remove guns from both of our apartments and store them, locked and unloaded, in a safe place." Sound okay? [4.12; 4.viii; SP.II]

Steve: Yes. That's okay (*nodding*).

Douglas: And, as Aaron said on the phone, he'll keep the whereabouts of the guns a secret. [4.viii; SP.II]

Steve: Right. That's good.

Douglas: Okay, so (*reading aloud*): "Three: Aaron won't tell me where the guns are stored." [4.12; 4.viii; SP.II]

Steve: Yes.

Douglas: Anything else that he would need to secure for you to feel really safe? Any other weapons? [4.T; 4.10; 4.12; 4.viii]

Steve: No. I mean, he's got like a knife collection, but I have a knife. I guess we could do that too. I mean, I haven't had thoughts about using a knife, but if you want to take that away.

Douglas: Well, the question is, what's going to make it possible for you to feel safe? [4.12]

If clients are going to embrace the safety plan, it has to feel like their creation, not something to which they are reluctantly agreeing. As much as possible, we want clients to experience us as consultants, rather than as unilateral decision makers.

Steve: I mean, I don't, you know, I could live without my knife for a while. I don't know how long we're talking about, but I mean, I am sure he would be okay with that.

Douglas: Okay, so we'll add that in (*reading aloud*): "Four: He'll also remove our knives." We'll call him back before he collects the guns and add to his list. What about your meds—your pills? [4.12; 4.viii; SP.II; SP.IV]

Steve: You know, I don't really think of them as something I would take to hurt myself. I just take them the way I'm supposed to take them. I guess, I know people take overdoses and you could kill yourself with pills, but really, that was not a thought I was having.

Douglas: So those feel safe? [4.12; SP.II]

Steve: To me they feel safe. When I was feeling so bad, I was really thinking about the gun.

Steve wasn't currently considering an overdose to be an option, but it could have become one for him if he was feeling desperate and had no access to guns. It's always better to anticipate and inquire about other possible means.

Douglas: Okay. You are going to go and stay at Aaron's place for the time being, and he is going to secure the guns and the knives—at both your place and his. [4.12; SP.II; SP.IV]

Steve: Right.

Douglas: If you started having thoughts about the pills, thoughts of taking an overdose, would you be up for telling Aaron that and giving him the bottles for safekeeping? [4.R; 4.11; 4.12; SP.II; SP.VII]

It might have been safer to also put Aaron in charge of Steve's medication, but at some point it would become untenable to expect Aaron to oversee and protect against every possible risk. If you start feeling like that will be necessary, then you should seriously consider the hospital as the most viable option. As we mentioned in Chapter 4, anytime the safety plan starts being overly complex or requires significant others to take on a level of care beyond what they can reasonably be expected to perform, then it needs to be reconsidered.

Steve: Yeah, sure. I don't think that would happen, but whatever.

Douglas: Does he have alcohol at his place? [3.M; 4.12]

Steve: He's not really a drinker, but he probably has some.

Douglas: You said earlier that you'll drink sometimes? Have you been drinking much lately? [3.M]

Steve: I did. I did. I drank—what's today? Wednesday?

Douglas: Wednesday, yeah.

Steve: I drank Monday night.

Douglas: And did you start the drinking in response to the thoughts? [3.M; 4.Q]

Steve: The anxiety was too much.

Douglas: Oh, so you drank to try to not feel so anxious? [2.G; 3.M]

Steve: I felt really anxious.

Douglas: I'm sure. Did the drinking help? [3.M]

Steve: Yeah, for a while maybe, but then the anxiety came back.

Douglas: How much did you drink? [3.M]

Steve: Five or six, maybe.

Douglas: Is that a typical amount? How often have you been doing that? [3.M]

Douglas should have asked for more details. Was Steve talking about five or six beers, or five or six mixed drinks with two or three ounces of whisky or vodka in each one?

Steve: Not very often. Maybe once or twice a week. More since I haven't been going to school.

Douglas: If you've been drinking, it increases the risk that you'll do something impulsive, so it makes sense to avoid it. And as you said, it doesn't really help, anyway. Would you be comfortable getting Aaron to secure the alcohol as well? [3.M; 3.N; 3.vi; 4.U; 4.12; 4.viii; SP.III]

Steve: I mean, we could ask him, but I imagine he would. Be okay with it, I mean.

Douglas: Okay (*writing and reading*), that's number five: "For the time being, I won't drink any alcohol." [3.M; 4.12; SP.III]

Steve: That's fine.

Douglas accepted his agreement without ensuring that Steve was capable of deciding not to drink. Gathering a more detailed history of his alcohol use (i.e., past history of abuse, withdrawal, etc.) would have helped to determine whether this part of the plan was achievable.

Douglas: So what if the thoughts were really getting to you and you started thinking about buying a gun or getting one some other way? [4.R; 4.T]

As we create the outlines of a safety plan, we start looking for holes, for ways that it could fail to protect.

Steve: Then I'd need more help.

This was a reassuring statement—it gave Douglas confidence that Steve would reach out for additional resources if the need arose.

Douglas: Right, more than Aaron could provide. It sounds like if you were at that level, you'd be looking at the hospital, because at that point you'd want to be in a place where you couldn't get a gun, no matter what. [4.12; SP.IV]

Steve: I don't want to feel like this. If that's what it takes, I could do that. I would do that.

Douglas: Would Aaron drive you? [2.iv; 4.viii; SP.II; SP.IV]

Steve: I'm sure he would.

Douglas: We'll ask him when he gets here—we'll go through the whole safety plan with him—but let's assume for now he will. So (*reading*): "If I get thoughts about looking for a gun or some other way of killing myself, I'll ask Aaron"—no let's make it that you'll *tell* him, not ask him— [4.viii; SP.VII]

Steve: Right.

Douglas: (*Resumes reading*) "I'll ~~ask~~ tell Aaron to take me to the hospital." Now I'm writing down the name and address and phone number of the hospital so you'll have it. [4.12; SP.IV]

Steve: Okay.

Douglas: If it got to that point, you could see yourself taking that step? [4.12]

Steve: If I had to. I mean, I don't know, do I have to do that now? I don't know.

Steve was still unnerved by the thoughts, so he wasn't certain that he didn't need to go to the hospital. The possibility was given serious consideration again, and they decided together that with the safety precautions put in place so far, it would be okay to continue exploring the possibility of safety outside the hospital. Douglas reassured Steve that they would think it all through again once the safety plan was finished and determine the best course of action.

Douglas: There's another step that I don't think needs to happen right now, but I think it would be important for us to talk about in terms of making the situation less dangerous. What do you think would be the first step towards letting your parents know what's been going on? [4.11; 4.12; SP.VII]

Steve: I thought I'd have to at some point tell my mom that I'm not going to school.

Douglas: And then she would tell your dad? [4.11]

Steve: Yeah.

Douglas: And that would be safer than telling both of them at the same time? [4.11; 4.12]

Steve: I think so. I don't think I could face my dad to tell him, but I think if he found out about it from my mom, it would be easier for him.

Douglas: Are you more protecting your dad or protecting yourself when you think about doing it that way? [2.H; 2.d; 4.11]

Steve: I don't know, maybe both of us.

Douglas: Would you want to do that on your own? Or bring them here and let Jennifer help you talk with them? [2.3; 2.iv; 4.11; 4.vii; 4.viii; SP.VII]

Steve: I like that idea. That would be better.

It probably wasn't essential for Steve to talk to his parents immediately, but given how integral their imagined (and possibly real) disapproval was to Steve's shame, Douglas wanted to make sure that the schism was addressed soon. Steve's acute safety needs had been covered, but for him to establish an enduring foundation of safety, he would need to be freed up from having to continue keeping his school failure a secret from his parents.

Douglas: This doesn't seem like a step that has to happen right now. But it's not one that you probably want to keep putting off for a very long time because then the longer you put it off, you're still dealing with worrying about the shame and worrying about your dad and worrying about your dealing with your dad, and so on. How soon do you think it will be important for you to let them know what's going on? [2.H; 4.11; SP.VII]

Steve: I think it would be easier to just wait and not deal with it, but harder to wait and not deal with it, I don't know. I like what you say. I've got to get it off my chest. But not right now. I can't.

Douglas: Excellent. That's what I am talking about, taking one step at a time. You can figure out the timing of that the next time you come here. [1.1; SP. VII]

Steve: Okay, when will that be?

Douglas: You're already scheduled to see Jennifer tomorrow, but I'm going to make sure you are able to see Dr. Gralnik, as well, while you're here. [2.3; 4.12; SP.VIII]

Steve: That would be good.

Close follow-up is not only ideal but necessary in this kind of situation. Steve's desire to be seen the next day helped Douglas feel still more confident with the plan.

Douglas: Maybe tomorrow you and Jennifer could talk about some ways to deal with the anxiety—meditation or self-hypnosis—and I'd like Dr. Gralnik to evaluate your medications. [2.G; 2.3; SP.III; SP.VIII]

Steve: Okay.

Douglas: Let's put that into the safety plan, too. [4.12; SP.VIII]

Steve: Okay.

Douglas: And then let's put in there that you'll also talk to Jennifer about talking to your parents, and maybe setting up a family session. [2.3; 4.11; 4.12; 4.i; SP.VII]

Steve: Okay.

Douglas: Given that they have guns at their house, and they don't know what's going on yet, I think we should put something in the safety plan about not going to see them until they know what you've been experiencing and they are willing and able to secure their guns, too. [4.11; 4.12; SP.II; SP.VII]

Steve: That's fine.

Douglas: (*Added all three points to the plan.*) Now, if at any time you are feeling panicky or unsafe, you know you can always call our crisis line. Even tonight you can talk to our on-call counselor. There's always somebody available, and it doesn't matter when you call. [2.3; 4.10; 4.12; SP.VIII]

As mentioned in Chapter 4, our clinic had a 24/7 crisis line, which helped us help our clients feel safe. Douglas also gave Steve the national number for suicide crisis calls, in case he was reluctant to call ours.

Steve: Yeah, Jennifer went over that with me, before.

Douglas: I'll put our number in the plan, along with another one: 1-800-SUICIDE. They're also available all the time and have caring people on call to talk with you. [4.11; 4.12; SP.VIII]

Steve: Okay.

Douglas: And if things feel really desperate, you can always call 9-1-1, and they'll send somebody to you, wherever you are. You know that already, but I'll write it down, anyway. [4.10; 4.11; 4.12; SP.VIII]

Steve: Okay.

Douglas: So you knew about our crisis line already, but you didn't call us last night. Do you think you would actually call one of these numbers if you were feeling unsafe? [1.1; 4.11; 4.12; SP.VIII]

A safety plan that isn't followed isn't safe. We never complete an RSA without having reconfirmed that the client is willing and able to endorse and participate in the plan.

Steve: I'm pretty sure I'd call if I needed to.

Douglas: So what are you thinking about going to the hospital right now? [4.12; SP.IV]

Steve: I don't think I need to. If things get bad, then maybe, but not right now.

Douglas: So the safety plan feels safe to you?

Steve: Yes, yes it does.

Douglas: Any part of it that needs to feel safer?

Steve: I don't think so.

Douglas: Let's walk through it together—make sure it feels doable and that we haven't left anything out.

Steve: Sure.

Going through the plan one more time served as a final step in Douglas's decision-making process, allowing him to juxtapose his professional understanding of risks and resources with his empathic, emotionally grounded grasp of Steve's experience. He took a second look at what he knew and what he felt, a second look at the integrity of and the inevitable gaps in the plan, a second look at Steve's engagement in the construction of the plan, a second look at Steve's commitment to protecting himself from his suicidality: The plan felt safe enough. No changes were made.

Douglas: It feels pretty safe to me, too. So let's find some times for your appointments tomorrow. I'll make a copy of the plan for me and give this one to you. [4.12; SP.VIII]

Steve: Sure.

Douglas: Tell you what—I'll make an extra copy so you'll have two. Maybe you can give one to Aaron or something.

Steve: That's fine.

As we discussed in the last chapter, we don't ask clients to sign the safety plan, because we don't consider it to be a no-self-harm or no-suicide contract. Why treat it as something the client needs to formally promise to adhere to when he or she helped to construct it in the first place? A sense of ownership follows naturally from being invited to invent, disagree with, change, and fine-tune the plan as it is being developed. The client's commitment to it is thus reflected in his or her participation in co-creating it, rather than by way of a signature on the bottom of it.

In the last chapter we also talked about the importance of keeping *yourself* safe, given this litigious society of ours, by thoroughly documenting every suicide assessment you conduct. Below you'll find a case note for Steve's assessment, which, in keeping with the recommendations made in Chapter 4, includes each of the following elements.

- A detailed description of the client's intra- *and* interpersonal risks *and* resources.
- The clinician's safety decision.
- The clinician's rationale for the safety decision—making clear how an understanding of the client's risks, resources, and possibilities for safety influenced the decision that was made.
- The steps taken to implement the safety decision.
- A copy of the safety plan.

To organize your thoughts in preparation for writing such a case note, you might find it helpful to first make a list of the client's risks and resources.[2] Here's a list for Steve:

STEVE'S RISKS AND RESOURCES

DISRUPTIONS AND DEMANDS

Risks:
- Failed a class and may have to repeat the year. May not continue in law school.
- Parents expect him to become a lawyer and are not aware of his struggles in school.
- Father says to just "study harder."
- Girlfriend broke up with him just as law school was about to start. Still thinks about what she thinks of him and how she would judge him now.

Resources:
- Reached out to close friend, Aaron, and stayed with him last night.
- Felt that staying with Aaron helped.
- Prior to today's session, he confided with Aaron about some of his school problems and emotional struggles.
- Doesn't want ex-girlfriend to think he's a loser, which she will if he ends his life.

SUFFERING

Risks:
- Depressed mood with suicidal thoughts.
- Specific thoughts (without intent) of shooting himself, which frighten him.
- Panic attacks.
- Insomnia (wakes up and can't fall back asleep).
- Trouble studying.
- Racing thoughts.
- Previous episode of depression with suicidal thoughts at the time his girlfriend broke up with him.
- Two aunts who were treated for depression.
- History of feeling guilty over his cousin's death.
- Ashamed to tell Aaron he might withdraw from school.
- Ashamed to tell parents he failed class—he believes parents will be disappointed either way (if he fails or if he ends his life). Worries about disappointing his father (a successful lawyer).

<u>Resources</u>:
- Initiated coming in today for a walk-in appointment—actively seeking help.
- Agrees to follow up in the very near future with his therapist and psychiatrist, and agrees with idea of re-evaluating medications with the implied idea of resuming them.
- Is an expert downhill skier whose racing experience might be able to come into play in response to racing thoughts and heart rate. When he was skiing a race, anticipatory thoughts about getting hurt would go away when he engaged in the activity.

TROUBLING BEHAVIORS

<u>Risks</u>:
- Drinking alcohol. Drank recently to reduce his anxiety—"five or six" drinks.
- Binge drinking on occasion.
- Stopped taking antidepressant medications "a few" days ago.

<u>Resources</u>:
- No thoughts of harming others.
- Agrees not to drink alcohol.
- No drug use since college (didn't like experience of LSD or marijuana).
- Agrees he will not go to his parents' house in the near future since he may have access to guns there. Will only go once they know about the suicidality and so secure guns.
- Agrees with the plan of a family session to help him communicate with his parents about the stressors he is facing, including difficulties at school (appointment not yet scheduled).

DESPERATION

<u>Risks</u>:
- Has difficulty maintaining hope—doesn't yet see an alternative career if he withdraws from law school.

- Intense desire for relief from depressed mood, panic attacks, racing thoughts, and "bad" (i.e., suicidal) thoughts.
- Thinks of death as a means of relief.
- Suicidal thoughts becoming more active compared to previous episode: "Maybe I should do something to not be here."
- Afraid he will act on the suicidal thoughts even though he doesn't want to.
- Guns are readily available to him at his parents' home.
- Has experience shooting guns.
- Has had "images" of shooting himself, which he struggles against.
- Possible family history of suicide (his aunt).
- Has not told his parents about his suicidal thoughts and hadn't told Aaron about them prior to today's session.
- Going to the hospital for suicidality could bring shame to his father, who is well known at hospitals in the area.

Resources:
- No history of suicide attempts and no mental-health hospitalizations.
- Low suicidal intent: "I don't want to die." Doesn't see himself actively trying to obtain a gun. States he is trying to stay safe.
- No thoughts or plans for other methods of suicide: "Not buying pills."
- Has some degree of hope: "An intellectual idea, I'm trying to believe it."
- Participated fully in developing and implementing a safety plan.
- His friend Aaron is reliable and supportive, and also participated fully in developing and implementing the safety plan.
- Agrees to eliminate access to guns and knives—Aaron has already removed them from each of their homes.
- Agrees to call our on-call therapist or emergency numbers, including 1-800-SUICIDE or 9-1-1, if needed.

- Volunteers the idea that if the suicidal thoughts reoc-
  curred, that would mean he would need more help,
  such as going to the hospital.

The case note for Steve's RSA doesn't mention all of these risks and resources, but it makes mention of those that contributed most to the safety decision.

CASE NOTE

Steve presented for a session at his request. He describes having "bad thoughts" (thoughts of shooting himself), which he states were triggered at least in part by his fears over failing a class that will probably necessitate repeating a year in law school. He feels ashamed, and he fears how his parents, particularly his father (a successful lawyer), will react to this news when they find out. He denies suicidal intent, stating he does not want to die. Nevertheless, the thoughts persist, despite his attempts to suppress them, so he is worried, he says, that this means he might act on the thoughts even though he does not want to. He describes recent insomnia and panic attacks (accompanied by racing thoughts) that are brought on by the bad thoughts. He has been drinking (sometimes heavily) as an attempt to deal with his anxiety and to facilitate sleep. He stopped taking his antidepressant two days ago because he thought it wasn't working. He denies auditory or visual hallucinations. He specifically denies command hallucinations and denies thoughts of harming or killing anyone else. He describes his mood as depressed and anxious.

He describes a previous episode of depression, with passive thoughts of suicide, at the beginning of law school, immediately following his girlfriend breaking up with him. The thoughts are more troubling and persistent now, compared to that episode, and he now has thoughts about acting on them, even though he asserts that he does not want to die. He denies any history of suicide attempts or previous psychiatric hospitalizations. There is a possible family history of suicide—a depressed aunt may have taken her life.

He denies thoughts or plans to use any other method to make an attempt, such as taking an overdose of medications. He has not obtained or sought out any means of taking his life, but he has access to guns in his parents' home. Prior to today's session, he had access to guns in his and Aaron's homes. He maintains an "intellectual idea" that things might get better, but has moments where he loses hope and intensely desires relief from his anxiety and shame.

We discussed treatment/safety options, including voluntary hospitalization. Steve agrees to keep this as an option should the need arise, but would prefer outpatient treatment at this time if possible (his father is well known professionally at several hospitals; Steve worries about shaming him if hospitalization for suicidality were to be necessary).

Steve collaborated in the development of a safety plan, including eliminating access to guns and staying away from his parents' house until they know about his suicidality and have removed weapons from their home. He agreed to stay with his friend Aaron, and to tell Aaron if the suicidal thoughts re-occur or intensify. He agrees to call our 24/7 crisis line if problems or questions arise, agrees to call 1-800-SUICIDE or 9-1-1 as needed, and agrees to go to the hospital for voluntary admission if necessary (e.g, if the suicidal thoughts become increasingly intense or persistent). I provided him with the number and address for Memorial Hospital. He also agrees not to drink alcohol for the time being (see safety plan, below). Follow-up is scheduled for tomorrow with his therapist, Jennifer, and with Dr. Gralnik.

I am concerned that Steve could be at significant risk for suicide in the near future, given the risks noted above. However, the risk is mitigated by Steve's (and Aaron's) full participation in the development of a workable safety plan (including Aaron's removal of weapons from both their homes); Steve's low suicidal intent; his having no history of suicide attempts or psychiatric hospitalizations; his agreement to continue with close outpatient follow-up for psychotherapy, family therapy, and medication management; and his agreement to access emergency services, including voluntary hospitalization if necessary. Taking into consideration Steve's risks and resources, along with the safety plan we developed (see below), I have decided that involuntary hospitalization is not necessary at this time. It is my judgment that Steve can be safely treated as an outpatient, with close follow-up as described in the safety plan. He is not currently a danger to self or others, and therefore hospitalization is not warranted at this time.

SAFETY PLAN FOR STEVE

1. I will stay at Aaron's until it feels safe to go back home.

2. Aaron will remove guns from both of our apartments and store them, locked and unloaded, in a safe place.

3. Aaron won't tell me where the guns are stored.

4. He'll also remove our knives.

5. For the time being, I won't drink any alcohol.

6. If I get thoughts about looking for a gun or some other way of killing myself, I'll ask tell Aaron to take me to the hospital—Memorial Hospital: 350 Smith Street 222-333-2000.

7. I will come here tomorrow for an appointment with Jennifer (to talk about ways of reducing anxiety) and Dr. Gralnik (for a medication evaluation).

8. Jennifer and I will talk tomorrow about what to tell my parents and when to tell them and how to tell them.

9. I won't go and visit my parents until they are informed and they have removed Dad's guns from their home.

10. If the thoughts are really bugging me, I'll call the clinic's 24/7 crisis line or the 24/7 suicide line: 1-800-SUICIDE.

11. If I need immediate help, I'll call 9-1-1.

In the actual case—the one on which this transcript is based—Aaron arrived at our clinic after having secured the guns and knives away from both his and Steve's apartments. By then the safety plan—in many respects, as we mentioned earlier, similar to the one presented here—was complete. Aaron was comfortable with all aspects of it. Safety plan in hand, Steve, feeling "safe enough," left to go home with his friend. He stayed with him for almost 2 weeks. During that time, he took a leave of absence from school and found a way to tell his mother what was going on. She then told his dad and, as Steve predicted, they both expressed significant disappointment in his performance. Although Steve struggled with shame, once he didn't have to maintain his secret, he no longer felt suicidal.

Over the next year, Steve continued to come into our center for scheduled appointments, and we continued to prioritize safety. After a leave of absence of several months, he returned to law school, and even though his studies did not go well, his depression and panic attacks improved. Eventually, he left school without graduating. When we last saw him—over a year after our suicide assessment—he gave us permission to include this transcript in our book. He told us that Aaron was still keeping his guns and knives in an undisclosed location.

NOTES

1 The transcript is a couple of steps removed from the interview that took place with Steve, so we want to explain how it came to be. We had sophisticated recording capabilities in our clinic. When therapists wanted to video-record their work with a client, they would show the equipment to the client, explain the measures we took to keep the digital file safe and the information protected, and then have him or her read through and sign an elaborate agreement form that the university's attorneys had drawn up. This was imposition enough on clients who were needing services but weren't desperate; it would have been entirely inappropriate and unethical to have a suicidal client go through such a process prior to our beginning an assessment.

This commitment not to make recordings of suicide assessments created a dilemma for us when we decided that we wanted to include an annotated transcript in our book to demonstrate the semistructured, extemporaneous process of an assessment interview. The solution we came up with wasn't ideal, but it preserved the integrity of our clients, and it allowed us to create a representative rendition of what our relational approach to suicide assessment actually looks like.

Steve had been coming to our Student Counseling Center, seeing Len for medication management, and Jennifer, one of the staff counselors, for individual therapy. In early December of that year, he booked an appointment with Jennifer for early January, but the day before his scheduled session, he called, sounding troubled and asking if he could be seen any sooner. Our operations manager, Mirna, following protocol, told him to come right in, and then she freed up Jennifer's and Len's schedules so that they could see him together.

Len conducted most of the assessment, but Jennifer, an experienced clinician who knew Steve well, also contributed to the process, filling Len in on details he might not know, asking Steve some questions, and participating in the development of the safety plan. After Steve left our center, Len and Jennifer, in keeping with the center's policies, apprised Douglas, the director, of the status of the case. During that conversation, it occurred to us that we had an opportunity to record an assessment that would fairly closely mirror what had just transpired.

For a year or two leading up to this time, we (Douglas and Len) had collaborated on training the clinical staff by occasionally coming to case-staffing meetings in the role of a troubled student. The staff would spend an hour or more conducting a team-based suicide assessment, with each clinician having an opportunity to make empathic statements, ask risk- and resource-based questions, come to a decision regarding the "client's" safety, and receive feedback on their contributions. Inspired by the role-playing success of such trainings, we scheduled a 2-hour meeting for the three of us—Len, Jennifer, and Douglas—a few days after Steve's assessment. When we got together, we turned on the recording equipment and Len "became" Steve, presenting with the same history and suicidality as had the real Steve a few days earlier.

Douglas had learned a little about Steve a few months earlier when Jennifer had presented the case at case-staffing meetings, and although he knew that Len hadn't facilitated an involuntary assessment of Steve at the hospital, he didn't know many of the details of the interview Len had conducted, and he didn't know what had gone into the safety plan. We decided that for the conversation to unfold as realistically as possible, Douglas shouldn't try to recreate what Len did but, rather, should conduct his own interview, even to the point of leaving open the possibility of coming to a different safety decision than Len. Jennifer, who knew Steve the best, contributed to the process in an invaluable way. When Douglas would ask "Steve" a question for which Len didn't know the answer, Jennifer, staying in role as Steve's counselor, would smoothly provide it, thus allowing Len, too, to stay in role and the assessment to proceed without interruption. When Douglas asked a question that neither Len nor Jennifer knew (such as the speed Steve would travel when engaged in competitive downhill skiing), "Steve" improvised an answer that we then later corrected.

Once we finished the recording, we had it transcribed, edited it for technical errors, and simplified it. For the purposes of a book, we thought it would be too complex to talk about how to conduct an assessment with two clinicians, so we took Jennifer's contributions in the role-play and dissolved them into both Douglas's questions and "Steve's" responses. We were scrupulous about leaving in Douglas's errors and omissions, as we didn't want the interview to appear more effective, streamlined, or organized than it actually was. Finally, we went through the transcript and wrote a commentary on what we saw occurring and what Douglas was experiencing and noticing. Some of the comments attributed to Douglas in the transcript reflect not only his experience in the role-play but also Len's experience in the actual interview. The safety plan, which Douglas and "Steve" developed in the role-play, is included at the end of the transcript; it actually bears a close resemblance to what Len, Steve, and Jennifer developed in the actual assessment.

Steve continued coming to our center for therapy and medication management for some months after the development of the safety plan, and then, for various reasons, he took a hiatus. Some months after that, a little over a year after the initial assessment, Steve, struggling with school but not suicidal, returned for a few follow-up visits. Len told him about our book and how we had created a transcript that protected his identity but captured something of the assessment that Len had originally conducted with him. Generous in his desire to help others, Steve gave us permission to include the transcript.

2 You could, if you wished, append the list to your case note.

APPENDIX

THE BACKPOCKET RSA

THE BACKPOCKET RSA is offered as a resource for you to keep beside you and to consult, as needed, throughout the suicide-assessment process. It is comprised of three guides:

- The Risk and Resource Interview Guide (RRIG) lists and organizes relevant topics to be addressed during a relational suicide assessment.
- The Safety Plan Construction Guide (SPCG) outlines eight key tasks to undertake when collaborating with a client on the construction of a safety plan.
- The Documentation Guide provides a checklist of what you should be sure to include when documenting a relational suicide assessment.

If you prefer to access the Backpocket RSA on a digital device, scan the QR code below or go to this URL: http://contextconsultants.com/Backpocket_RSA/

RISK AND RESOURCE INTERVIEW GUIDE

The RRIG provides a research-informed architecture for organizing assessment interviews with your clients. All topics of inquiry are arrayed within 2 × 2 tables under four categories of suicidal experience: *disruptions and demands, suffering, troubling behaviors,* and *desperation.* Use the RRIG to help ensure that you—

- address, at some point during your assessments, current and past challenges and successes within all four of the categories.
- inquire about the topics within these categories that, given the idiosyncratic circumstances and mindset of each client, you deem pertinent.
- keep your interview balanced, so that you're attending not only to clients' *risks,* but also to their *resources;* not only to their *intra*personal experience, but also to their *inter*personal relationships; not only to issues of *danger,* but also to possibilities for *safety.*

As a *semistructured* interview guide, the RRIG is designed to assist you in conducting assessments that your clients will experience as *conversations.* This means that the order in which you address topics will be determined not by the structure of the RRIG tables but by the unfolding interactive pattern of each unique dialogue.

For you to make a sound clinical decision and, if appropriate, to construct an effective safety plan, you must be thorough; however, avoid being exhaustingly exhaustive. For a particular client at a particular time, some, or perhaps even many, of the topics of inquiry won't be relevant.

If you only ask questions, your assessments will feel more like interrogations than conversations. Balance your queries with frequent empathic statements—reflections that capture both the content and emotional nuances of what clients are telling you. This will help keep clients from recoiling from your curiosity and help them trust that you're getting an accurate sense of who they are and what they've been going through. Take care in broaching sensitive issues and delve, when warranted, into issues of concern and possibility.

Throughout your interviews, pay close and ongoing attention to how clients interact with you. Make note of their speech, mood, appearance, forthrightness, eye contact, consistency of response, commitment to safety, orientation to surroundings, and responsiveness to empathic statements and therapeutic possibilities. However, take the context of the interview into account. Those who are meeting with you at someone else's request may appear more withdrawn, evasive, or dismissive than they would otherwise be.

RRIG

1. DISRUPTIONS AND DEMANDS

		Client		Client's Significant Others
Risks	A) B) C) D) E)	Loss/Failure of relationship Overwhelming expecta- tions/obligations Loss of social position/fi- nancial status Legal/Disciplinary troubles Abuse/Bullying/Peril	a) b) c)	Distressing expectations/demands of the client Abandoning the client Abuse/Bullying of the client
Resources	1) 2)	Effective problem solving Positive personal/spiritual connections	i) ii)	Reasonable expectations/encour- agement of the client Helping the client meet obligations

2. SUFFERING

		Client		Client's Significant Others
Risks	F) G) H) I) J) K)	Depressed/Manic mood Anxiety/Anger/Obsessive thinking Conflicted identity/Shame/ Burdensomeness Hallucinations/Delusions Insomnia/Nightmares Pain/Illness/Injury	d) e)	Viewing the client as flawed/a burden Limited awareness of/Unhelpful response to the client's suffering
Resources	3) 4) 5)	Engagement in medical/ mental health treatment Variability in psychologi- cal/physical symptoms Effective response to suffer- ing	iii) iv)	Empathic response to the client's suffering Supporting the client's medical/ mental health treatment

© 2013 Douglas Flemons, Ph.D., & Leonard M. Gralnik, M.D., Ph.D.

RRIG

3. TROUBLING BEHAVIORS

		Client		Client's Significant Others
Risks	L) M) N) O)	Withdrawing from activities/relationships Substance abuse/Disordered eating Impulsive/Compulsive actions Harming self/others		f) Participating in the client's troubling behaviors g) Unhelpful attempts to regulate the client's troubling behaviors
Resources	6) 7) 8)	Engaging in activities/relationships Participating in therapy/rehab Finding alternative behaviors		v) Reaching out to the client vi) Facilitating recovery/safety

4. DESPERATION

		Client		Client's Significant Others
Risks	P) Q) R) S) T) U)	Hopelessness Intense desire for relief Intention/Plan to act on suicidal thoughts Communicating about suicidality Having/Gaining access to means Preparing for/Attempting suicide		h) Suicidality i) Ignorance/Denial of the client's suicidality j) Dismissive response to the client's suicidality
Resources	9) 10) 11) 12)	Hope/Reasons for living Variability in suicidality Willingness not to conceal suicidality Active participation in developing and implementing a safety plan		vii) Compassionate response to the client's suicidality viii) Active participation in a safety plan

SAFETY PLAN CONSTRUCTION GUIDE

When possible and appropriate, draw on the possibilities listed below to collaboratively construct with the client (and significant others, if available) a specific point-form safety plan for how the client and significant others will, in response to the current danger, address acute risks and enhance safety. Write down the details you work out with the client as you proceed. Stay attuned to the participation of the client, ensuring that he or she remains engaged and that you are offering adequate opportunities for him or her to contribute. Once you have completed articulating the plan, go back over it, point by point, asking the client to add anything you've left out and ensuring with the client that it isn't too elaborate or asking too much of him or her. Make a copy for your file and give the original to the client.

I. Identify resourceful significant others who could assist in implementing relevant details of the safety plan. If they are in the waiting room, bring them into the session. If not, phone them. Determine their willingness and ability to help, and engage them accordingly.

II. Work out how the client and resourceful significant others can prevent and/or restrict access to means for making a suicide attempt. Put measures in place to safeguard against any method the client has been considering (e.g., shooting, hanging, jumping, overdosing, suffocation, carbon monoxide or pesticide poisoning, cutting, drowning, crashing a car or stepping in front of a vehicle, electrocution).

III. Identify troubling behaviors the client has been using to cope with distress (e.g., withdrawing from activities/relationships, substance abuse, disordered eating, impulsive/compulsive actions, harming self/others), and, if appropriate, explore temporary alternatives (e.g., walking, exercise, music, meditation, prayer, reading, writing, reaching out).

IV. Identify safe havens the client could, if necessary, access for a limited time (include contact information, if relevant):
   • In the client's, a family member's, or a friend's home
   • In the hospital

V. Consider enlisting the client's work supervisors and/or school administrators to at least temporarily alter the client's schedule, reducing his or her workload, and/or granting a leave of absence.

© 2013 Douglas Flemons, Ph.D., & Leonard M. Gralnik, M.D., Ph.D.

SPCG

VI. Determine, if warranted and appropriate, if the client would consider initiating, resuming, or continuing relevant treatment:
   • Therapy
   • Medication(s)
   • Detox/rehab
   • Inpatient or outpatient program(s)

VII. Generate a list of personal resources the client could call if necessary (include contact information for each):
   • Family members and/or friends
   • Members of the client's religious or spiritual community
   • Peers and/or mentors

VIII. Identify emergency resources the client could access if necessary (include contact information for each):
   • Doctor(s)
   • Therapist(s)
   • Crisis line(s) and 9-1-1
   • Nearby emergency room and/or hospital

DOCUMENTATION GUIDE

A case note describing a relational suicide assessment should minimally include the following:

1. A detailed description of the client's intra- *and* interpersonal risks *and* resources.
2. The safety decision you arrived at, for example, whether you decided
   - to hold off on developing a safety plan;
   - to involve the client in constructing and implementing a safety plan; or
   - to arrange for the client's immediate admission to a hospital.
3. A rationale for your safety decision that makes clear how the information you gathered—regarding risks, resources, and safety—influenced the decision you made.
4. The steps you took to implement the safety decision, such as
   - contacting other clinicians and/or clinical facilities
   - scheduling dates for follow-up appointments
   - enlisting the help of significant others in implementing a safety plan
   - providing emergency contact numbers to the client
   - facilitating hospitalization
5. A copy of the safety plan (if you and the client constructed one).

REFERENCES

Adams, D. M., & Overholser, J. C. (1992). Suicidal behavior and history of substance abuse. *American Journal of Drug and Alcohol Abuse, 18*(3), 343–354. DOI: 10.3109 /009529992 09026071

Aish, A. M., & Wasserman, D. (2001). Does Beck's Hopelessness Scale really measure several components? *Psychological Medicine: A Journal of Research in Psychiatry and the Allied Sciences, 31*(2), 367–372. DOI: 10.1017/ s0033291701003300

American Association of Suicidology. (2008). *Recognizing and responding to suicide risk: Essential skills for clinicians.* Washington, DC: Author.

American Psychiatric Association, Work Group on Suicidal Behaviors. (2003). *Practice guideline for the assessment and treatment of patients with suicidal behaviors.* Washington, DC: Author.

Anderson, H., & Goolishian, H. (1992). The client is the expert. In S. McNamee & K. Gergen (Eds.), *Therapy as social construction* (pp. 25–39). Newbury Park, CA: Sage.

Anderson, P. L., Tiro, J. A., Price, A. W., Bender, M. A., & Kaslow, N. J. (2002). Additive impact of childhood emotional, physical, and sexual abuse on suicide attempts among low-income African American women. *Suicide and Life-Threatening Behavior, 32*(2), 131–138. DOI: 10.1521/suli.32.2.131.24405

Andover, M. S., Zlotnick, C., & Miller, I. W. (2007). Childhood physical and sexual abuse in depressed patients with single and multiple suicide attempts. *Suicide and Life-Threatening Behavior, 37*(4), 467–474. DOI: 10.1521/suli.2007.37.4.467

Angst, F., Stassen, H. H., Clayton, P. J., & Angst, J. (2002). Mortality of patients with mood disorders: Follow-up over 34–38 years. *Journal of Affective Disorders, 68*(2–3), 167–181. DOI: 10.1016/s0165-0327(01)00377-9

Appleby, L., Shaw, J., Amos, T., McDonnell, R., Harris, C., McCann, K., et al. (1999). Suicide within 12 months of contact with mental health services: National clinical survey. *British Medical Journal, 318*(7193), 1235–1239. DOI: 10.1136/ bmj.318.7193.1235

Apter, A., Kotler, M., Sevy, S., Plutchik, R., Brown, S. L., Foster, H., et al. (1991). Correlates of risk of suicide in violent and nonviolent psychiatric patients. *American Journal of Psychiatry, 148*(7), 883–887.

Axelsson, R., & Lagerkvist-Briggs, M. (1992). Factors predicting suicide in psychotic patients. *European Archives of Psychiatry and Clinical Neuroscience, 241*(5), 259–266. DOI: 10.1007/bf02195974

Bagley, C., & Tremblay, P. (2000). Elevated rates of suicidal behavior in gay, lesbian, and bisexual youth. *Crisis: The Journal of Crisis Intervention and Suicide Prevention, 21*(3), 111–117. DOI: 10.1027//0227-5910.21.3.111

Balázs, J., Benazzi, F., Rihmer, Z., Rihmer, A., Akiskal, K. K., & Akiskal, H. S. (2006). The close link between suicide attempts and mixed (bipolar) depression: Implications for suicide prevention. *Journal of Affective Disorders, 91*(2), 133–138. DOI: 10.1016 /j. jad. 2005.12.049

Bateson, G. (1979). *Mind and nature: A necessary unity*. New York: Dutton.

Bateson, G. (1991). *Sacred unity: Further steps to an ecology of mind* (R. Donaldson, Ed.). New York: HarperCollins.

Bateson, G. (2000). *Steps to an ecology of mind*. Chicago: University of Chicago Press.

Bateson, M. C. (1994). *Peripheral visions*. New York: HarperCollins.

Beautrais, A. L. (2003). Subsequent mortality in medically serious suicide attempts: A 5-year follow-up. *Australian and New Zealand Journal of Psychiatry, 37*(5), 595–599. DOI: 10.1046/j.1440-1614.2003.01236.x

Beautrais, A. L., Joyce, P. R., & Mulder, R. T. (1997). Precipitating factors and life events in serious suicide attempts among youths aged 13 through 24 years. *Journal of the American Academy of Child and Adolescent Psychiatry, 36*(11), 1543–1551. DOI: 10.1016/ S0890-8567(09)66563-1

Beck, A. T., Brown, G. K., Berchick, R. J., Stewart, B. L., & Steer, R. A. (1990). Relationship between hopelessness and ultimate suicide: A replication with psychiatric outpatients. *American Journal of Psychiatry, 147*(2), 190–195.

Beck, A. T., Brown, G. K., & Steer, R. A. (1997). Psychometric characteristics of the scale for suicide ideation with psychiatric outpatients. *Behaviour Research and Therapy, 35*(11), 1039–1046.

Beck, A. T., Kovacs, M., & Weissman, A. (1975). Hopelessness and suicidal behavior: An overview. *Journal of the American Medical Association, 234*(11), 1146–1149. DOI: 10.1001/ jama.234.11.1146

Beck, A. T., Kovacs, M., & Weissman, A. (1979). Assessment of suicidal intention: The Scale for Suicide Ideation. *Journal of Consulting and Clinical Psychology, 47*(2), 343–352. DOI: 10.1037/0022-006x.47.2.343

Beck, A. T., & Steer, R. A. (1991). *Beck Scale for Suicide Ideation: Manual*. San Antonio, TX: Psychological Corporation.

Beck, A. T., Steer, R. A., Kovacs, M., & Garrison, B. (1985). Hopelessness and eventual suicide: A 10-year prospective study of patients hospitalized with suicidal ideation. *American Journal of Psychiatry, 142*(5), 559–563.

Beck, A. T., Weissman, A., Lester, D., & Trexler, L. (1974). The measurement of pessimism: The Hopelessness Scale. *Journal of Consulting and Clinical Psychology, 42*(6), 861–865. DOI: 10.1037/h0037562

Berg, I. K., & Miller, S. (1992). *Working with the problem drinker: A solution-focused approach*. New York: Norton.

Bernert, R. A., & Joiner, T. E. (2007). Sleep disturbances and suicide risk: A review of the literature. *Neuropsychiatric Disease and Treatment, 3*(6), 735–743. DOI: 10.2147 /ND TS 1248

Besman-Albinder, S. (2006). *The impact of trauma work on resilient therapists and their partners*. Unpublished doctoral dissertation. Nova Southeastern University, Fort Lauderdale, FL.

Blaauw, E., Winkel, F. W., & Kerkhof, A. J. F. M. (2001). Bullying and suicidal behavior in jails. *Criminal Justice and Behavior, 28*(3), 279–299.

Bode, S., He, A. H., Soon, C. S., Trampel, R., Turner, R., & Haynes, J. D. (2011). Tracking the unconscious generation of free decisions using ultra-high field fMRI. *PLoS ONE, 6*(6), e21612. DOI: 10.1371/journal.pone.0021612

Bongar, B. (2002). *The suicidal patient: Clinical and legal standards of care* (2nd ed.). Washington, DC: American Psychological Association.

Borges, G., Angst, J., Nock, M. K., Ruscio, A. M., & Kessler, R. C. (2008). Risk factors for the incidence and persistence of suicide-related outcomes: A 10-year follow-up study using the National Comorbidity Surveys. *Journal of Affective Disorders*, *105*(1), 25–33. DOI: 10.1016/j.jad.2007.01.036

Bostwick, J. M., & Pankratz, V. S. (2000). Affective disorders and suicide risk: A reexamination. *American Journal of Psychiatry*, *157*(12), 1925–1932. DOI: 10.1176 /appi. ajp. 157.12.1925

Breed, W. (1972). Five components of a basic suicide syndrome. *Suicide and Life-Threatening Behavior*, *2*(1), 3–18. DOI: 10.1111/j.1943-278X.1972.tb00451.x

Brent, D. A. (2001). Firearms and suicide. *Annals of the New York Academy of Sciences*, *932*(1), 225–240. DOI: 10.1111/j.1749-6632.2001.tb05808.x

Brent, D. A., & Mann, J. J. (2005). Family genetic studies, suicide, and suicidal behavior. *American Journal of Medical Genetics Part C: Seminars in Medical Genetics*, *133*C(1), 13–24. DOI: 10.1002/ajmg.c.30042

Brent, D. A., & Melhem, N. (2008). Familial transmission of suicidal behavior. *Psychiatric Clinics of North America*, *31*(2), 157–177. DOI: 10.1016/j.psc.2008.02.001

Brent, D. A., Oquendo, M., Birmaher, B., Greenhill, L., Kolko, D., Stanley, B., et al. (2002). Familial pathways to early-onset suicide attempt: Risk for suicidal behavior in offspring of mood-disordered suicide attempters. *Archives of General Psychiatry*, *59*(9), 801–807. DOI: 10.1001/archpsyc.59.9.801

Brent, D. A., Perper, J. A., Allman, C. J., Moritz, G. M., Wartella, M. E., & Zelenak, J. P. (1991). The presence and accessibility of firearms in the homes of adolescent suicides. *Journal of the American Medical Association*, *266*(21), 2989–2995. DOI: 10.1001/ jama. 1991.03470210057032

Brent, D. A., Perper, J. A., Moritz, G., & Baugher, M. (1993). Stressful life events, psychopathology, and adolescent suicide: A case control study. *Suicide and Life-Threatening Behavior*, *23*(3), 179–187. DOI: 10.1111/j.1943-278X.1993.tb00178.x

Breslau, N., Schultz, L. R., Johnson, E. O., Peterson, E. L., & Davis, G. C. (2005). Smoking and the risk of suicidal behavior: A prospective study of a community sample. *Archives of General Psychiatry*, *62*(3), 328–334. DOI: 10.1001/ archpsyc.62.3.328

Brezo, J., Paris, J., Vitaro, F., Hébert, M., Tremblay, R. E., & Turecki, G. (2008). Predicting suicide attempts in young adults with histories of childhood abuse. *British Journal of Psychiatry*, *193*(2), 134–139. DOI: 10.1192/bjp.bp.107.037994

Broadhead, W. E., Leon, A. C., Weissman, M. M., Barrett, J. E., Blacklow, R. S., Gilbert, T. T., et al. (1995). Development and validation of the SDDS-PC screen for multiple mental disorders in primary care: A pilot study. *Archives of Family Medicine*, *4*, 211–219. DOI: 10.1001/archfami.4.3.211

Brodsky, B. S., Groves, S. A., Oquendo, M. A., Mann, J. J., & Stanley, B. (2006). Interpersonal precipitants and suicide attempts in borderline personality disorder. *Suicide and Life-Threatening Behavior*, *36*(3), 313–322. DOI: 10.1521/suli. 2006.36.3.313

Brown, G. K., Henriques, G. R., Sosdjan, D., & Beck, A. T. (2004). Suicide intent and accurate expectations of lethality: Predictors of medical lethality of suicide attempts. *Journal of Consulting and Clinical Psychology*, *72*(6), 1170–1174. DOI: 10.1037/0022 -006x. 72.6. 1170

Bullman, T. A., & Kang, H. K. (1996). The risk of suicide among wounded Vietnam veterans. *American Journal of Public Health*, *86*(5), 662–667. DOI: 10.2105/ ajph.86.5.662

Busch, K. A., & Fawcett, J. (2004). A fine-grained study of inpatients who commit suicide. *Psychiatric Annals*, *34*(5), 357–364.

Cade, B., & O'Hanlon, W. H. (1993). *A brief guide to brief therapy*. New York: Norton.

Charmaz, K. (2006). *Constructing grounded theory: A practical guide through qualitative analysis*. Thousand Oaks, CA: Sage.

Coffey, A., & Atkinson, P. (1996). *Making sense of qualitative data.* Thousand Oaks, CA: Sage.

Conner, K. R., Cox, C., Duberstein, P. R., Tian, L., Nisbet, P. A., & Conwell, Y. (2001). Violence, alcohol, and completed suicide: A case-control study. *American Journal of Psychiatry, 158*(10), 1701–1705. DOI: 10.1176/appi.ajp.158.10.1701

Cooper, S. L., Lezotte, D., Jacobellis, J., & DiGuiseppi, C. (2006). Does availability of mental health resources prevent recurrent suicidal behavior?: An ecological analysis. *Suicide and Life-Threatening Behavior, 36*(4), 409–417. DOI: 10.1521/ suli.2006.36.4.409

Cooper-Patrick, L., Crum, R. M., & Ford, D. E. (1994). Identifying suicidal ideation in general medical patients. *Journal of the American Medical Association, 272*(22), 1757–1762. DOI: 10.1001/jama.1994.03520220051030

Cornelius, J. R., Salloum, I. M., Mezzich, J., Cornelius, M. D., Fabrega , H., Jr., Ehler, J. G., et al. (1995). Disproportionate suicidality in patients with comorbid major depression and alcoholism. *American Journal of Psychiatry, 152*(3), 358–364.

Csorba, J., Rózsa, S., Vetro, A., Gadoros, J., Makra, J., Somogyi, E., et al. (2001). Family- and school-related stresses in depressed Hungarian children. *European Psychiatry, 16*(1), 18–26. DOI: 10.1016/s0924-9338(00)00531-9

Cull, J. G., & Gill, W. S. (1982). *Suicide Probability Scale (SPS) manual.* Los Angeles: Western Psychological Services.

D'Augelli, A. R., Grossman, A. H., Salter, N. P., Vasey, J. J., Starks, M. T., & Sinclair, K. O. (2005). Predicting the suicide attempts of lesbian, gay, and bisexual youth. *Suicide and Life-Threatening Behavior, 35*(6), 646–660. DOI: 10.1521/suli.2005. 35.6.646

Deisenhammer, E. A., Ing, C. M., Strauss, R., Kemmler, G., Hinterhuber, H., & Weiss, E. M. (2009). The duration of the suicidal process: How much time is left for intervention between consideration and accomplishment of a suicide attempt? *Journal of Clinical Psychiatry, 70*(1), 19–24. DOI: 10.4088/JCP.07m03904

Dervic, K., Oquendo, M. A., Grunebaum, M. F., Ellis, S., Burke, A. K., & Mann, J. J. (2004). Religious affiliation and suicide attempt. *American Journal of Psychiatry, 161*(12), 2303–2308. DOI: 10.1176/appi.ajp.161.12.2303

de Shazer, S. (1985). *Keys to solution in brief therapy.* New York: Norton.

De Wilde , E. J., Kienhorst, I. C. W. M., Diekstra, R. F. W., & Wolters, W. H. G. (1994). Social support, life events, and behavioral characteristics of psychologically distressed adolescents at high risk for attempting suicide. *Adolescence, 29*(113), 49–60.

Dey, I. (1990). *Qualitative data analysis.* New York: Routledge.

Diamond, G. M., Diamond, G. S., Levy, S., Closs, C., Ladipo, T., & Siqueland, L. (2012). Attachment-based family therapy for suicidal lesbian, gay, and bisexual adolescents: A treatment development study and open trial with preliminary findings. *Psychotherapy, 49*(1), 62–71. DOI: 10.1037/a0026247

Druss, B., & Pincus, H. (2000). Suicidal ideation and suicide attempts in general medical illnesses. *Archives of Internal Medicine, 160*(10), 1522–1526. DOI: 10.1001/archinte.160.10. 1522

Dumais, A., Lesage, A. D., Alda, M., Rouleau, G., Dumont, M., Chawky, N., et al. (2005). Risk factors for suicide completion in major depression: A case-control study of impulsive and aggressive behaviors in men. *American Journal of Psychiatry, 162*(11), 2116–2124. DOI: 10.1176/appi.ajp.162.11.2116

Dutton, M. A., & Rubinstein, F. L. (1995). Working with people with PTSD: Research implications. In C. R. Figley (Ed.), *Compassion fatigue: Coping with secondary traumatic stress disorder in those who treat the traumatized* (pp. 82–100). New York: Routledge.

Eisenberg, M. E., & Resnick, M. D. (2006). Suicidality among gay, lesbian and bisexual youth: The role of protective factors. *Journal of Adolescent Health, 39*(5), 662–668. DOI: 10.1016/j.jadohealth.2006.04.024

Erickson, M. H. (1980). Further clinical techniques of hypnosis: Utilization techniques. In
    E. L. Rossi (Ed.), *The collected papers of Milton H. Erickson: Vol. 1* (pp. 177–205). New York:
    Irvington.
Erickson, M. H., & Rossi, E. L. (1980). Varieties of double bind. In E. L. Rossi (Ed.), *The
    collected papers of Milton H. Erickson: Vol. 1* (pp. 412–429). New York: Irvington.
Esposito-Smythers, C., Spirito, A., Kahler, C. W., Hunt, J., & Monti, P. (2011). Treatment
    of co-occurring substance abuse and suicidality among adolescents: A randomized trial.
    Journal of Consulting and Clinical Psychology, 79(6), 728–739. DOI: 10.1037/a0026074
Evans, E., Hawton, K., & Rodham, K. (2004). Factors associated with suicidal phenomena
    in adolescents: A systematic review of population-based studies. *Clinical Psychology Re-
    view, 24*(8), 957–979. DOI: 10.1016/j.cpr.2004.04.005
Fanous, A. H., Prescott, C. A., & Kendler, K. S. (2004). The prediction of thoughts of
    death or self-harm in a population-based sample of female twins. *Psychological Medicine,
    34*(2), 301–312. DOI: 10.1017/S0033291703008857
Fay, A. (1891). *Music-study in Germany: From the home correspondence of Amy Fay.* Charleston,
    SC: Nabu Press.
Figley, C. R. (1995). Compassion fatigue as secondary traumatic stress disorder: An over-
    view. In C. R. Figley (Ed.), *Compassion fatigue: Coping with secondary traumatic stress disorder in
    those who treat the traumatized* (pp. 1–20). New York: Routledge.
Finn, S. E. (2007). *In our clients' shoes: Theory and techniques of therapeutic assessment.* New York:
    Routledge.
Finn, S. E. (2009). *What are the core values of therapeutic assessment?* [Web page]. Retrieved from
    http://therapeuticassessment.com/about4.html
Finn, S. E., & Tonsager, M. E. (2002). How therapeutic assessment became humanistic. *The
    Humanistic Psychologist, 30*(1–2), 10–22. DOI: 10.1080/08873267.2002. 9977019
Fisch, R., Weakland, J. H., & Segal, L. (1982). *The tactics of change: Doing therapy briefly.* San
    Francisco, CA: Jossey-Bass.
Flannery, D. J., Singer, M. I., & Wester, K. (2001). Violence exposure, psychological
    trauma, and suicide risk in a community sample of dangerously violent adolescents.
    Journal of the American Academy of Child and Adolescent Psychiatry, 40(4), 435–442. DOI:
    10.1097/ 00004583-200104000-00012
Flemons, D. (1991). *Completing distinctions.* Boston: Shambhala.
Flemons, D. (2002). *Of one mind: The logic of hypnosis, the practice of therapy.* New York: Nor-
    ton.
Flemons, D., & Green, S. (2007). Just between us: A relational approach to sex therapy. In
    D. Flemons & S. Green (Eds.), *Quickies: The handbook of brief sex therapy* (Rev. and expanded
    ed., pp. 126–150). New York: Norton.
Florida Statewide Office of Suicide Prevention. (2008). *Suicide prevention: Statewide Office of
    Suicide Prevention annual report.* Tallahassee: Author. Retrieved from http://www.florida
    suicideprevention.org/sosp.htm
Frances, R. J., Franklin, J., & Flavin, D. K. (1986). Suicide and alcoholism. *Annals of the New
    York Academy of Sciences, 487*(1), 316–326. DOI: 10.1111/j.1749-6632. 1986.tb27910.x
Franko, D. L., & Keel, P. K. (2006). Suicidality in eating disorders: Occurrence, correlates,
    and clinical implications. *Clinical Psychology Review, 26*(6), 769–782. DOI: 10.1016 /j.
    cpr. 2006.04.001
Fulkerson, J. A., Story, M., Mellin, A., Leffert, N., Neumark-Sztainer, D., & French, S. A.
    (2006). Family dinner meal frequency and adolescent development: Relationships with
    developmental assets and high-risk behaviors. *Journal of Adolescent Health, 39*(3), 337–345.
    DOI: 10.1016/j.jadohealth.2005.12.026
Garvey, K. A., Penn, J. V., Campbell, A. L., Esposito-Smythers, C., & Spirito, A. (2009).

Contracting for safety with patients: Clinical practice and forensic implications. *Journal of the American Academy of Psychiatry and the Law Online*, 37(3), 363–370.

Gaudiano, B. A., Dalrymple, K. L., & Zimmerman, M. (2009). Prevalence and clinical characteristics of psychotic versus nonpsychotic major depression in a general psychiatric outpatient clinic. *Depression and Anxiety*, 26(1), 54–64. DOI: 10.1002/da.20470

Gibbs, J. T. (1997). African-American suicide: A cultural paradox. *Suicide and Life-Threatening Behavior*, 27(1), 68–79. DOI: 10.1111/j.1943-278X.1997.tb00504.x

Glasser, B. G., & Strauss, A. L. (1967). *The discovery of grounded theory: Strategies for qualitative research*. Chicago: Aldine.

Goldstein, T. R., Bridge, J. A., & Brent, D. A. (2008). Sleep disturbance preceding completed suicide in adolescents. *Journal of Consulting and Clinical Psychology*, 76(1), 84–91. DOI: 10.1037/0022-006x.76.1.84

Greenleaf, E. (1994). *A Sunday lecture on the unconscious mind*. Unpublished workshop transcript.

Groholt, B., Ekeberg, Ø., & Haldorsen, T. (2006). Adolescent suicide attempters: What predicts future suicidal acts? *Suicide and Life-Threatening Behavior*, 36(6), 638–650. DOI: 10.1521/suli.2006.36.6.638

Grossman, D. C., Soderberg, R., & Rivara, F. P. (1993). Prior injury and motor vehicle crash as risk factors for youth suicide. *Epidemiology*, 4(2), 115–119. DOI: 10.1097/00001648 - 199303000-00006

Guze, S. B., & Robins, E. (1970). Suicide and primary affective disorders. *British Journal of Psychiatry*, 117(539), 437–438. DOI: 10.1192/bjp.117.539.437

Haley, J. (1993). *Jay Haley on Milton H. Erickson*. New York: Brunner/Mazel.

Hall, R. C. W., Platt, D. E., & Hall, R. C. W. (1999). Suicide risk assessment: A review of risk factors for suicide in 100 patients who made severe suicide attempts: Evaluation of suicide risk in a time of managed care. *Psychosomatics*, 40(1), 18–27. DOI: 10.1016/S0033-3182(99)71267-3

Harris, E. C., & Barraclough, B. (1997). Suicide as an outcome for mental disorders: A meta-analysis. *British Journal of Psychiatry*, 170(3), 205–228. DOI: 10.1192/bjp.170.3.205

Harriss, L., Hawton, K., & Zahl, D. (2005). Value of measuring suicidal intent in the assessment of people attending hospital following self-poisoning or self-injury. *British Journal of Psychiatry*, 186(1), 60–66. DOI: 10.1192/bjp.186.1.60

Hastings, M. E., Northman, L. M., & Tangney, J. P. (2002). Shame, guilt, and suicide. In T. Joiner & M. D. Rudd (Eds.), *Suicide science: Expanding the boundaries* (pp. 67–79). New York: Kluwer Academic.

Hawton, K. (2002). United Kingdom legislation on pack sizes of analgesics: Background, rationale, and effects on suicide and deliberate self-harm. *Suicide and Life-Threatening Behavior*, 32(3), 223–229. DOI: 10.1521/suli.32.3.223.22169

Hawton, K., Sutton, L., Haw, C., Sinclair, J., & Deeks, J. J. (2005). Schizophrenia and suicide: Systematic review of risk factors. *British Journal of Psychiatry*, 187(1), 9–20. DOI: 10.1192/bjp.187.1.9

Hawton, K., Zahl, D., & Weatherall, R. (2003). Suicide following deliberate self-harm: Long-term follow-up of patients who presented to a general hospital. *British Journal of Psychiatry*, 182(6), 537–542. DOI: 10.1192/bjp.182.6.537

Henden, J. (2008). *Preventing suicide: The solution-focused approach*. New York: Wiley.

Hendin, H., & Haas, A. P. (1991). Suicide and guilt as manifestations of PTSD in Vietnam combat veterans. *American Journal of Psychiatry*, 148(5), 586–591.

Hendin, H., Maltsberger, J. T., & Szanto, K. (2007). The role of intense affective states in signaling a suicide crisis. *Journal of Nervous and Mental Disease*, *195*(5), 363–368. DOI: 10.1097/NMD.0b013e318052264d

Henriques, G., Beck, A. T., & Brown, G. K. (2003). Cognitive therapy for adolescent and young adult suicide attempters. *American Behavioral Scientist*, *46*(9), 1258–1268. DOI: 10.1177/0002764202250668

Hill, R. M., Castellanos, D., & Pettit, J. W. (2011). Suicide-related behaviors and anxiety in children and adolescents: A review. *Clinical Psychology Review*, *31*(7), 1133–1144. DOI: 10.1016/j.cpr.2011.07.008

Høyer, E. H., Mortensen, P. B., & Olesen, A. V. (2000). Mortality and causes of death in a total national sample of patients with affective disorders admitted for the first time between 1973 and 1993. *British Journal of Psychiatry*, *176*(1), 76–82. DOI: 10.1192 / bjp.176.1.76

Huey, S. J., Jr., Henggeler, S. W., Rowland, M. D., Halliday-Boykins, C. A., Cunningham, P. B., Pickrel, S. G., et al. (2004). Multisystemic therapy effects on attempted suicide by youths presenting psychiatric emergencies. *Journal of the American Academy of Child and Adolescent Psychiatry*, *43*(2), 183–190. DOI: 10.1097/00004583-200402000-00014

Huth-Bocks, A. C., Kerr, D. C. R., Ivey, A. Z., Kramer, A. C., & King, C. A. (2007). Assessment of psychiatrically hospitalized suicidal adolescents: Self-report instruments as predictors of suicidal thoughts and behavior. *Journal of the American Academy of Child and Adolescent Psychiatry*, *46*(3), 387–395. DOI: 10.1097/chi.0b013e31802b9535

Ilgen, M. A., Harris, A. H. S., Moos, R. H., & Tiet, Q. Q. (2007). Predictors of a suicide attempt one year after entry into substance use disorder treatment. *Alcoholism: Clinical and Experimental Research*, *31*(4), 635–642. DOI: 10.1111/j.1530-0277.2007.00348.x

Ilgen, M. A., Zivin, K., McCammon, R. J., & Valenstein, M. (2008). Pain and suicidal thoughts, plans and attempts in the United States. *General Hospital Psychiatry*, *30*(6), 521–527. DOI: 10.1016/j.genhosppsych.2008.09.003

Irving, J. (2012). *In one person*. New York: Simon & Schuster.

Isacsson, G., Bergman, U., & Rich, C. L. (1996). Epidemiological data suggest antidepressants reduce suicide risk among depressives. *Journal of Affective Disorders*, *41*(1), 1–8. DOI: 10.1016/0165-0327(96)00050-x

Isometsä, E. T., Henriksson, M. M., Aro, H. M., & Lönnqvist, J. K. (1994). Suicide in bipolar disorder in Finland. *American Journal of Psychiatry*, *151*(7), 1020–1024.

Ivanoff, A., & Jang, S. J. (1991). The role of hopelessness and social desirability in predicting suicidal behavior: A study of prison inmates. *Journal of Consulting and Clinical Psychology*, *59*(3), 394–399. DOI: 10.1037/0022-006x.59.3.394

Jobes, D. A. (2006). *Managing suicidal risk: A collaborative approach*. New York: Guilford Press.

Joiner, T. E., Jr. (2005). *Why people die by suicide*. Cambridge, MA: Harvard University Press.

Joiner, T. E., Jr., Pettit, J. W., Walker, R. L., Voelz, Z. R., Cruz, J., Rudd, M. D., et al. (2002). Perceived burdensomeness and suicidality: Two studies on the suicide notes of those attempting and those completing suicide. *Journal of Social and Clinical Psychology*, *21*(5), 531–545. DOI: 10.1521/jscp.21.5.531.22624

Joiner, T. E., Jr., Sachs-Ericsson, N. J., Wingate, L. R., Brown, J. S., Anestis, M. D., & Selby, E. A. (2007). Childhood physical and sexual abuse and lifetime number of suicide attempts: A persistent and theoretically important relationship. *Behaviour Research and Therapy*, *45*(3), 539–547. DOI: 10.1016/j.brat.2006.04.007

Joiner, T. E., Jr., Voelz, Z. R., & Rudd, M. D. (2001). For suicidal young adults with comorbid depressive and anxiety disorders, problem-solving treatment may be better than treatment as usual. *Professional Psychology: Research and Practice*, *32*(3), 278–282. DOI: 10. 1037/ 0735-7028.32.3.278

Joiner, T. E., Jr., Walker, R. L., Rudd, M. D., & Jobes, D. A. (1999). Scientizing and routinizing the assessment of suicidality in outpatient practice. *Professional Psychology: Research and Practice, 30*(5), 447–453. DOI: 10.1037/0735-7028.30.5.447

Jurich, A. P. (2001). The nature of suicide. *Clinical Update: Suicidal Ideation and Behavior, 3*(6), 1–7. Washington, DC: American Association for Marriage and Family Therapy.

Kahneman, D. (2011). *Thinking, fast and slow.* New York: Farrar, Straus & Giroux.

Kang, H. K., & Bullman, T. A. (2010, January). *The risk of suicide among U.S. war veterans: Vietnam war to Operation Iraqi Freedom.* Paper presented at the Department of Defense/Veterans Administration Suicide Prevention Conference: Building Strong and Resilient Communities, Washington, DC. Retrieved from http://www.dcoe.health.mil

Keilp, J. G., Sackeim, H. A., Brodsky, B. S., Oquendo, M. A., Malone, K. M., & Mann, J. J. (2001). Neuropsychological dysfunction in depressed suicide attempters. *American Journal of Psychiatry, 158*(5), 735–741. DOI: 10.1176/appi.ajp. 158.5.735

Kellermann, A. L., Rivara, F. P., Somes, G., Reay, D. T., Francisco, J., Banton, J. G., et al. (1992). Suicide in the home in relation to gun ownership. *New England Journal of Medicine, 327*(7), 467–472. DOI: 10.1056/NEJM199208133270705

Kelly, K. T., & Knudson, M. P. (2000). Are no-suicide contracts effective in preventing suicide in suicidal patients seen by primary care physicians? *Archives of Family Medicine, 9*(10), 1119–1121. DOI: 10.1001/archfami.9.10.1119

Kendler, K. S., Karkowski, L. M., & Prescott, C. A. (1998). Stressful life events and major depression: Risk period, long-term contextual threat, and diagnostic specificity. *Journal of Nervous and Mental Disease, 186*(11), 661–669. DOI: 10.1097/00005053-199811000-00001

Kienhorst, C. W. M., De Wilde, E. J., Diekstra, R. F. W., & Wolters, W. H. G. (1992). Differences between adolescent suicide attempters and depressed adolescents. *Acta Psychiatrica Scandinavica, 85*(3), 222–228. DOI: 10.1111/j.1600-0447. 1992.tb08599.x

Kim, Y. S., & Leventhal, B. (2008). Bullying and suicide: A review. *International Journal of Adolescent Medicine and Health, 20*(2), 133–154. DOI: 10.1515/ IJAMH.2008.20.2.133

Kirsch, I. (1990). *Changing expectations: A key to effective psychotherapy.* Pacific Grove, CA: Brooks/Cole.

Kotler, M., Iancu, I., Efroni, R., & Amir, M. (2001). Anger, impulsivity, social support, and suicide risk in patients with posttraumatic stress disorder. *Journal of Nervous and Mental Disease, 189*(3), 162–167. DOI: 10.1097/00005053-200103000-00004

Kreitman, N. (1976). The coal gas story: United Kingdom suicide rates, 1960–71. *British Journal of Preventive and Social Medicine, 30*(2), 86–93. DOI: 10.1136/jech. 30.2.86

Kuo, W. H., & Gallo, J. J. (2005). Completed suicide after a suicide attempt. *American Journal of Psychiatry, 162*(3), 633–633. DOI: 10.1176/appi.ajp.162.3.633

Kvale, S. (1996). *InterViews: An introduction to qualitative research interviewing.* Thousand Oaks, CA: Sage.

Lakoff, G., & Johnson, M. (1980). *Metaphors we live by.* Chicago: University of Chicago Press.

Lakoff, G., & Johnson, M. (1999). *Philosophy in the flesh: The embodied mind and its challenge to Western thought.* New York: Basic Books.

Lapierre, S., Dubé, M., Bouffard, L., & Alain, M. (2007). Addressing suicidal ideations through the realization of meaningful personal goals. *Crisis: The Journal of Crisis Intervention and Suicide Prevention, 28*(1), 16–25. DOI: 10.1027/0227-5910. 28.1.16

Lehrer, J. (2009). *How we decide.* New York: Houghton Mifflin Harcourt.

Lester, D. (1997). The role of shame in suicide. *Suicide and Life-Threatening Behavior, 27*(4), 352–361. DOI: 10.1111/j.1943-278X.1997.tb00514.x

Lester, D. (1998). The association of shame and guilt with suicidality. *Journal of Social Psychology, 138*(4), 535–536. DOI: 10.1080/00224549809600407

Lewis, G., & Sloggett, A. (1998). Suicide, deprivation, and unemployment: Record linkage study. *British Medical Journal, 317*(7168), 1283–1286. DOI: 10.1136/ bmj.317.7168.1283

Lewis, L. M. (2007). No-harm contracts: A review of what we know. *Suicide and Life-Threatening Behavior, 37*(1), 50–57. DOI: 10.1521/suli.2007.37.1.50

Lieberman, E. J. (1993). Suicidal ideation and young adults. *American Journal of Psychiatry, 150*(1), 171.

Lincoln, Y. S., & Guba, E. G. (1985). *Naturalistic inquiry.* Newbury Park, CA: Sage.

Linehan, M. M., Goodstein, J. L., Nielsen, S. L., & Chiles, J. A. (1983). Reasons for staying alive when you are thinking of killing yourself: The Reasons for Living Inventory. *Journal of Consulting and Clinical Psychology, 51*(2), 276–286. DOI: 10.1037/0022- 006x. 51.2.276

Linehan, M. M., & Nielsen, S. L. (1981). Assessment of suicide ideation and parasuicide: Hopelessness and social desirability. *Journal of Consulting and Clinical Psychology, 49*(5), 773–775. DOI: 10.1037/0022-006x.49.5.773

Linehan, M. M., & Nielsen, S. L. (1983). Social desirability: Its relevance to the measurement of hopelessness and suicidal behavior. *Journal of Consulting and Clinical Psychology, 51*(1), 141–143. DOI: 10.1037/0022-006x.51.1.141

Loftus, E. F., & Palmer, J. C. (1974). Reconstruction of automobile destruction: An example of the interaction between language and memory. *Journal of Verbal Learning and Verbal Behavior, 13*, 585–589.

Luoma, J. B., & Pearson, J. L. (2002). Suicide and marital status in the United States, 1991–1996: Is widowhood a risk factor? *American Journal of Public Health, 92*(9), 1518–1522. DOI: 10.2105/ajph.92.9.1518

Malone, K. M., Oquendo, M. A., Haas, G. L., Ellis, S. P., Li, S., & Mann, J. J. (2000). Protective factors against suicidal acts in major depression: Reasons for living. *American Journal of Psychiatry, 157*(7), 1084–1088. DOI: 10.1176/appi.ajp. 157.7.1084

Mandrusiak, M., Rudd, M. D., Joiner, T. E., Berman, A. L., Van Orden, K. A., & Witte, T. (2006). Warning signs for suicide on the Internet: A descriptive study. *Suicide and Life-Threatening Behavior, 36*(3), 263–271. DOI: 10.1521/suli.2006.36.3.263

Mann, J. J., Bortinger, J., Oquendo, M. A., Currier, D., Li, S., & Brent, D. A. (2005). Family history of suicidal behavior and mood disorders in probands with mood disorders. *American Journal of Psychiatry, 162*(9), 1672–1679. DOI: 10.1176/ appi.ajp.162.9.1672

Marion, M. S., & Range, L. M. (2003). African American college women's suicide buffers. *Suicide and Life-Threatening Behavior, 33*(1), 33–43. DOI: 10.1521/ suli.33.1.33.22780

Martin, G., Bergen, H. A., Richardson, A. S., Roeger, L., & Allison, S. (2004). Sexual abuse and suicidality: Gender differences in a large community sample of adolescents. *Child Abuse and Neglect, 28*(5), 491–503. DOI: 10.1016/j.chiabu. 2003.08.006

Marttunen, M. J., Aro, H. M., & Lönnqvist, J. K. (1993). Precipitant stressors in adolescent suicide. *Journal of the American Academy of Child and Adolescent Psychiatry, 32*(6), 1178–1183. DOI: 10.1097/00004583-199311000-00010

McAuliffe, C., Corcoran, P., Keeley, H. S., & Perry, I. J. (2003). Risk of suicide ideation associated with problem-solving ability and attitudes toward suicidal behavior in university students. *Crisis: The Journal of Crisis Intervention and Suicide Prevention, 24*(4), 160–167. DOI: 10.1027//0227-5910.24.4.160

McCann, I. L., & Pearlman, L. A. (1990). Vicarious traumatization: A framework for understanding the psychological effects of working with victims. *Journal of Traumatic Stress, 3*(1), 131–149.

McGee, D., Del Vento, A., & Bavelas, J. B. (2005). An interactional model of questions as therapeutic interventions. *Journal of Marital and Family Therapy, 31*(4), 371–384. DOI: 10.1111/j.1752-0606.2005.tb01577.x

Meichenbaum, D. (2005). 35 years of working with suicidal patients: Lessons learned. *Canadian Psychologist, 46*(2), 64–72. (Visit www.melissainstitute.org to read other related papers on suicide by Meichenbaum.)

Meichenbaum, D. (2006). Trauma and suicide: A constructive narrative perspective. In T. E. Ellis (Ed.), *Cognition and suicide: Theory, research, and therapy* (pp. 333–353). Washington, DC: American Psychological Association.

Meichenbaum, D. (2010). *35 years of working with suicidal patients: Lessons learned.* Retrieved from http://www.melissainstitute.org/

Meichenbaum, D. (2012). *Roadmap to resilience: A toolkit for returning service members and their family members.* Clearwater, FL: Institute Press. Retrieved from www.copingaftercombat .com/PDF/friday_handout.pdf

Miles, M. B., & Huberman, A. M. (1994). *Qualitative data analysis: An expanded sourcebook* (2nd ed.). Thousand Oaks, CA: Sage.

Miller, M., & Hemenway, D. (1999). The relationship between firearms and suicide: A review of the literature. *Aggression and Violent Behavior, 4*(1), 59–75. DOI: 10.1016/s1359-1789(97)00057-8

Minkoff, K., Bergman, E., Beck, A. T., & Beck, R. (1973). Hopelessness, depression, and attempted suicide. *American Journal of Psychiatry, 130*(4), 455–459.

Mitchell, A. M., Kim, Y., Prigerson, H. G., & Mortimer-Stephens, M. (2004). Complicated grief in survivors of suicide. *Crisis: The Journal of Crisis Intervention and Suicide Prevention, 25*(1), 12–18. DOI: 10.1027/0227-5910.25.1.12

Möller, H. J. (1989). Efficacy of different strategies of aftercare for patients who have attempted suicide. *Journal of the Royal Society of Medicine, 82*(11), 643–647.

Morrison, R., & O'Connor, R. C. (2008). A systematic review of the relationship between rumination and suicidality. *Suicide and Life-Threatening Behavior, 38*(5), 523–538.

National Center for Injury Prevention and Control, Division of Violence Prevention. (n.d.). *Suicides due to alcohol and/or drug overdose: A data brief from the National Violent Death Reporting System.* Retrieved from Centers for Disease Control and Prevention website: http://www.cdc.gov/ViolencePrevention/pdf/ NVDRS_Data_Brief-a.pdf

Nock, M. K., Joiner, T. E., Gordon, K. H., Lloyd-Richardson, E., & Prinstein, M. J. (2006). Non-suicidal self-injury among adolescents: Diagnostic correlates and relation to suicide attempts. *Psychiatry Research, 144*(1), 65–72. DOI: 10.1016/ j.psychres.2006.05.010

Norton, P. J., Temple, S. R., & Pettit, J. W. (2008). Suicidal ideation and anxiety disorders: Elevated risk or artifact of comorbid depression? *Journal of Behavior Therapy and Experimental Psychiatry, 39*(4), 515–525. DOI: 10.1016/j.jbtep. 2007.10.010

O'Hanlon, B., & Beadle, S. (1997). *A guide to possibility land: Fifty-one methods for doing brief, respectful therapy.* New York: Norton.

Oquendo, M. A., Friend, J. M., Halberstam, B., Brodsky, B. S., Burke, A. K., Grunebaum, M. F., et al. (2003). Association of comorbid posttraumatic stress disorder and major depression with greater risk for suicidal behavior. *American Journal of Psychiatry, 160*(3), 580–582. DOI: 10.1176/appi.ajp.160.3.580

Ösby, U., Brandt, L., Correia, N., Ekbom, A., & Sparén, P. (2001). Excess mortality in bipolar and unipolar disorder in Sweden. *Archives of General Psychiatry, 58*(9), 844–850. DOI: 10.1001/archpsyc.58.9.844

Ostamo, A., & Lönnqvist, J. (2001). Excess mortality of suicide attempters. *Social Psychiatry and Psychiatric Epidemiology, 36*(1), 29–35. DOI: 10.1007/ s001270050287

Owens, D., Horrocks, J., & House, A. (2002). Fatal and non-fatal repetition of self-harm. *British Journal of Psychiatry, 181*(3), 193–199. DOI: 10.1192/bjp.181.3.193

Oyefeso, A., Ghodse, H., Clancy, C., & Corkery, J. M. (1999). Suicide among drug addicts in the UK. *British Journal of Psychiatry, 175,* 277–282. DOI: 10.1192/ bjp.175.3. 277

Palmer, B. A., Pankratz, V. S., & Bostwick, J. M. (2005). The lifetime risk of suicide in schizophrenia: A reexamination. *Archives of General Psychiatry, 62*(3), 247–253. DOI: 10.1001/ archpsyc.62.3.247

Papadopoulos, F. C., Ekbom, A., Brandt, L., & Ekselius, L. (2009). Excess mortality, causes of death and prognostic factors in anorexia nervosa. *British Journal of Psychiatry, 194*(1), 10–17. DOI: 10.1192/bjp.bp.108.054742

Patsiokas, A. T., & Clum, G. A. (1985). Effects of psychotherapeutic strategies in the treatment of suicide attempters. *Psychotherapy: Theory, Research, Practice, Training, 22*(2), 281–290. DOI: 10.1037/h0085507

Paykel, E. S., Myers, J. K., Lindenthal, J. J., & Tanner, J. (1974). Suicidal feelings in the general population: A prevalence study. *British Journal of Psychiatry, 124*(582), 460–469. DOI: 10.1192/bjp.124.5.460

Pearlman, L. A., & Saakvitne, K. W. (1995). Treating therapists with vicarious traumatization and secondary traumatic stress disorder. In C. R. Figley (Ed.), *Compassion fatigue: Coping with secondary traumatic stress disorder in those who treat the traumatized* (pp. 150–177). New York: Routledge.

Petronis, K. R., Samuels, J. F., Moscicki, E. K., & Anthony, J. C. (1990). An epidemiologic investigation of potential risk factors for suicide attempts. *Social Psychiatry and Psychiatric Epidemiology, 25*(4), 193–199. DOI: 10.1007/bf00 782961

Pirkis, J., Burgess, P., & Jolley, D. (1999). Suicide attempts by psychiatric patients in acute inpatient, long-stay inpatient and community care. *Social Psychiatry and Psychiatric Epidemiology, 34*(12), 634–644. DOI: 10.1007/s001270050186

Pollock, L. R., & Williams, J. M. G. (1998). Problem solving and suicidal behavior. *Suicide and Life-Threatening Behavior, 28*(4), 375–387. DOI: 10.1111/j.1943-278X.1998.tb00973.x

Pompili, M., Amador, X., Girardi, P., Harkavy-Friedman, J., Harrow, M., Kaplan, K., et al. (2007). Suicide risk in schizophrenia: Learning from the past to change the future. *Annals of General Psychiatry, 6*(1), 10.

Pompili, M., Mancinelli, I., Girardi, P., Ruberto, A., & Tatarelli, R. (2004). Suicide in anorexia nervosa: A meta-analysis. *International Journal of Eating Disorders, 36*(1), 99–103. DOI: 10.1002/eat.20011

Pompili, M., Ruberto, A., Girardi, P., & Tatarelli, R. (2005). Suicide risk during pregnancy. *European Journal of Obstetrics, Gynecology, and Reproductive Biology, 120,* 121–123; author reply, 124.

Pompili, M., Vanacore, N., Macone, S., Amore, M., Petriconi, G., Tonna, M., et al. (2007). Depression, hopelessness and suicide risk among patients suffering from epilepsy. *Ann Ist Super Sanità, 43*(4), 425–429.

Prigerson, H. G., Frank, E., Kasl, S. V., Reynolds, C. F., Anderson, B., Zubenko, G. S., et al. (1995). Complicated grief and bereavement-related depression as distinct disorders: Preliminary empirical validation in elderly bereaved spouses. *American Journal of Psychiatry, 152*(1), 22–30.

Prochaska, J. O., DiClemente, C. C., & Norcross, J. C. (1992). In search of how people change: Applications to addictive behaviors. *American Psychologist, 47*(9), 1102–1114. DOI: 10.1037/0003-066x.47.9.1102

Qin, P., Mortensen, P. B., & Pedersen, C. B. (2009). Frequent change of residence and risk of attempted and completed suicide among children and adolescents. *Archives of General Psychiatry*, *66*(6), 628–632. DOI: 10.1001/archgen psychiatry.2009.20

Radomsky, E. D., Haas, G. L., Mann, J. J., & Sweeney, J. A. (1999). Suicidal behavior in patients with schizophrenia and other psychotic disorders. *American Journal of Psychiatry*, *156*(10), 1590–1595.

Range, L. M. (2005). The family of instruments that assess suicide risk. *Journal of Psychopathology and Behavioral Assessment*, *27*(2), 133–140. DOI: 10.1007/ s10862-005-5387-8

Remafedi, G., French, S., Story, M., Resnick, M. D., & Blum, R. (1998). The relationship between suicide risk and sexual orientation: Results of a population-based study. *American Journal of Public Health*, *88*(1), 57–60. DOI: 10.2105/ajph.88.1.57

Resnick, M. D., Bearman, P. S., Blum, R. W., Bauman, K. E., Harris, K. M., Jones, J., et al. (1997). Protecting adolescents from harm: Findings from the National Longitudinal Study on Adolescent Health. *Journal of the American Medical Association*, *278*(10), 823–832. DOI: 10.1001/jama.278.10.823

Rice, K. G., Leever, B. A., Christopher, J., & Porter, J. D. (2006). Perfectionism, stress, and social (dis)connection: A short-term study of hopelessness, depression, and academic adjustment among honors students. *Journal of Counseling Psychology*, *53*(4), 524–534. DOI: 10.1037/0022-0167.53.4.524

Richman, J. (1979). The family therapy of attempted suicide. *Family Process*, *18*(2), 131–142. DOI: 10.1111/j.1545-5300.1979.00131.x

Rogers, C. R. (1980). *A way of being*. Boston: Houghton Mifflin.

Rogers, C. R. (1987). Rogers, Kohut, and Erickson: A personal perspective on some similarities and differences. In J. K. Zeig (Ed.), *The evolution of psychotherapy* (pp. 179–187). New York: Brunner/Mazel.

Rucci, P., Frank, E., Kostelnik, B., Fagiolini, A., Mallinger, A. G., Swartz, H. A., et al. (2002). Suicide attempts in patients with bipolar I disorder during acute and maintenance phases of intensive treatment with pharmacotherapy and adjunctive psychotherapy. *American Journal of Psychiatry*, *159*(7), 1160–1164. DOI: 10.1176/appi.ajp.159.7.1160

Rudd, M. D. (2006). *The assessment and management of suicidality*. Sarasota, FL: Professional Resource Press.

Rudd, M. D., Berman, A. L., Joiner, T. E., Nock, M. K., Silverman, M. M., Mandrusiak, M., et al. (2006). Warning signs for suicide: Theory, research, and clinical applications. *Suicide and Life-Threatening Behavior*, *36*(3), 255–262. DOI: 10.1521/suli.2006.36.3.255

Rudd, M. D., Mandrusiak, M., & Joiner, T. E., Jr. (2006). The case against no-suicide contracts: The commitment-to-treatment statement as a practice alternative. *Journal of Clinical Psychology*, *62*(2), 243–251. DOI: 10.1002/jclp.20227

Runeson, B., Tidemalm, D., Dahlin, M., Lichtenstein, P., & Långström, N. (2010). Method of attempted suicide as predictor of subsequent successful suicide: National long-term cohort study. *British Medical Journal*, *341*(7765), 186. DOI: 10.1136/bmj.c3222

Salkovskis, P. M., Atha, C., & Storer, D. (1990). Cognitive–behavioural problem solving in the treatment of patients who repeatedly attempt suicide: A controlled trial. *British Journal of Psychiatry*, *157*, 871–876. DOI: 10.1192/bjp.157.6.871

Sareen, J., Cox, B. J., Afifi, T. O., de Graaf, R., Asmundson, G. J. G., ten Have, M., et al. (2005). Anxiety disorders and risk for suicidal ideation and suicide attempts: A population-based longitudinal study of adults. *Archives of General Psychiatry*, *62*(11), 1249–1257. DOI: 10.1001/archpsyc.62.11.1249

Schotte, D. E., & Clum, G. A. (1987). Problem-solving skills in suicidal psychiatric patients. *Journal of Consulting and Clinical Psychology*, *55*(1), 49–54. DOI: 10.1037/0022 -006x. 55.1.49

Shaffer, D., Scott, M., Wilcox, H., Maslow, C., Hicks, R., Lucas, C. P., et al. (2004). The Columbia Suicide Screen: Validity and reliability of a screen for youth suicide and depression. *Journal of the American Academy of Child and Adolescent Psychiatry, 43*(1), 71–79. DOI: 10.1097/00004583-200401000-00016

Shahar, G., Bareket, L., Rudd, M. D., & Joiner, T. E. (2006). In severely suicidal young adults, hopelessness, depressive symptoms, and suicidal ideation constitute a single syndrome. *Psychological Medicine, 36*(7), 913–922. DOI: 10.1017/ S0033291706007586

Shea, S. C. (2002). *The practical art of suicide assessment: A guide for mental health professionals and substance abuse counselors.* Hoboken, NJ: Wiley.

Sher, L. (2006). Alcohol consumption and suicide. *QJM: An International Journal of Medicine, 99*(1), 57–61. DOI: 10.1093/qjmed/hci146

Shneidman, E. S. (1998). *The suicidal mind.* New York: Oxford University Press.

Silver, J. M., Kramer, R., Greenwald, S., & Weissman, M. (2001). The association between head injuries and psychiatric disorders: Findings from the New Haven NIMH Epidemiologic Catchment Area Study. *Brain Injury, 15*(11), 935–945. DOI: 10.1080/ 02699050110065295

Simon, R. I. (2006). Imminent suicide: The illusion of short-term prediction. *Suicide and Life-Threatening Behavior, 36*(3), 296–301. DOI: 10.1521/suli.2006.36.3.296

Simon, R. I. (2007). Gun safety management with patients at risk for suicide. *Suicide and Life-Threatening Behavior, 37*(5), 518–526. DOI: 10.1521/suli.2007.37.5.518

Simon, R. I. (2011). *Preventing patient suicide: Clinical assessment and management.* Washington, DC: American Psychiatric Association.

Simon, T. R., Swann, A. C., Powell, K. E., Potter, L. B., Kresnow, M. J., & O'Carroll, P. W. (2001). Characteristics of impulsive suicide attempts and attempters. *Suicide and Life-Threatening Behavior, 32*, 49–59. DOI: 10.1521/suli.32.1.5.49.24212

Simpson, G., & Tate, R. (2002). Suicidality after traumatic brain injury: Demographic, injury, and clinical correlates. *Psychological Medicine, 32*(4), 687–697. DOI: 10.1017/ S0033291702005561

Sjöström, N., Hetta, J., & Waern, M. (2009). Persistent nightmares are associated with repeat suicide attempt: A prospective study. *Psychiatry Research, 170*(2), 208–211. DOI: 10.1016/ j.psychres.2008.09.006

Sjöström, N., Wærn, M., & Hetta, J. (2007). Nightmares and sleep disturbances in relation to suicidality in suicide attempters. *Sleep: Journal of Sleep and Sleep Disorders Research, 30*(1), 91–95.

Soon, C. S., Brass, M., Heinze, H. J., & Haynes, J. D. (2008). Unconscious determinants of free decisions in the human brain. *Nature Neuroscience, 11*(5), 543–545. DOI: 10.1038/ nn.2112

Spradley, J. P. (1979). *The ethnographic interview.* New York: Holt, Rinehart & Winston.

Stack, S. (2001). Occupation and suicide. *Social Science Quarterly, 82*(2), 384–396. DOI: 10.1111 /0038-4941.00030

Stack, S., & Wasserman, I. (2007). Economic strain and suicide risk: A qualitative analysis. *Suicide & Life-Threatening Behavior, 37*(1), 103–112. DOI: 10.2307/2136676

Stanley, B., Gameroff, M. J., Michalsen, V., & Mann, J. J. (2001). Are suicide attempters who self-mutilate a unique population? *American Journal of Psychiatry, 158*(3), 427–432. DOI: 10.1176/appi.ajp.158.3.427

Sterud, T., Hem, E., Lau, B., & Ekeberg, O. (2008). Suicidal ideation and suicide attempts in a nationwide sample of operational Norwegian ambulance personnel. *Journal of Occupational Health, 50*(5), 406–414. DOI: 10.1539/joh.L8025

Strakowski, S. M., McElroy, S. L., Keck, P. E., Jr., & West, S. A. (1996). Suicidality among patients with mixed and manic bipolar disorder. *American Journal of Psychiatry, 153*(5), 674–676.

Stravynski, A., & Boyer, R. (2001). Loneliness in relation to suicide ideation and parasuicide: A population-wide study. *Suicide and Life-Threatening Behavior, 31*(1), 32–40. DOI: 10.1521/suli.31.1.32.21312

Strong, T. (2003). Getting curious about meaning-making in counselling. *British Journal of Guidance and Counselling, 31*(3), 259–273. DOI: 10.1080/0306988031000 147875

Strosahl, K. D., Linehan, M. M., & Chiles, J. A. (1984). Will the real social desirability please stand up?: Hopelessness, depression, social desirability, and the prediction of suicidal behavior. *Journal of Consulting and Clinical Psychology, 52*(3), 449–457. DOI: 10.1037/0022-006x.52.3.449

Suominen, K., Isometsä, E., Henriksson, M., Ostamo, A., & Lönnqvist, J. (1998). Inadequate treatment for major depression both before and after attempted suicide. *American Journal of Psychiatry, 155*(12), 1778–1780.

Suominen, K., Isometsä, E., Suokas, J., Haukka, J., Achte, K., & Lönnqvist, J. (2004). Completed suicide after a suicide attempt: A 37-year follow-up study. *American Journal of Psychiatry, 161*(3), 562–563. DOI: 10.1176/appi.ajp.161.3.562

Swann, A. C., Dougherty, D. M., Pazzaglia, P. J., Pham, M., Steinberg, J. L., & Moeller, F. G. (2005). Increased impulsivity associated with severity of suicide attempt history in patients with bipolar disorder. *American Journal of Psychiatry, 162*(9), 1680–1687. DOI: 10.1176/appi.ajp.162.9.1680

Szanto, K., Prigerson, H., Houck, P., Ehrenpreis, L., & Reynolds, C. F. (1997). Suicidal ideation in elderly bereaved: The role of complicated grief. *Suicide and Life-Threatening Behavior, 27*(2), 194–207. DOI: 10.1111/j.1943-278X.1997. tb00291.x

Taliaferro, L. A., Rienzo, B. A., Miller, M. D., Pigg, R. M., & Dodd, V. J. (2008). High school youth and suicide risk: Exploring protection afforded through physical activity and sport participation. *Journal of School Health, 78*(10), 545–553. DOI: 10.1111/j.1746-1561.2008.00342.x

Tang, N. K. Y., & Crane, C. (2006). Suicidality in chronic pain: A review of the prevalence, risk factors and psychological links. *Psychological Medicine, 36*(5), 575–586. DOI: 10.1017/S0033291705006859

Tanskanen, A., Tuomilehto, J., Viinamäki, H., Vartiainen, E., Lehtonen, J., & Puska, P. (2001). Nightmares as predictors of suicide. *Sleep: Journal of Sleep and Sleep Disorders Research, 24*(7), 844–847.

Tarrier, N., & Gregg, L. (2004). Suicide risk in civilian PTSD patients: Predictors of suicidal ideation, planning, and attempts. *Social Psychiatry and Psychiatric Epidemiology, 39*(8), 655–661. DOI: 10.1007/s00127-004-0799-4

Teasdale, T. W., & Engberg, A. W. (2001). Suicide after traumatic brain injury: A population study. *Journal of Neurology, Neurosurgery, and Psychiatry, 71*(4), 436–440. DOI: 10. 1136/ jnnp.71.4.436

Tesch, R. (1990). *Qualitative research: Analysis types and software tools.* Abingdon, UK: Routledge Falmer.

Tiet, Q. Q., Finney, J. W., & Moos, R. H. (2006). Recent sexual abuse, physical abuse, and suicide attempts among male veterans seeking psychiatric treatment. *Psychiatric Services, 57*(1), 107–113. DOI: 10.1176/appi.ps.57.1.107

Tomm, K. (1987). Interventive interviewing: Part I. Strategizing as a fourth guideline for the therapist. *Family Process, 26*(1), 3–13. DOI: 10.1111/j.1545-5300.1987. 00003.x

Tomm, K. (1988). Interventive interviewing: Part III. Intending to ask lineal, circular, strategic, or reflexive questions? *Family Process, 27*(1), 1–15. DOI: 10.1111/ j.1545-5300. 1988.00001.x

Tondo, L., Hennen, J., & Baldessarini, R. J. (2001). Lower suicide risk with long-term lithium treatment in major affective illness: A meta-analysis. *Acta Psychiatrica Scandinavica, 104*(3), 163–172. DOI: 10.1034/j.1600-0447.2001.00464.x

Tondo, L., Isacsson, G., & Baldessarini, R. J. (2003). Suicidal behaviour in bipolar disorder: Risk and prevention. *CNS Drugs, 17*(7), 491–511. DOI: 10.2165/ 00023210–200317070 - 00003

Trout, D. L. (1980). The role of social isolation in suicide. *Suicide and Life-Threatening Behavior, 10*(1), 10–23. DOI: 10.1111/j.1943-278X.1980.tb00693.x

Turvey, C., Stromquist, A., Kelly, K., Zwerling, C., & Merchant, J. (2002). Financial loss and suicidal ideation in a rural community sample. *Acta Psychiatrica Scandinavica, 106*(5), 373–380. DOI: 10.1034/j.1600-0447.2002.02340.x

Waern, M., Rubenowitz, E., Runeson, B., Skoog, I., Wilhelmson, K., & Allebeck, P. (2002). Burden of illness and suicide in elderly people: Case-control study. *British Medical Journal, 324*(7350), 1355. DOI: 10.1136/bmj.324.7350.1355

Walker, J., Waters, R. A., Murray, G., Swanson, H., Hibberd, C. J., Rush, R. W., et al. (2008). Better off dead: Suicidal thoughts in cancer patients. *Journal of Clinical Oncology, 26*(29), 4725–4730. DOI: 10.1200/jco.2007.11.8844

Watzlawick, P., Weakland, J., & Fisch, R. (1974). *Change: Principles of problem formation and problem resolution.* New York: Norton.

Weiss, R. S. (1994). *Learning from strangers.* New York: Free Press.

Weissman, M. M., Klerman, G. L., Markowitz, J. S., & Ouellette, R. (1989). Suicidal ideation and suicide attempts in panic disorder and attacks. *New England Journal of Medicine, 321*(18), 1209–1214. DOI: 10.1056/NEJM198911023211801

Whitehead, A. N. (1953). *Science and the modern world.* New York: Free Press. (Original work published 1925)

Whitlock, J., & Knox, K. (2007). The relationship between self-injurious behavior and suicide in a young adult population. *Archives of Pediatrics and Adolescent Medicine, 161*(7), 634–640. DOI: 10.1001/archpedi.161.7.634

Wilcox, H. C., Storr, C. L., & Breslau, N. (2009). Posttraumatic stress disorder and suicide attempts in a community sample of urban American young adults. *Archives of General Psychiatry, 66*(3), 305–311. DOI: 10.1001/archgenpsychiatry. 2008.557

Wilk, J. (1975). Ericksonian therapeutic patterns: A pattern which connects. In J. K. Zeig (Ed.), *Ericksonian psychotherapy: Vol. 2. Clinical applications* (pp. 210–233). New York: Brunner/Mazel.

Wojnar, M., Ilgen, M. A., Wojnar, J., McCammon, R. J., Valenstein, M., & Brower, K. J. (2009). Sleep problems and suicidality in the National Comorbidity Survey Replication. *Journal of Psychiatric Research, 43*(5), 526–531. DOI: 10.1016/j.jpsychires.2008.07.006

Zeig, J. K. (1994). Advanced techniques of utilization: An intervention metamodel and the use of sequences, symptom words, and figures of speech. In J. K. Zeig (Ed.), *Ericksonian methods: The essence of the story* (pp. 295–314). New York: Brunner/Mazel.

INDEX

Rucci, P., 97
Rudd, M. D., 82, 121, 123, 159

sadness, tracking, 44
safe havens, identifying, xii, 166–69, 177, 221
safer alternatives to troubling behaviors, explor-
    ing with client, 163–64
safety, 113, 136–73
    appreciating clients' risks and potential for,
        65
    change within context of finding and main-
        taining possibilities for, 15
    coming to a safety decision, 138–44
    engaged, relational, intersubjective position-
        ing around, 52
    establishing, listening for individual charac-
        teristics and, 55–56
    facilitating, 117–18, 176, 220
    juxtaposing professional knowledge with cli-
        ent information, 145
    juxtaposing your emotional response with
        your knowledge of the "facts," 145–46
    of therapist, ensuring, 172
    thinking twice about your safety decision,
        146–47
safety decision
    coming to, 11–12, 138–44
    data-analysis procedures of ethnographers
        and, 143
    defined, 136
    thinking twice about, 146–47
Safety Plan Construction Guide (SPCG), 160,
    161–72, 174, 177, 221–22
    in Backpocket RSA, 217, 221–22
    Guideline I, 162, 177, 221
    Guideline II, 162–63, 177, 221
    Guideline III, 163–66, 177, 221
    Guideline IV, 166–69, 177, 221
    Guideline V, 169–70, 177, 221
    Guideline VI, 170–71, 177, 222
    Guideline VII, 171, 177, 222
    Guideline VIII, 171–73, 177, 222
safety plan(s), 64, 174, 195, 216n1
    abbreviations as mnemonic for construction
        of, xii, 173n1
    active participation in developing/imple-
        menting, 129–30, 176, 208, 213, 220
    active participation of significant others in,
        133–35, 176, 202, 211
    brainstorming elements of, 200, 202
    collaborative creation of, 128, 202
    complexity of, 138, 203
    constructing, 159–61
    detailed, collaboratively developing, 12–13,
        200–208

establishing significant others as resources
    for, 180, 181, 182
hospitals included in, 169
looking for holes in, 204
necessary and possible, 148–51
no-harm contract vs., 136, 159, 208
real-world testing of, 161
in Relational Suicide Assessment, 214
taking a second look at, 207–8
when it is not enough, 151–58
when none is needed, 147–48
Salkovskis, P. M., 82
Scale for Suicide Ideation (SSI), 2
schizoaffective disorder, 94
schizophrenia, hallucinations/delusions and, 94
Shneidman, E. S., 92
school
    connectedness to, reduced rates of suicidal
        ideation and, 83
    leave of absence from, 169
school phobia, 39, 40
screening devices, general, 2
Segal, L., 149
self-harming behaviors, 9
self-hypnosis, 99, 206
self-injurious behavior, suicidality and, 109–10
self-report inventories, 2, 4
semistructured clinical interviews, 2
semistructured interview approach, 68
sensations, as relational processes, 16, 18
sexual abuse
    history of, 9
    risk of suicidality and, 80–81, 85
sexual intimacy with client, notion of a slippery
    slope and, 33, 53n8
sexual orientation, conflicted, risk of suicidality
    and, 9, 91, 92, 131
Shahar, G., 121
shame, 129, 130, 175, 182, 183, 184, 194, 196,
    205, 209, 212, 213, 219
    confounding effects of social desirability
        and, 119
    possible questions, 93–94
    risk of suicidality and, 91–93
Shea, S. C., 3, 9, 123
Sher, L., 106
shifting relationships that constitute the prob-
    lem, 37–38
significant-other resources
    Desperation category, 59, 132–35, 176, 220
    Disruptions and Demands category, 58, 86–
        88, 175, 219
    Suffering category, 58, 102–4, 175, 219
    Troubling Behaviors category, 59, 116–18,
        176, 220